MW00535395

Praise for *Alabama Grandson*

With heart-wrenching vulnerability, Cedrick Bridgeforth has crafted a beautiful and riveting narrative. It reveals how personal integrity and character develop through Black gay self-acceptance and deep, nurturing, love by family. This spiritually enlivening journey contains both excruciating, betrayal-filled life lessons and awe-inspiring examples of his non-judgmental, compassionate care for others.

—TRACI C. WEST, PhD, Professor of Christian Ethics
and African American Studies

Alabama Grandson reviews more than just a gay man's coming out experience. It's the story of how family heritage passes along values and approaches to life that remain vivid, relevant, and powerful under the most challenging conditions. It's a powerful story of the South, of love, of black men and oppression, and of self-realization that leaves readers thinking long after Bridgeforth's story concludes, with another powerful letter to his grandmother celebrating his journey.

—DIANE DONAVON, Midwest Book Review

My brother Cedrick comes out of the closet like an educational cyclone with this book. After reading it you will be both blown away and enlightened. With each chapter I clutched my pearls, busted a gut laughing, and wept with his pain. This book is a must-read for all who seek to embrace and understand our LGBTQIA brothers and sisters. Once you read it, you cannot remain the same.

—DR. SHERON PATTERSON, Senior Pastor of
Hamilton Park United Methodist Church in Dallas, TX
and author of *The Blessings and Bling*

I have known Cedrick for many years but never knew the level of silent suffering he was experiencing in hiding as a Black, gay minister. I applaud the courage demonstrated on the pages of *Alabama Grandson* and hope this book will encourage others suffering from the fear of rejection and humiliation to embrace life fully while taking steps to live in the open. The truth is always the right thing to speak and this book is a manifesto of love and truth.

—DR. RUDY RASMUS, pastor, humanitarian and
author of *Love. Period. When All Else Fails*

Cedrick's writing is full of compelling stories that give you a lens into what it's like carrying a secret in silence. His stories capture each moment in a way that lets you inside his mind, heart and soul. This book is a courageous journey of healing in the pursuit of freedom and wholeness. Cedrick refers to it as a "passage out of hiding" but it's that and much more. *Alabama Grandson* is an example of what the rite of passage to freedom can look like when you can't hide any longer. It's both a powerful testimony and invitation for you to do the kind of inner-work that leads to healing for yourself and encouragement for others.

—ROMAL TUNE, author of *Love Is an Inside Job:
Getting Vulnerable with God*

Alabama Grandson

ALABAMA GRANDSON

A Black, Gay Minister's Passage Out of Hiding

CEDRICK D. BRIDGEFORTH

PRECOCITY PRESS

Copyright © 2021 by Cedrick D. Bridgeforth

All rights reserved. No part of this book may be used or reproduced in any manner without written permission from the author and publisher.

Editors: Ruth Mullen and Sara Volle
Creative Director and Cover Design: Susan Shankin
Book Design and Layout: Andrea Reider
Cover Art: Linda Furtado
Photo credit: Charles Loeb
Precocity Press, Venice, CA

This book contains material protected under International and Federal Copyright Laws and Treaties. No part of this publication may be reproduced, distributed, or transmitted in any form or by any means, including photocopying, recording, or other electronic or mechanical methods, without the prior written permission of the author, except in the case of brief quotations embodied in critical reviews and certain other noncommercial uses permitted by copyright law. For permission requests, email the publisher at: susan@precocitypress.com

This book is memoir. It reflects the author's present recollections of experiences over time. Some names and characteristics have been changed, some events have been compressed, and some dialogue has been recreated. The book was not intended to hurt anyone. Both my publisher and I regret any unintentional harm resulting from the publishing and marketing of *Alabama Grandson*.

ISBN: 978-1-7373539-5-9
Library of Congress Control Number: 2021915022
First edition printed in the United States of America

*To every person who was not always certain
that truth was the right thing to speak.*

CONTENTS

PREFACE

Dear Grandma,

I have some secrets I need to share with you. I'm on my way to the cemetery to spend time with you as I do each time I return to Alabama. Yet this time is different. Now, more than three decades after your passing, we face a global pandemic, civil unrest, and economic collapse. The current climate is so unlike any other I have known that leaving anything undone seems careless.

On the short walk from my car to your gravesite across the ankle-high Kentucky bluegrass and Bermuda strands, I'm consumed with anguish. Would you appreciate who I have become? Would you accept me or would you rebuff me? You were a wife, mother, grandmother, great-grandmother, sister, aunt, cousin; you were Southern Baptist, working class, conservative. You had a sixth-grade education. You were a seamstress, a midwife, and a great cook. You were impeccable with housework, a wiz in the garden, thrifty, a generous giver. Yet you never came across as a complex person. You were settled and secure in who you were.

I crave a similar clarity and confidence in my own life. But instead, I have struggled to embrace my own identities and celebrate my existence. I learned to lie about who I am. I learned to hide in plain sight. I faltered in intimate relationships and felt like an imposter in my professional realm. And finally, it all caught up with me. Several "dark nights of the soul" experiences culminated on a single day in 2015 and my whole world came tumbling down. I felt abandoned by the church and by close friends. All I had left was my faith in God and my hope that my life experiences and your imparted wisdom would sustain me.

Now, your voice melds back into my memories as I look across the great expanse of what was a pasture during my youth and a cotton field during yours. You were the most influential person in my life. Yet as much as I admired and appreciated you, I did not trust you enough to say to you: "I am gay."

I look down at the little plot of clay that holds your body and imagine introducing myself to you and filling in the blanks of who I have become. I hear your voice say, "Don't get that red clay on those white soles of your shoes unless you want everybody to know where you've been." I stoop down and scoop up a handful of that red earth and cup it in the palms of my hands. I let it sift between my fingers like sand through an hourglass. You lived over seventy years and yet never traveled farther than about a hundred miles from this place on earth where you now rest. Your world was so small and yet you knew so much about life.

The slow movement of the falling soil marks the end of the time spent at your gravesite. And in that moment, I make a decision: I commit to share who I am with you and with the world. The road to claim my intersecting and sometimes conflicting identities begins with what I learned from watching you and listening to the wisdom that flowed from your experiences. Now it is time to build a bridge back to you, a bridge from where I came to where I am.

Your grandson,
Cedrick

Fall from Grace with Dignity

In 2017, I flew to Texas to deliver a speech at a United Methodist conference. The audience knew me as a candidate for bishop just one year prior. My resume also included president of a national advocacy group, multiple high-level leadership roles in my denomination, consistent voice in the global conversation about the intersecting harm being done to LGBTQIA+ and people of color, and presumptive future leader in the church.

No one in that room knew I was currently a Lyft driver and a substitute teacher. Eighteen months had passed since this group first reached out to invite me to come. My life had been turned upside down from the time I received the invitation until the moment I walked to the podium to deliver that speech.

My world began to unravel one day in late 2015. I was driving to my church office. It seemed a normal Thursday morning. NPR was playing on the radio. I had a bag of midmorning snacks on the passenger seat of the car beckoning for some early attention. Traffic was slow and congested so when my phone buzzed, I took the call. It was a colleague, Bishop Dale.

"Hey, Doc! How are you this morning?"

"I'm doing alright for a Black man," I said. "I'm just heading to the office for a bit."

He got to the point. "Doc, I hope I am not catching you at a bad time but I have something I need to ask you about."

I was now approaching the on-ramp to the freeway and my eyes scanned the traffic ahead.

"Do you know someone by the name Shannon Davis?"

Without hesitation, I responded, "I do know Shannon. How do you know Shannon?"

"I received an email this morning from Shannon and it detailed some accusations about you that are not painting you in the best light."

My heart sank. "What? An email? I don't understand."

"Yeah, Doc. It showed up this morning in my in-box. I have no idea who else received it."

"What did it say?"

The next words that came through the phone crushed my spirit. Someone I had known and trusted for over a decade sent an unsolicited email about my sexuality and sexual activity to someone who had no idea I was gay. And I instantly understood that my colleague was not the only recipient. The email had been written in anger, and it was intended to hurt me. In most professions, an employee's sexual orientation and choice of partners has little or no bearing on their standing within the organization or company. In the church, that is not the case. As an unmarried ordained person, I was expected to be celibate. And there were additional prohibitions against non-heteronormative relationships.

I didn't say very much by way of admitting or discounting the litany of charges in the email. My discomfort was obvious. Before we ended the call, Bishop Dale said, "I don't know Shannon. I know you. I love you. I trust you. I am here to support you, so you tell me what you need. You may not know right now, but know I am here for you, Doc."

Holding back tears, I said, "Thank you. I appreciate you thinking enough of me to let me know about this."

I completed that call as I heard the voice of Steve Inskeep signing off for NPR's *Morning Edition*. The morning had barely begun, yet my whole world had come apart. I wanted and needed to scream, cry, and have someone pinch me so I could know if this was all a nightmare or if my career was about to be on the chopping block.

For almost eight years prior to this phone call, I served as a District Superintendent within the United Methodist Church, which meant I handled such accusations when they were levied against a clergyperson under my supervision. I saw what happened to these individuals, their families, and the churches they served when someone filed formal charges against them or even insinuated some impropriety was taking place. I had been in enough mediations and supervisory meetings to know that when someone was accused of multiple breaches of ordination vows and edicts of the church, the way back from that was tumultuous and painful, if it happened at all. Most walked away from the church without putting up much fight. Theirs were situations of infidelity, sexual misconduct, or abuse of power. But what was contained in that email about me were those three accusations—and more. I was devastated, tossed about in a tornado of emotions that began with fear, anger, and disgust and spiraled into shame, guilt, and worry.

I pulled over to catch my breath and then turned around and drove back home. As I passed through the picturesque gates of my apartment complex, I felt like I was being dragged into the public square for all the world to see, to judge, to despise and to cast aside. I wanted nothing to do with anyone that day, but hiding was not an option. I was gay. I had broken my vows and violated a sacred trust. I was in a relationship with a man. I was cohabitating with that man. I at least owed my partner the courtesy of informing him of how my life was about to be upended and how his would also be impacted.

I loved him and he loved me. He said, "This is bad, but we will get through this because we will go through this together."

His reassurance gave me the courage I needed to call my supervising bishop to request a meeting so I could confess what I needed to confess and debunk what I could. The remainder of that day my thoughts were like most days in the San Francisco Bay area—a gray fog of confusion. I never made it to my office, nor did I do any work. I could not stop catastrophizing about all the possibilities of how this scenario could play out. I wondered whether I had enough fight in me to even enter the battle. Whether I chose fight or flight, no matter what, I would have to confess to being gay and that was a chargeable offense on its own. Everything that was true in the email was enough to bring me down if not handled with justice and compassion.

My work—ensuring that emancipated youth had permanent housing, low-income families had secure places to live, immigrant families had thriving preschools and Head Start programs in their communities, re-imagined community-church partnerships that fed thousands each month, and projects to destigmatize mental health and HIV/AIDS in African American church communities—could be erased. My life and livelihood could be undone by one person's description of me in one email. The more I ruminated about it the more I resolved to at least try to center my defense in the context of my full story, a narrative of travail and triumph from weathering my parent's divorce to learning my true paternity, exploring my sexual identity, and trying to serve the world in ways that mattered beyond financial gains.

When I arrived at the bishop's office the next morning, I was directed into a large conference room. The bishop sat on one side of the table and I sat on the other. The room was arranged for twenty people and they just as well had been there with us because I felt totally exposed and vulnerable. I had a great working relationship with the bishop and trusted this to be a collegial and supportive conversation. My goal was preemptive: I did not want him to learn about the email or its contents from anyone other than me.

I got straight to the point. "I want you to know that there is an email floating around that makes some pretty horrific accusations against me." The bishop leaned forward and stopped me mid-sentence. "I know about the email. I received it yesterday."

Every motor function I had ground to a halt. "You know?"

"Yes, and this is a very serious matter."

"Well, if you are treating it as a serious matter, then I think it best that I refrain from volunteering information."

"Oh! No need for that, my brother. This is serious and we will work through this together."

I felt relieved and I trusted what was spoken in that room that day. I departed after a few hours of conversation about possible outcomes and steps I needed to take.

I would spend the next few months going through the church's equivalent of depositions and inquiries into the intimate details of my relationships, travels, and psychological well-being. All of that was required so that I could clear my name, hold on to my job, and maintain a sense of dignity and self-respect—even if the church determined I was too great a liability for its roster.

I decided to own my truth, admit the wrongs I had done, and accept the missteps I had taken that led to this awful situation. I was a same-gender-loving man who was in a committed cohabitational relationship with a man. I had to own it if I was to be open and transparent with the church, my family, my partner, and myself. My choice to hide in plain sight of the church's prohibitions had not served me well. Now I would go public about how I violated my vows. I felt naked in my humiliation. What would come of me and the hopes and dreams I held so dearly and the reputation I had crafted so meticulously?

PART ONE

HIDING IN PLAIN SIGHT

CHAPTER 1

TRUST YOUR GUT

Try Something New

It was always the simplest of things with her. My grandmother worked miracles almost every day. A minimally educated woman, she was an avid reader of the Bible and other literature related to the Bible. She made everything seem so easy, planned, and purposeful. When she was not toiling on the small family farm with my grandfather, she worked as a domestic for white families in the area. She cooked and cleaned for them and often served as the primary caregiver for their children. By all accounts, she also made sure her own children never felt neglected or second-rate.

Grandma made the most out of what she had, whether that was using the plums that had overripened on the tree and fallen to the ground to make wine and preserves or mixing herbal elixirs that she swore would cure any ailment. There was a Houdini-like quality about her too. She could make dresses that looked like something she saw in the window of Cato's Dress Shop while walking down Main Street or in the pages of her JCPenney or Sears catalogs.

If Las Vegas is the venue for magicians to perform their magic, then my grandma's kitchen was the stage where she truly demonstrated her sleight of hand. One of my fondest memories of early childhood relates to my experience of going to Head Start. It was held in the lone remaining building of what had been the Morgan County Training School, our local Black high school prior to desegregation and where my mother completed high school. As a three- or four-year-old child, I would not have known that historic connection or its significance.

At Head Start, we were served cinnamon toast for our midmorning snack. I don't recall anything as delicious as that bread toasted just enough to make a crunchy sound, covered with sprinkled bursts of cinnamon and sugar. My teachers knew they could get me to do almost anything if they bartered with that cinnamon toast.

It was so good that one day when Head Start was not in session and my siblings and I were at grandma's house while our parents were at work, I asked, "Grandma, can you make that sweet toast we have at school?"

She said, "When my stories go off, I can make you any kind of toast you want."

"Stories" is what the old Black women called daytime soap operas.

True to her word, somewhere in between the escapades of Mrs. Chancellor and Victor Newman on *The Young and the Restless* and the whirlwind love affair between Luke and Laura on *General Hospital*, she made that sweet toast.

She called for us to come into the kitchen. We ran as quickly as we could.

"Y'all sit down and grandmama gonna serve y'all this sweet toast."

I was so excited. Since Grandma could make my favorite toast, I did not have to go back to school. The three of us kids sat at the round Formica table with its design of roses and carnations encircled by a red and yellow ring at the center. We could only see half of the flower design because grandma used the other half of that table to stack boxes of canned goods, preserves she stockpiled for the winter months, and old paper bags.

Grandma served her toast on small yellow dessert plates, one for each of us. "Here ya go! Y'all go on and eat so you can get outside and play before my other stories come on."

I stared at my plate in dismay. "This ain't like the toast they make at school."

Her head seemed to swivel around on her neck as she asked, "What is wrong with it? Didn't you ask for sweet toast?"

"Yes ma'am, but not this color."

"What do you mean? It's sweet. Grandma put extra sugar on it for you."

"The school lady makes hers brown. Yours is white."

"Oh! They probably use brown sugar and I used white sugar. Baby, it's ok. It's all sugar. You will like my white one better."

Grandma encouraged me to take one bite to determine if I liked it. I took a tiny bite and it tasted like sugar. I took another bite, and another, until the toast was gone.

By the time I finished, I was a fan of grandma's version of sweet toast. It wasn't what I imagined but it opened me to the idea that there are multiple means of achieving a goal.

She was an authority in the kitchen and she did not eat everybody's cooking. During church potluck suppers she would tell us to get in line behind her and we were only allowed to take food from the containers that she took from. I was in my early teens before I realized that she was only taking food from the containers she brought. I attended church potlucks regularly from as early as I can remember until I left for the Air Force at age eighteen, and I do not know how any of the other church ladies' cooking tasted.

One of her dessert specialties was sweet potato pie. Most everyone who tried her pies said they were the best they had ever had. She would make ten to fifteen at a time—six or seven would go to the church, four or five to neighbors, and the others were for our Sunday dinner and snacks.

On one occasion she was responsible for baking pies for an event. She spent most of the day in the kitchen boiling sweet potatoes and prepping all the ingredients. It was a true treat to be there when the pies came out of the oven, but it was even more advantageous to be nearby when the first one was cool. Grandma would always give us a sliver of warm pie and a glass of milk.

That night, she placed five small dessert plates on the table along with forks and paper napkins. My brother climbed up to retrieve five Mason jars from the cupboard for our milk. As I poured the milk, he took a first bite of his pie. "Grandma! Something is soggy in here."

My grandfather looked at him with disgust. He took a bite and his face changed. "There is something wrong with this pie," he said.

My grandma was beside herself. "Y'all know those are the best pies you have ever tasted. Stop messing around. I'm done with this."

My mom took a bite. "Mama, did you buy this crust?"

Grandma was quite indignant as she responded, "I sure did."

Mom said, "Ma'am, you left the wax paper on the bottom of the crust. You can't serve this."

Grandma used to say that "shortcuts will do you in every time." And sometimes she'd add: "If you do it right the first time, you won't have to do it again." Those words come to mind as I think about the day she tried to use premade crust to make her prized pies. My mom had to go to several grocery stores to find enough of the right type of sweet potatoes for grandma to make a new batch of pies.

Don't Tell Lies

As a high school student, I worked at Sonic Drive-In. I would like to say that was my first job, but it was not. Prior to Sonic, I worked briefly as a dishwasher at Quincy's Family Steakhouse. I was fired because I lied about my age to get the job. If I were sixteen years old and in possession of a work permit, I could work part-time.

When the manager who interviewed me saw my last name, he asked, "Do you know Greg Bridgeforth?"

I said, "Yes. He is one of my dad's younger brothers."

He said, "Great! I went to school with Greg. How's he doing?"

I was not in regular communication with my Uncle Greg. But, as Hamilton says in the musical, "I was not throwing away my shot." I realized this was an opportunity I could not waste, so I responded, "He is doing great!" To cement our connection, I added, "He's my cool uncle."

He said, "You are from a good family. So, when can you start?"

That would have been a good time to let him know that I was not yet sixteen. Instead, I replied, "Right away!"

He broke out a stack of forms for me to complete and asked, "Did you bring your work permit with you?"

It hadn't occurred to me that I would have to produce it right away. But with the prospect of employment right in front of me, I decided I would try to get through the summer and acquire a permit as soon as I turned sixteen, in the fall.

I said, "No. I will bring it to you."

And so, in a matter of minutes I went from being scared and jobless to being a confidently employed teen riding on a lie. That's what happens when a child goes out into the world thinking he knows how the world works.

That charade only lasted a few weeks. It was a Friday, payday for the employees, and the second busiest shift of the week. (The busiest, of course, was after church on Sunday afternoons.) I arrived a few minutes early and was hanging out in the parking lot with Frank, a coworker. He was going into tenth grade at one of the large high schools in Decatur. That fateful Friday, we sat listening to music in Frank's brown sedan with vanity plates that read "ROOM4U."

I should have known there was an issue right away. On this particular day, after Frank and I finished listening to his cassette tape in the car his grandfather had given him and it was time to go inside and clock in, he told me to go in first and he would be along later. That was odd. But I made my way across the parking lot that was slowly filling with families, baseball and softball teams, and others who fancied nothing more on a Friday night in Decatur, Alabama, than the less-than-fresh all-you-can-eat salad bar, over-cooked baked potatoes, and sub-par steaks. As I approached the timeclock, the manager poked his head out of the office. He said, "I need to talk to you before you clock in."

Every day he'd made a point of asking me for my permit. I'd concocted an assortment of responses: "I forgot again," "My mom has it," or "I may have to call the school to get another copy." But this time, he shut the door behind us, raised his hand as if he were silencing a crowd, and announced: "I cannot allow you to work here."

I responded indignantly. "I told you I will get the permit to you, and I will."

He said, "No. Stop. You have lied to me and I cannot let that slide."

I crumpled my face so as to present an image to him of some-one who was confused. I asked him, "What's the problem? I haven't been late or missed a day of work and I'm doing a good job. You said so yourself!"

He stood behind his paper-ridden desk and said, "I have spo-ken with your uncle. He said you are a good kid. A smart kid. But he told me you are fifteen. You said you had a work permit and you don't. I think I've known that all along, but out of respect for your uncle, I wanted to give you the benefit of the doubt. I can't trust people once they lie to me. If you lied about this, how do I know you wouldn't steal or lie about something else?"

"But Uncle Greg told you that I was a good person. I don't understand why you can't just let me work." In the same way that I thought I knew enough to get by on a lie, I was also mistaken to believe the manager's admiration for my uncle would outweigh my missing credentials.

I pleaded, "Give me another chance."

He said, "That's not possible. It is against the law for you to work without the permit. And other employees, like Frank, know you don't have a permit."

Still fighting to hold onto my first job, I said, "I can tell Frank not to say anything to anybody about it."

The manager said, in a paternalistic tone, "Frank is my nephew. He needs to know that I will do the right thing even when it is difficult to do it."

I was beside myself. I quickly went from feeling great strength to fight for my dishwashing job at Quincy's Family Steakhouse, which filed for bankruptcy a few years later, to hanging my head in shame as the manager wrote out one last check for the hours I had worked.

I rushed out of the office with my check, wondering how many of the other employees knew I lied and had been fired. I walked past the time clock with all the little yellow cards with our names and employee numbers on them, past the heavy metal racks that held the large pans of foil-wrapped potatoes, and over to the dishwasher area where I came face to face with Frank. He looked at me and said, "I'm sorry, man, but you should have told the truth." I could not argue with him. This was a lesson my grandma had tried to instill in us. She would say, "If a person lies, they will cheat. If they cheat, they will steal. If they steal, they will kill. If they will kill, there is no reason to stick around."

That was a lot for a young person to comprehend and apply when there seemed to be so many different types of lies. Did she mean even little white lies, like about one's weight or age? Did her aphorism include Santa Claus, the Easter Bunny, and the Tooth Fairy?

This question about which lies mattered would become even more convoluted as I grew older and realized that my grandmother did not give birth to my mom's youngest brother, although she loved and scolded him the same as she did her other children. My grandparents never divorced or separated. My grandfather was unfaithful to her at a point in their marriage and they remained together. How had they managed that transgression? What did he know to say to get a second chance that I could not conjure in that manager's office to get a second chance? She was a woman who knew the necessity of boundless grace for others and an unrelenting faith in God. He was a man who knew the character of the woman he wed at age seventeen and remained married to until his body succumbed to cancer nearly eleven years after she died.

When I sat at his funeral in August 1999, I thought about my grandparents and wondered how one truly regains respect from others after violating their trust. The question brought pain because the better part of my own life was a lie. I hid my sexuality from most people by not talking about it and from myself by telling myself that one day I would wake up and no longer be gay. I hid my Black consciousness even though my actual blackness is something I never escaped or eluded in any way—not even when I thought I was blending in with my white friends and lovers. My religion, politics, economics, education, marital status, and sexual proclivities were hidden and closeted until or unless I released them. I had mastered hiding in plain sight.

Leaving Is Sometimes Best

I often say the best thing my parents ever did for us, for themselves, and for the world was to decide to divorce. We lived about twenty miles away from my grandparents until I was ten years old. Up to that point we lived on my dad's family farm, surrounded by my dad's family. As a child I noted differences between the two sides of my family. On my dad's side, most of his twelve siblings lived within the confines of or adjacent to the family farm. All his adult brothers had some function on the farm. Three of his five sisters provided support for the farm at various times. Most of them completed college. There was a mystique and pride that came with the Bridgeforth name in that region and family gatherings were always large and extended. Yet, I did not feel completely a Bridgeforth. My facial features, hair texture, and eye color were not like theirs, and that made me suspicious of them and of my own reality.

My mom's seven siblings lived relatively far from each other. Most of them worked in factories. Only my mom's oldest sister attended and graduated from college. The bloodlines and storylines were not always clear on that side of the family. It was difficult to decipher who was or was not a relative and how I was related to them. We never had a family reunion and there were multiple sets of Griffins in the world. Yet I seemed to connect more with my mom's side and I felt more welcomed and included.

When my parents met and married, they worked together at a spark plug manufacturing plant in Decatur. They lived with my paternal great-grandmother until they built their first home on the plot of land my paternal grandfather gifted to each of his children upon adulthood. Within two years my mom gave birth to my brother, Marcus. I came along almost three years later, and my sister Quanza was born four years after me. My father had four other children, three of whom grew up with me. In their nearly sixteen years of marriage, my parents separated at least three times that I recall. There was verbal abuse, excessive alcohol use, and various financial disruptions. The arguments were repetitive and more vicious than violent. Infidelity was a third party in their marriage.

One late night my mom got me out of bed and told me to get in the car.

We drove for what seemed like a hundred miles to a seven year old. As we passed along dark and narrow streets, I heard dogs barking in the distance. The houses were not as nice as ours. There were towels or sheets serving as curtains, living room furniture on front porches, and cars parked on the lawns.

My mom slowly pulled up in front of a house that had lights on. I could see people dancing through the windows. She said, "Go knock on that door and tell your daddy you kids need lunch money for tomorrow."

I don't know why he hadn't left the money on the counter in the kitchen in the three stacks that were usually there each morning. As I walked across this stranger's lawn, I heard music and laughter. I wondered who lived in this house—could it belong to one of my cousins, uncles, or aunts?

When I stepped on the porch, a dog lying in front of the door rose to its feet. A few years earlier I had run from a dog—my grandfather's Doberman, Red. He chased me the quarter mile from grandfather's house to ours. I was terrified he would eat me alive. As I ran inside and slammed the door behind me, Mom asked what was wrong.

I breathed out the words, "Red. Chase. Bit. Ran."

I touched the back of my pants and felt a hole. My pocket had been ripped. I screamed and cried even louder until my mom told me I was fine. She said, "Next time, don't run. Just stand there and don't look him in the eye. Just stand still."

Recalling her words, I tried to charm this dog. Speaking soothingly in the same voice I would use to quiet my sister to get her to go to sleep, I took another step toward the door. I saw his tail begin wagging and I knew that meant I was not in danger of being mauled.

Just then, the door opened as a woman's voice said, "Whose car is that sitting in front . . . ?"

The woman paused when she saw me standing at the edge of the porch. She shooed the dog away and asked, "Boy, what are you doing on my porch?"

I pointed in the direction of our car and said, "I'm here to get lunch money from my daddy."

"Who is your daddy? What's his name?"

"George, ma'am."

"I got at least two of those in here." She flung the door completely open and I could see into the large front room. "Do you see him?"

I pointed. "That's him in the green John Deere cap."

"Oh! You Bridgeforth's son."

"I'm one of his sons. I have two older brothers and three younger sisters."

"That's nice, baby. Who is in that car?"

"My mama. She said we need lunch money for tomorrow so she sent me up here to get it."

The lady was tall and pretty. She looked a lot like my Aunt Rose but I had never seen this woman before. She motioned for me to come in.

The presence of a seven-year-old boy did not slow down the festivities. As I approached the table where my dad was engrossed in a card game, he looked in my direction. He looked back at the cards in his hand and then back at me as if he could not believe his eyes. He said, "Hey, hey! Wait! I know she didn't. What are you doing here?"

"Mama said we need lunch money for tomorrow."

He threw his cards down on the table and guided me by my shoulders toward the front door and onto the porch. Once outside, he removed his hand from my shoulder and advanced quickly toward the car. The dog looked up with just as much confusion as I felt in that moment. He joined me on the steps and I rubbed his head. I could hear a familiar rhythm and cadence in my mom and dad's exchange. I did not need to know the words. I had most likely heard them before.

After a few minutes, Dad called me over. When I got in the car, he slammed the door and walked away. I saw money on the floor. I picked it up as we drove home. That was not the last time I made a drive like that with my mom. It was not the last time I rubbed the head of that dog. I saw other neighborhoods that did not look like the family farm where we lived. I encountered other dogs of all types and sizes. I stepped in some mud puddles and was offered fried chicken. No matter where we went to find him, the woman who opened the door was always nice to me.

When my parents divorced, we moved from Tanner to Hartselle, three miles from my mom's parents. I was elated. That move changed everything for me. I had developed a reputation as a less-than-average student, and moving to a new school gave me a fresh start. The pressure to work on the farm was eliminated. I no longer had to listen to my parents argue about everything. I could spend more time with my grandparents. I could remake my entire existence. And that is what I did.

Prayer Changes Things

Jackson was my favorite male cousin because he was mild-mannered, stylish, and had a thing for sports cars. He also engaged me differently than others did. It was as though he saw me and he heard me. Jackson was not dismissive. He resembled my grandma in that way. I could ask him ten times to take me for a ride around the block on his motorcycle and he would do it. Jackson worked at one of the large manufacturing plants along the Tennessee River and we were proud of him for landing that job. Many people prayed for him to find a good job and he did.

My grandparents' house sat near the corner of a dead-end street. Everyone who came or went on McGaugh Street had to pass their house. The polite Southern thing to do whenever a car or pedestrian passed was to wave and offer a verbal acknowledgment. Exchanges were not lengthy, and they had a cadence that guided them.

"Hi, Mr. and Mrs. Griffin."

"Hey, baby! How are you doing? Alright?"

"Yes'm. How y'all doing?"

"We are doing alright. How's the family?"

"Everybody's doing good."

All of that would ensue without the pedestrian slowing their stride or my grandparents pausing in their pea-shelling, corn-shucking, or fence-painting. If we were eating, food would be offered: "You better come have some." The common response was, "No thank you, but it does look good." Everyone knew the unwritten rule: never, ever pass people on the porch or in the yard without acknowledging their presence. If you did, you were considered rude and you would hear about it. My grandmother would recall at the end of the day all those who passed and any information she'd learned about them and include it in her prayers and future inquiries.

That front yard was a sanctuary for those who rested in its reach in the same way that little house expanded to provide shelter to whoever needed it for however long they needed it. The maple tree was a modern-day brush harbor, like where the slaves would steal away for respite and revival from the brutality of the work and life they endured. It was where many secrets were shared and truths spoken that transformed people's lives, one prayer or one conversation at a time.

One sweltering afternoon we were sitting in that small front yard eating watermelon under the expansive canopy of the large maple tree. Just as grandma never missed an opportunity to pray or to share some wisdom with others, granddaddy never missed a plot of dirt he could transform into a garden. He particularly loved to grow watermelons. He'd put that fresh watermelon in a green ice chest and cover it with ice. It would take approximately three hours for the watermelon to cool in that ice chest. At least, that is what we were told by both grandparents and because they said it, it was true.

We would nearly lose our minds when we would see that green cooler sitting under the tree in the front yard because it meant watermelon joy was imminent. When I was a child waiting for watermelon to chill, there was not much that could distract my attention, except the presence of my cousin Jackson.

His arrival at grandma's by motorcycle was not received any differently than if he'd strolled past the house on foot, ridden a bike, or pushed a lawnmower. If I was ever going to have competition for who was my grandparents' favorite grandchild, it would be Jackson. I am sure he was always a close second. It could have been because he was the oldest male grandchild, but it was most likely because grandma served as the midwife who helped bring him into this world. Not only was she a skilled and revered midwife, she also had canine-like hearing.

Long before anyone else heard or saw a motorcycle, she said, "That can't be nobody but Jackson."

My grandfather asked, "What? Where is Jackson? I don't see him."

She said, "I hear that loud music coming. It has to be him."

A few moments later my cousin Jackson's sporty motorcycle rounded the curve that led to McGaugh Street.

The volume of the music lowered quickly as he approached my grandparents' house. They were not opposed to loud music; they just didn't want it in front of their house.

Jackson parked on the street and walked around the white clapboard fence wearing navy blue coveralls like those other men in my family wore to work on the farm, fix cars, or help a neighbor repair a leaky faucet. Unlike theirs, Jackson's were official because there was a rectangular white patch above the right pocket with "Jackson" stitched in red. Most people called him by his last name for most of his life, so as an adult he lived into that moniker. If you met him when he was five years old or twenty-five years old, he was Jackson and he always had a million-dollar smile.

His smile that day was as bright as I had ever seen it. As he hugged grandma and granddaddy, gave me a playful push on my left shoulder, and picked up my little sister and spun her around, it was obvious he was excited, happy, or preparing to make a monumental request.

Grandma asked, "What's going on with you today? Get you some of this watermelon. Daddy just cut it."

Granddaddy added, "You have a good day at work? I like those new tires."

It was not uncommon for them to team up on you with a dual prosecutorial approach, questions and statements woven together before you could offer a full response. I am not sure if that is a southern thing or something they did because they had been together so long or if it was just their way of speaking. I heard other relatives enter and maneuver conversations the same way, but I do not know if that came from generations before, or if my grandparents were the masters and propagators of the technique.

Jackson replied, "I have some good news to share."

"Really?"

"Yes! I came directly here from the plant so I could tell you first."

"You know better than to leave us in the dark. What's done happened?"

"They made me the shift supervisor."

Granddaddy said, "You're going to be in charge of the whole plant? I'm guessing it's just your department."

Grandma added, "Son, that is great. We are proud of you."

Jackson said, "Grandma, I have to give God all the credit. God did it. God did that for me."

Grandma turned all the way around so she could look him directly in the eye. She asked, "You say God did that for you?"

"Yes ma'am. God is the only one who could have made that happen."

She said, "Well, just imagine if you lived right."

Grandma was vicious when it came to the art, discipline, and practice of prayer. She wanted us to know that God was always working on our behalf and if we bothered or tried to live better and more faithful lives, God would do even more for us. It was sharp to the ear and piercing to the soul to be challenged in that way, but we knew we could always do better.

Power in Prayer

I first learned the power of prayer one hot summer day when I was nine years old. My mom worked long hours in a factory and it was obvious the work was hard on her physically and mentally. She was like my grandma in that when she asked for something to be done there was not an expectation of a discussion, negotiation, or vote—it was as good as done. One day she asked me to wash the dishes before going outside to play. I chose to go outside for a little while, with the anticipation of getting the dishes done before she woke from her nap. Not long into my play period and her alleged nap, the front screen door swung open. She yelled, "Didn't I tell you to wash those dishes before you could go outside?"

"Yes ma'am."

"Why are you outside and there are dishes in the sink?"

"I was gonna wash them in a minute."

"Well, I am gonna show you something in a minute. Go get me a switch."

I began to cry and run toward the porch instead of toward the hedgerow of plum bushes and blackberry vines where we would normally go to retrieve a branch that would be used to inflict punishment upon us. My crying turned to wailing when I reached the front porch only to watch her bound off, saying, "You wait right here. I will go get it."

There were three brick steps that led up to the porch. At that moment they became pillows for my limp body as I collapsed onto them and allowed my tears to consecrate the porch as my altar. I clasped my hands and began to pray, "God, help me. Please let something happen to her. Don't let her whoop me today. I'm sorry. I was gonna wash the dishes, God. Please help me."

As I sat with my eyes closed, tears flowing, and prayed, I heard loud screams from the direction of the hedge. I stood to my feet but was too short to see over the berm where the trees were. It was my mom. She was running and screaming, "Lord help me! Lord Jesus, help me!" She ran past me into the house and slammed the door behind her. I looked to see if there was a bandit or a Doberman, but I did not see anyone. I went inside. She was nestled on the floor in between the tufted light blue sofa and white marble coffee table. This was odd because no one ever went into that room. It was for show only.

I asked her, "What happened? What's wrong?"

She continued to shake and cry. I knelt next to her.

"Did I do something else bad? Why are you crying?"

"There was a snake wrapped around that tree."

"A snake?"

"He hissed at me."

I looked up toward Heaven and said, "Thank you, God."

Be Your Own Advocate

Prayer was a key concept but equally as powerful for me was self-advocacy, which I learned during my junior year of high school when Boys State came onto my radar. By then I was already well versed in the finer points of challenge and debate. Jamie, the love of my life—along with Janet Jackson, the pop star, and Rosemary, my high school girlfriend—returned from Boys State and told me I should apply to attend the following year. I asked my guidance counselor, Mr. Dawson, to provide me with an application. He did, and he also volunteered the information that no one else from our school had applied.

Each school could send two rising seniors to the event. The fact that no one else from my school had applied made me a shoo-in. In fact, this was so far removed from anyone's awareness at my school that Mr. Dawson had to call the local American Legion Post to get the registration forms and submission dates. He suggested I let others know of the opportunity, so I told someone who I thought would also be interested and able to go.

Jack was not my best friend but he was certainly a good one. We were both on the football team and the yearbook staff, and loved to make people laugh. When I explained the purpose and potential of Boys State to him, he expressed moderate interest. Jack thought it wise to discuss it with his parents before he went too far with the idea. In my mind, that seemed a definite "no." I reasoned they would respond negatively because I projected my mom's reaction onto his mom and dad. That being the case, I moved on to my second choice, Jason Edendale.

I'd known Jason since sixth grade. From the first time I laid eyes on him, I thought he was cute. He was always kind to me and exuded creativity and mystery at the same time. We were friendly and the idea that we would get to travel to Birmingham for time away from our families was something magical. That is the best way to describe the fantasies I conjured in my mind. Although I knew I was gay, I was not sure about him. This could be our chance to become even closer and learn more about each other. Jason was a little less enthusiastic about Boys State than Jack had been but he did not have any concerns about whether his parents would support the idea.

A few weeks passed. The next thing we heard was when Mr. Dawson informed me that I had not been selected as one of the two representatives from our school. My heart sank. To be told that the two individuals I encouraged to apply would be going and I would not was devastating. They were both good students with great promise and potential, but had I not brought the idea to them, they would never have known about it.

My protests were immediate and unrelenting. Every teacher who would listen heard from me. The principal, vice principal, and my coaches were made aware of what happened and how it happened. Eventually, Jason withdrew his application and the decision was made to send me as one of our school's two representatives.

My excitement upon arriving at Boys State on the campus of Samford University quickly turned into horror when I saw a brown sedan parked outside the dormitory with "ROOM4U" vanity plates. A full year had passed since I was fired from Quincy's Family Steakhouse. I quickly told Jack an abbreviated version of the story, slanted to make me sound more like the victim than the perpetrator. I don't know if it worked.

Jack asked, "What are you gonna do? Is he someone you want to be around?"

I said, "I don't really know. I didn't do anything to him, so it should be fine. I just don't want him telling other people about it."

Jack laughed and assured me that he had my back. He and I were both on our school's fledgling football team. We were not burly athletic types and were often underestimated when it came to strength, speed, and ability to reason our way out of most situations.

As it turned out, Jack and I were assigned to different dorms and I only saw him a few times that week. Boys State is designed to give rising seniors an opportunity to learn more about civic government and policymaking. Each dormitory was a "city" and within each city there were districts. Each city had elected officials who served in leadership. Other participants served in state-level offices. I chose to run for state party chairman. I did not have signs printed or buttons to pass out. I was not aware of the amount of pre-planning that many put into Boys State before arriving.

To be elected as chairman I had to give an impromptu two-minute speech to the entire assembly. Since I had a speaking role in church on most Sundays, I was not nervous about being on the stage but I was nervous about what to say. In the church there are key phrases that move things along and get a response regardless of who says them or how they are spoken. This was different. In my mind everyone in that auditorium knew more than me and deserved to be there more than me. In my mind none of them came from families that struggled financially or had deep dark secrets. In my mind all of them had prepped for this moment and knew exactly what to say to sway the crowd to vote for them.

When they called for all who were interested in the chairman's position to go backstage, the adult chaperone for my city nudged me and said, "You have to go now." Uncertain, I said, "I don't know." He said, "I do. Go!"

I went backstage and took my position in line with the other contestants. One by one they went onstage to make their speech and then returned backstage to handshakes and affirmation. I was the final candidate to speak. When I returned backstage, I received handshakes and affirmation just as every other candidate had received. With that, I started to feel more like one of them. I felt like I fit in. A hand vote was taken in the auditorium and the field was narrowed to two of us. We were asked to return to the stage and offer a one-minute speech before the final vote. My opponent ended his speech by mimicking Oral Roberts' infamous claim that God would call him home if he did not raise eight million dollars for his university. The audience laughed vigorously.

While they were still laughing, I took the microphone and said, "There is no way God would take *me* from here because I am the one you need to lead this party to victory!" The crowd roared with applause. I went on to describe what I believed I could offer by way of ideas and leadership. After that, the vote was taken and I was elected.

In addition to our elected and appointed roles, we engaged in sports, music, and art as extracurricular activities. I chose to run track and sing in the choir as my activities. One of my track mates and dorm mates was Chris Granberry. He lived in the Birmingham area and was the fastest white boy I had ever competed against, but that was not what struck me most about him. What drew me to Chris was the fact that he was also a church boy. He spoke fervently about his faith and did not express any of the hesitancy or shame that I sometimes felt when speaking about church, God, or my beliefs when outside of the congregational context. We would stay up past curfew most nights, sharing stories about our families and friends. We dreamed aloud of his future vocation as a missionary and mine as an architect.

Just before lights out on the last night of Boys State, he pulled me aside and said he wanted to have a talk with me about my life. As it turned out, he wanted to ask whether I was really a Christian. Although he didn't say so, it was glaringly obvious that his questioning was because I had disclosed to him, in a moment of vulnerability and comfort, that I was attracted to men. When the words came out of my mouth, they floated as clouds through the sky—effortless and natural. Chris seemed to take what I said in stride and we moved through the days that followed without a mention.

That last night, we stayed out so late the chaperone assigned to our dorm came out to check on us about every half hour until finally he said, "Boys, it is two o'clock in the morning. I want to sleep and both of you have to pack in the morning and head out. Exchange numbers and you can talk to each other for the rest of your lives." Oddly enough, I was the one who responded, "We will get to bed right after we pray with each other. We promise." The chaperone acquiesced and walked away. Chris and I held hands while sitting on the steps in front of our dorm and we prayed for and with each other. As we closed the prayers, we embraced for what seemed an eternity. My disclosure to Chris began a near seven-year hiatus before I would share such information with anyone other than a potential partner or sojourner within the gay sphere.

Pray Without Ceasing

I learned a different aspect of prayer at the end of my fourth and final year of service in the Air Force. The church I attended was committed to prayer and the power that could come when the whole church banded together to "touch and agree" on a matter. Their persistence and commitment mirrored that of my grandmother.

I did not have a plan for what I would do after the Air Force beyond enrolling in college and staying near Cheyenne so I would not be far from my church family. I stood up in service one Friday night in early 1992 and shared my desire with the congregation. "When I am discharged from the Air Force, I am going to college. I ask that all of you join me in prayer about that. I want to know where I should go. I need a scholarship."

Everyone began to pray. They did not pray as I had on that porch—not that I still believed God put that snake there to save me that day. They did not pray for bad things to happen. I trusted they had my best interest at heart.

Shortly after I submitted my application to Colorado State University, all of New Kingdom Church began to pray that I would be accepted and that I would receive a sizable scholarship. They also prayed that I would receive an early release from the Air Force because at the time there was a freeze on discharges due to the military buildup for Desert Storm—the first Gulf War. After a while they expanded the prayer to include a good-paying job and a place to live. It took some time but eventually answers to those prayers began to appear.

The first answer came when I received my acceptance letter and clearance to enroll in the Occupational Therapy program at Colorado State University. The second answer came from the Air Force when I was approved for early release. The third answer came when I was awarded a sizable scholarship and an on-campus job with benefits. Another answer came when I was informed there was space available in a dormitory that housed nontraditional older students.

The pastor called me to stand in front of the congregation. He put his arm around my shoulder and said, "God has answered every prayer we prayed for you. God did more than we ever imagined." The church was elated.

A few days before I was to move from Francis E. Warren Air Force Base to my dorm at Colorado State, I began to feel uneasy. When I was in high school and I decided to attend Boys State and run for class president, those decisions had a lasting impact on my life—but I did not know they were life-changing decisions at the time. They were easy. The decision to enlist in the Air Force was more monumental but I was able to make it without much concern.

Now that I was faced with what to do after the Air Force, I was stalled, just days before I was to start down the new path.

I felt confused. I believed God was telling me to "go home." But why would God answer the prayers for college admission, scholarships, housing, and a job, if I was not supposed to take that path? Second, I had heard people say that God "spoke" to them. I wasn't hearing a clear voice—my experience was more like an inaudible prompting, a deep sense of knowing.

Feeling foolish, I reached out to my pastor and explained how I was struggling. He said, "Son, only you can know if God is speaking to you. You have to let go of pride, ego, and even what you want to truly hear God. The most important thing here is not that you get what you want or that you feel God gave you what you asked for when you prayed. What matters right now is whether you will do what God wants you to do." Those were wise and hard words to hear.

I hadn't told him everything. I had been in a passionate intimate relationship that suddenly turned deeply painful. My sexuality was secret and my identities were compartmentalized then, and so there was no one I could talk to about what I was going through. That dam would not break until much later.

Now I simply felt lost. I could not eat or sleep. My anxiety increased by the day. I called my mom and told her I believed God was telling me to come home. She asked, "Do you have time to do that before classes start?" She, like me, did not get it either. I told her that I was struggling because I felt the urge was not about a temporary visit. She said, "You listen to God and everything will be fine. Whatever you decide, I will be right here."

After days of praying and agonizing, I told my pastor and the congregation that after all that prayer and celebration, after all that we believed God had provided, I was going to walk away from it all. I was to return to Alabama without a vision, plan, or prospects.

CHAPTER 2

DO THE RIGHT THINGS

Swim in the Daytime

I was never a hard drug user or drinker, but pills of any kind—uppers, downers, it did not matter—were my drug of choice during my senior year of high school. No one suspected because I was the model student, scholar, athlete, and son. I was an avid church leader. I was revered by my peers and elders as one "all youth could look up to." I taught a Sunday School class; I was president of our Youth Fellowship. I even traveled with the family singing group my grandparents started. Why would anyone suspect me?

The secret that I would take any pill anyone gave me was safely held within a small group of close friends and football teammates who also had their demons on display. We would tell our parents we were going to the library to do research for a school project, but we would actually go buy beer and find somewhere to hang out in Decatur, which was the nearest city to our school and where we lived. It was also where the regional library was located. The convenient fact that also drew us there was that Decatur had recently voted to become a "wet" city. That meant alcohol could now be sold legally within the city limits. Prior to legalized liquor sales, the only ways to get alcohol were to drive about thirty miles to the Madison County line, risk being shot at by a bootlegger, or make your own home brew, all of which were problematic options for teens. A few of my friends knew some local bootleggers and moonshiners but being their customers was too risky. The newly elected sheriff was keen on shutting them down and we didn't want to be there when a raid was taking place.

Ironically or poetically, I was the only African American in my immediate group of friends who would make this regular trek to Decatur. We would go to the Black area and target one of the winos hanging around the liquor store. We would tell him what to buy for us and give him extra money to buy what he wanted for himself. We were crafty country kids trying to play a big-city game.

One of our hangouts was a ruined plantation house out on the edge of town. It was an abandoned property that still had a semblance of what it once was. Situated far off the main road, it stood two stories and spanned at least fifty feet across the front. There were floor-to-ceiling windows in every room. The façade was painted white, and the outline of what was once a wraparound porch could be seen by the brown band of unpainted wood where the porch supports once held the porch in place. The interior was even more mesmerizing. There was a spiral staircase to the second floor and delicate floral patterns still intact on the wallpaper throughout the grand foyer and what must have been the living room. I don't remember who told us about the place, but we were hooked on it. We would often run into students from rival high schools also carousing out there.

As marvelous as the dilapidated plantation house was, our most frequented hangout was Rhodes Ferry Park. It was nestled along the Tennessee River Bridge and was large enough for us to secure a secluded space, away from others. It was also easier to get to than the plantation house. We'd meet at the library, find a wino to buy our beer and wine coolers, and drive to the park, where we drank, played on the swing set and jungle gym, and walked along the unused train tracks that ran between the park and the river.

One night we were at the park drinking and a barge was anchored in the middle of the river. Larry and Ted, the only other guys in this group of six or seven teenagers, dared each other to swim out and touch the barge. We pleaded with them, "Don't do it, guys. That is not safe."

The current and undertow in this stretch of the Tennessee River was always rough, but with the recent opening of the Tennessee-Tombigbee Waterway that connected the two rivers, it was even more unpredictable. Boats would capsize and those enjoying the river for recreational purposes were often caught off guard and drowned. The passage of large vessels, like that barge, and the pollutants added by nearby manufacturing plants was a man-made recipe for disaster, made even worse by the darkness that covered us. Larry and Ted had no rationale other than ego and alcohol for being in that river.

They refused to back down. They stripped down to their underwear and jumped into the water. We were all screaming for them to turn around. We knew what they were doing was dangerous but we were also laughing at them. After all, we were a group of teenagers drinking at the park on a school night. While I was staring out at the water, shouting at those guys who could have been drowning, I realized one of the girls in our group didn't seem bothered by what was happening.

I asked, "What is going on with you?"

She said, "I don't feel a thing."

"What do you mean?"

"I don't care what they are doing."

That was a strange comment coming from her because I knew she had a major crush on Ted. She looked dreamy, as though she were in another world. As I turned away from her and back in the direction of the water, I felt her hand cup mine very gently. She leaned in and said, "Take this and join me," as she placed something very small in the palm of my hand. I looked up at her. She giggled as she brought her index finger to her lips to quiet my next words. My gaze shifted from her glassy eyes to the little black pill. I whispered, "What is this?" She said, "Black beauty."

I wasn't sure if she had dealt a racial slur or if that was the actual name. I trusted her and besides, I wasn't racially conscious enough to have offered a righteous response if it was a slur. I popped the black beauty into my mouth and washed it down with a Bartles & Jaymes strawberry wine cooler.

This wasn't my first experience with pills. For football practice and games, we would take a little pink pill that one of the linebackers provided. He told us they were for pain. I would take one and act like I was a pro athlete—almost invincible. That was until we learned the pills were for menstrual cramps.

That night I took my first black beauty, and just like that, black beauties, a form of speed, became the pill of choice.

It wasn't long before we could no longer see Larry or Ted in the dark water. We could no longer hear them splashing. We had no idea if they had drowned or if they were just too far away from shore or if the rumble of cars crossing the bridge was covering every confident stroke that moved them closer and closer to that barge. Suddenly, a bright light from the barge cast lumens upon the water that rivaled that of a midday sun. We could see their wet, white bodies in the water. We heard a voice coming from a speaker on the barge: "The authorities have been dispatched. Do not attempt to come aboard this vessel. You will be apprehended."

We started laughing because we did not know what to do. The police were on their way. We had two friends in the water. One of them was our driver. We were all underage and drinking, and at least two of us were also under the influence of black beauties. When the police arrived, we had tossed the beer cans and wine cooler bottles in the trash and made a seat out of the ice chest we'd brought with us. We sat there as calmly as we could. The police cars swarmed into the park like a SWAT unit descending upon Mayberry. They approached us and asked if we were alright or if we were in any danger. The girls spoke up and let them know we were fine.

The taller of the two officers shined the flashlight in my direction and asked, "What are y'all doing out here?"

I was the only Black in the group.

One of the girls spoke up, "We are . . ."

She was interrupted by the officer. "I asked him."

I found the courage to reply. "Nothing. We are just here."

There was a lot of commotion in other sections of the park as they were trying to figure out what was happening in the river. The policeman said, "If I look in that ice chest, will I find anything I should not find?"

I said, "No sir. You won't."

My black beauty culprit spoke up. "We are just waiting for our friends to get back and then we are going home. We have school in the morning."

"What school y'all attend?"

We responded in unison, "Danville."

He laughed. "Why are y'all all the way out here if y'all live in Danville?"

"We came to study at the library and decided to stop by the park before going back."

Out of the corner of my eye I saw two wet, white bodies slinking across the park surrounded by no fewer than six police officers.

The shorter of the two officers with us asked, "Are those the friends you were waiting for?"

"Yes!"

One of the officers accompanying Larry and Ted said, "Sergeant, these two smell of alcohol. What are we going to do about that?"

The sergeant said, "This is serious but no one will get into any trouble here tonight if you all tell us the truth. Have any of you sitting here been drinking?"

We nodded in the affirmative.

He asked, "Is that what the ice chest was for?"

We nodded in the affirmative again.

He gave us a long lecture about the perils of drinking while underage. He pointed out the absurdity of the feat undertaken by the two swimmers. At this point, I just knew we were going to jail. We had confessed to drinking and none of us were even close to legal drinking age.

He concluded, "If you all promise us you will not come to this park and drink or swim in the river at night, we will let you all head on home. Do we have a deal?"

"Yessir!" We grabbed the ice chest, tossed it in the back of Ted's truck, piled into our two vehicles, and drove away as quickly as we could without breaking the speed limit. We could not believe they let us drive away from the scene of what was an actual crime while committing another crime—driving while intoxicated. All of us had been drinking. They knew it and they let us drive away.

That was not the last time we went to that park. That was not the last time I took a black beauty. That was not the last time I drove a car under the influence or rode in one with a driver who had been drinking. There was a reckless spirit unleashed in me—an inward rage that was playing itself out through self-destructive actions.

Take Care of Your Friends

Those unhealthy urges came to a head the day I gave my friend Kevin four Flexeril pills, which were very strong muscle relaxers that I had stolen from my grandmother's medicine cabinet. That morning before first period, I was talking with Kevin and I told him I had some Flexeril. Neither of us were sure what it was. But I told him they were kept on grandma's top shelf and that meant she didn't want anyone to mess with them. He took two and I took one.

In between first and second periods, Kevin came to my locker. He said, "Man, those didn't do anything. I don't feel a thing. Give me two more."

I asked, "Are you sure? Maybe you need to give it time to kick in?"

He said, "Give them to me." I gave him two more pills and we went our separate ways.

My second period class was geometry with Mrs. Flack. She was a no-nonsense teacher who insisted that every student give their absolute best every single day. About halfway through the period there was a knock at the door. She shouted "Come in!" from her perch on a wooden stool next to the overhead projector. Jack, a student office assistant during that period, entered the classroom and told Mrs. Flack that my presence was needed elsewhere.

It was not uncommon for me to be summoned to participate in some function. I was senior class president. I was sometimes called upon to intervene in matters involving my sister, who also attended the school. But this time, when I entered the hallway, Jack whispered urgently, "We have to get whatever you gave Kevin out of your locker now." I immediately went into panic mode. How did Jack know I had given Kevin something? If he knew, others might know too.

As we picked up the pace to my locker, which was adjacent to his, I asked, "What is going on?"

He said, "I'm not sure. All I know is that Kevin's second period typing teacher reported his strange behavior to the principal. They sent me to help get him from class and into the office. When they asked him what was wrong, he mumbled your name."

I opened my locker and gave Jack the sandwich bag that still had five or six pills in it. My heart was racing and it sped up even more when Jack said, "He told them you gave him something this morning and I heard the principal say he would need to search your locker."

Jack took that proactive step to forewarn me of what was happening. He went back to the office and I returned to geometry class. When I reentered the room, Mrs. Flack asked, "Was everything alright?"

I replied, "Yes ma'am. Everything is fine."

About ten minutes later there was another knock at the door. Again, Mrs. Flack adjusted herself on that stool and shouted, "Come in!"

She was not amused when she saw that it was Jack. He said, "Principal Owens wants to see Cedrick in the office."

She looked at him and back at me and said, "I don't know what y'all got going on out there, but this better be the last time you interrupt this class."

I tried to act nonchalant as I got up and walked out of the room.

On the way to the office, Jack told me that Principal Owens and Coach Ellis, the vice principal and our football coach, were in the office with Kevin. I thanked Jack for his support and entered the office with my shoulders held high and a smile on my face. I could see Kevin sitting in the corner and he looked out of it. I quickly adopted an air of concern. "What's wrong with you? What happened?" As I was delivering this award-worthy performance, the principals told me to have a seat and to cut the act.

In very stern tones, they began cross-examining me. Mr. Owens said, "It is obvious Kevin is under the influence of something. He says you gave it to him. You say you didn't." I continued to lie, deny, and try to return the focus to Kevin's well-being.

Finally, Coach Ellis said, "We have given you an opportunity to come clean with us. We don't know what else to do. So, the two of you are under three-day suspension unless you get your mothers to come see us before the three days are up."

My mouth hit the floor. I was the senior class president and I was suspended? Thankfully it was Friday, so I had the weekend to come up with a plan to get this resolved.

Just as the Decatur police allowed us to drive ourselves home from Rhodes Ferry Park under the influence of alcohol, our principals let us leave school at the conclusion of that meeting and drive home. Kevin did not have a car. I was given the responsibility of driving a drug-influenced classmate home and they had the nerve to accuse me of negligence.

On the way home, I rolled down all the windows to try to sober Kevin a bit before we got to his house. I asked him repeatedly, "Why did you tell them it was me?" But I understood he'd been in no state to conjure up a lie after taking four muscle relaxers, or to understand the trouble I was now in. My perfect, protected world was spinning out of control quickly.

I made it to Sunday night without telling anyone about the suspension. Now, I needed to tell my mom and try to get her to intercede and save me from having to miss three days of school. My mom had a set nightly routine. Every night she would check the front and back doors to ensure they were locked. Then she would set the thermostat in the hallway. She would brush her teeth and tie up her hair in her bathroom, kneel by her bedside to pray, set her alarm for 5:30 a.m., and say, "Goodnight, y'all!"

I figured the best time to interrupt the flow was immediately after her prayer.

As soon as she rose from her knees and reached for the clock, she looked up and saw me standing in her bedroom doorway. I said, "I have to tell you something."

She said, "Please don't do this to me right now. You know I have to get up to go to work in the morning."

"Yes ma'am, I do, but I have to tell you something."

"What is it? You need money for something? I don't have any."

"No. I don't need money. I need you to come to the school with me tomorrow and talk to Mr. Owens. If you don't, I will be suspended for three days."

"Suspended for three days? For what? What did you do?"

"He thinks I gave Kevin some pills on Friday and he says we can't come back for three days unless our mamas come talk to him and Coach Ellis."

"What did you do?"

"I didn't do anything, mama."

"I know they did not just make this up, so I'm gonna ask you again."

"I gave Kevin some aspirin and he got sick. They thought he was high or something."

She looked at me with a potent combination of disgust, disdain, and visceral anger. She grabbed the alarm clock, set it to 5:30

a.m., and said, "I'm not missing time from work. You figure this one out. Goodnight, y'all!"

Seek Parental Support

I don't know if I slept that night or not. I do know I was extremely scared of what would become of my reputation if it got around that I was involved in something illicit. At that point I knew family and community members who had turned to crack and other drugs. Several of them had been good students who got caught up in the fast life and dropped out of school. I did not want to be one of those people. I did not want this situation with Kevin to limit my options in life.

The next morning's routine was as predictable as every school morning that preceded it. At approximately 6 a.m., my mom banged on my door frame and said, "Get up! It is time to get ready for school. I gotta go to work." She said the same thing every morning, Monday through Friday. Following her declaration, she would then start a daily search for her car keys. We would shuffle out of our beds and join the search. They were usually found in what my mom would refer to as "the last place I put them."

She left that morning and I sobbed like a baby. My sister came into my room because she heard me crying. She asked, "What's wrong?" I told her I was fine and insisted she get ready so we would not be late for school.

Before we left the house, I called Kevin to see if he'd convinced his mom to go to the school. He told me they were about to walk out the door. I decided I would go to the office and see if the fact that Kevin's mom came would suffice for both of us. It was my only hope.

When I arrived, Kevin and his mom were already in the principal's office with Mr. Owens and Coach Ellis. The office had a glass door that allowed full view of anyone inside the office. Since my attention was so focused on the office door, it took me a minute to realize that my mom was seated in the outer office in the same chair I sat in that Friday before going in to face the principals. I said to her, "I didn't think you were coming." She said, "I didn't either, but I at least want to know what you did."

When Coach Ellis saw us in the waiting area, he opened the door and invited us to join them in the office. As we walked in, my mom greeted Kevin's mom. Suddenly I felt a sense of power and courage come over me. Our moms had known each other since high school. They were on the same cheerleading squad. They had deep ties and connections even though they were not friends in their current lives.

As soon as the niceties subsided, Kevin's mom broke out with a spirited defense of her son. "I know my child. My child did not do what y'all accusing him of. He is a good child and y'all know it." She let them have it.

My mom just sat there and listened. Finally, Mr. Owens asked, "Ms. Bridgeforth, do you have any information to add to this conversation?"

She said, "Mr. Owens, I do." I leaned back in my chair and began to utter a prayer for my principals because God only knew the fire my mom was about to rain down on them. My chest swelled with pride. I knew my suspension was about to evaporate.

She said, as she clutched her purse into her stomach, "Y'all got us in here talking about whether or not these two had some drugs at this school. Y'all seem convinced that they did. So, let me say this one time and one time only. If y'all think my son here is doing drugs, selling drugs, or knows where drugs are, call the police. Don't call me about that."

My mouth dropped to the floor. She did not parrot the "I have a good child" speech. She riffed one out on her own—one of those improvisational interludes that overshadowed the song before it and the one that followed. She stood up and moved toward the door. "I have to go to work. Do whatever you feel is best." She walked out of the office and never looked back.

Kevin's mom looked at me with deep compassion for what she could see I was feeling. She asked, "What are we going to do about this?"

Mr. Owens said, "Ms. Stokely, we don't have hard evidence here—just Kevin's word. The truth is that no matter where he got whatever he took on Friday, he was wrong for taking it and he was doubly wrong for doing so while at school. But since we don't have anything and y'all came to talk with us, we have to let them back in."

They dismissed us from the office and gave us passes to our second period classes. When I walked in, Mrs. Flack looked shocked to see me.

I moped around the better part of that week in disbelief of what I had done and how far I had allowed this saga play out. I knew the impact drug use could have on a person and my family. I knew I was not doing what was best for me or for my future. I could see how my decision to take those pills, share them with others, and lie about it had the potential to be my undoing. Yet I continued down that path until I found myself backed up against this wall. I risked everything.

I had heard that scars, wounds, and residue do not always go away—even when an activity has ceased, apologies have been offered, and reconciliation, or at least an understanding, has been achieved. But I had to try. My misdeeds required an intentional response. As soon as school dismissed, I drove to the grocery store and bought food to prepare for dinner. Stevie Wonder and Ray

Charles could see what I was doing. I had been working for over two years and had never bought groceries to prepare a family meal. Since I worked at Sonic, I would occasionally bring home burgers for us, but that was a rarity.

When my mom got home from work, she was visibly upset. Normally she would enter the house, kick off her shoes by the door, and ask, "Did anybody check the mail?"

Since the time one of us misplaced her income tax refund check, we were forbidden from checking the mail. Her daily inquiry was more of an examination than anything. Our collective response was always, "No ma'am."

She would slide into some slippers and make her way across the street to the mailbox. The amount and type of mail determined her pace back to the house. If it was a personal card, letter, or check, she would open it while standing next to the mailbox or as she slowly walked back. Bills and notices of a negative nature were opened inside, to eventually land in the kitchen drawer by the laundry room. That mail doubled as our dustpan when we would sweep the kitchen floor.

On this particular day when she inquired if we had checked the mail, we responded, "No ma'am." Instead of making her predictable about-face pilgrimage to the mailbox, she told my sister to go check the mailbox. My sister was as stunned as I was. My mom came into the kitchen where I was cooking. She asked, "What are you making?"

I said, "I am making us some spaghetti before I go to work."

"It smells good. Did you go buy the stuff to make it?" This small talk stirred nerves in me and I was suspicious of her disposition. First, she sent my sister to the mailbox. Why had she plotted to get me alone in the house? Second, she had not mentioned the pill incident. I knew it had to be a setup.

My sister ran back into the house and said, "There wasn't any mail out there."

My mom thanked her and said, "If you got your homework done, you can go over to Tracy's."

That was all my sister needed to hear. She bolted out of the house like lightning. While stirring the spaghetti sauce, I was careful not to look directly at my mom, who had taken a seat at the dining room table. It was neatly decorated with a white lace tablecloth and small orange and yellow vases strategically placed at the center. It was much quainter and more refined than we were. The next few minutes would definitely reveal that truth.

After a few minutes of nothing but the clanging of the spoon in the saucepan and the percussive patting of her feet, she broke through that chorus. "What did you give Kevin? Don't lie to me. I have to know."

I felt shame and guilt. I knew as soon as I offered the truthful response to her question, I would be exposed to the one person I never wanted to see me in a negative light—grandma. Tears welled up in my eyes and my throat began to tighten. I said, "Flexeril."

She sat up straight and looked directly at me. "Flexeril? Where did you get it? I don't have any of those here."

That was where it got tough. "I got them from grandma."

"You mean she gave them to you or you took them from her cabinet?"

"I took them from her cabinet."

My tears were flowing into the sauce by then. My mom said, "You ought to be ashamed. You know this is going to break her heart."

"I know. I know I shouldn't have done it. I am sorry."

"I think you should cut the stove off and go over there and tell her what you did before you go to work today."

"I will call her and tell her. If I drive over there, I will be late for work."

"Nope. You will not call. You will go over there."

Grace Is Real

Although my grandparents only lived about three miles away, I took at least twenty minutes to get there. I rehearsed what I would say and what she would offer in response. I went over it and over it in my head. When I came around the curve off Milner Street, I could see my grandparents sitting in the front yard under the tree. The only thing that I could imagine being worse than having to tell my grandmother that I had taken something from her without permission was to have to do that in the presence of my godfather, Uncle JuJu. To my horror, Uncle JuJu's white work truck was parked in front of their house.

He and my godmother, Miss Betty, lived two streets over. They did not visit my grandparents' home frequently. Uncle JuJu would drive past, tender greetings, and keep rolling. That had been the routine for years. The major exception was when we were younger: grandma would call him to come over or send us to him so he could discipline us when we were acting up. Of all days, why was he at their house today? But once I'd turned that corner, there was no way to avoid going to their house. They never missed a car or a pedestrian on that street.

As I parked and walked toward them, I felt the weight of the moment. I saw the high hopes they had for me fading before my eyes. They saw me as a good kid, a rule follower. I did what I was told. I'd gone to great lengths to conceal my misdeeds but now I had to reveal a gross violation in front of three people who had done nothing but encourage me and believe in me. I was about to crush their dreams. At least, that is what I thought. I was quite full of myself to believe that they had no idea that I was not perfect.

I thought about telling the truth—my whole truth, as I knew it. I figured since I was opening a door, perhaps I might invite them all the way in. I could tell them about the time my girlfriend asked if I was "shooting off yet" and I had no idea what she meant, but later that night my cousin Roger taught me to masturbate and I discovered I was doing that thing she asked about. But I had not gotten her pregnant that day, as my brother did a few months later. I could tell them that despite my very public relationship with Rosemary, I had a boyfriend. I could tell them that some nights after work I went home with one of the older women and had intercourse with her. I could tell them I am not convinced my dad is my biological father and that not knowing is at the core of why I am acting out like this.

As I walked those twelve paces from my car to the center of the yard where they were seated, I noticed the patches of clover mingled in the blades of Bermuda grass; I couldn't raise my eyes. How could they ever trust me again?

Uncle JuJu was still in his work uniform, seated with his arms resting upon the wooden gate of the fence that ran along the yard. If there had been a sidewalk on McGaugh Street, that fence would have separated the yard from the sidewalk. My grandmother's back was to me as I approached. Was that foreshadowing what was to come?

My grandfather said, "Hey son! Where are you on your way to? Work, I suppose."

Uncle JuJu, with a firm and direct tone, said, "Don't come dragging your feet in this yard like everything is alright. Sit down."

My grandfather never took his eyes off me and my grandmother never turned around. I sat in the green metal chair that had once been my stepstool to help me climb the maple tree that was now creating a low and dark canopy over us. I wanted to scramble up in that tree and hide from the world. Would it still hold me? Could I get as high as I used to? Was my red and white Coca-Cola shirt still tied to one of the branches up there? That green chair held memories of years past. Now it would need to be a confessional. I had truths to share that needed a safe and compassionate place to be held.

I began, "Grandma, I took something from you and I am sorry."

She looked up from whatever she was knitting or reading. She looked confused.

I continued, "I took some of your medicine out of the cabinet and . . ."

My grandfather, who rarely engaged controversies, interrupted. "Why would you take her medicine?"

"I don't know. I just took it."

Uncle JuJu spoke up again and now I understood why he was there. My mom told him what happened. He said, "You do know. Tell them. The way you are telling it makes it sound like you were sick and you took one of her pills. Tell them what you did."

I went into detail about how I took the pills to school and gave some to a friend, and we got high. I truncated the story because the more I spoke, the worse I felt about the whole thing. Uncle JuJu let out a little chuckle when I got to the part about what my mom said to the principal about calling the police instead of calling her. When I finished my account of the events that led me to that green metal chair, my grandmother stared fiercely at me as she seemingly sized me up. All four of us sat there in silence for a few moments.

Grandma finally spoke. "What pills did you steal from me?"

"Flexeril."

"Boy, do you even know what that is?"

"No ma'am."

"It is a very strong muscle relaxer. Don't you know you are lucky y'all didn't hurt yourselves or someone else? Those things are dangerous. You don't ever take other people's medicine and as long as you live, don't you ever steal from me or anyone else."

My grandfather asked, "Which one of those knuckleheads did you give that stuff to?

"My friend Kevin."

Grandma said, "And your so-called friend is the one who told on you?"

"Yes. He told."

She looked with great intensity into my eyes and uttered words I had heard a hundred times before, but this time they reached a deeper place and took up residence in the marrow of my being: "Don't fool with people who don't have as much as or more than you to lose." Grandma cleared her throat and lowered her voice at least two octaves and continued, "He was not wrong for telling, because that will probably save you from doing it again."

I was in deep shock that they were willing to sit with me and talk it through. Neither of them condemned me or ridiculed me. Instead, they seemed to draw closer to me in that painful moment.

Pay it Forward

In August 1999, eleven years after I was almost suspended from school and found out my grandma had a heart of gold, I was brought into a moment of reckoning where I had a choice: condemn someone who had done a terrible thing or be as merciful and compassionate as grandma was toward me.

I was applying to ministerial graduate programs and was invited to participate in scholarship interviews at Claremont

School of Theology. I was excited because it was my first visit to California and it was a way for me to get out of the winter weather in Birmingham. When I received the plane ticket in the mail, I was certain the travel agent had made a mistake. The itinerary showed my travel from Birmingham to Ontario. The only Ontario I had ever heard of was in Canada. I called the Admissions Director right away. "I received my plane ticket in the mail today and it is wrong," I said.

He asked, "What is wrong with it? I checked those before they were mailed."

"Well, it has me flying to Ontario. I thought the school was in California."

He burst into laughter. "Ontario *is* in California. It is the closest airport to the school. LAX is too far away and too congested."

When I arrived on campus from the airport, I saw three Black men sitting on the wall in front of a tall white building across from a large grassy area. I had not seen more than one Black man at any of the schools I'd visited.

I walked across the quad to reach the trio. They were in a deep theological or philosophical conversation as I approached. The one in the middle addressed me first. "What up, Black man! Are you here for the visitation weekend?"

"Yes. I just got here from the airport. Are y'all students here?"

The one on the right asked, "Why would you ask us that? Don't we look like students?"

"I don't know. I was just excited when I saw three Black men sitting together. That's why I came over."

The one in the middle said, "We're just messing with you. We are students here. I am Salim. This is Gary and Franklin."

"I am Cedrick. I'm from Alabama."

Franklin asked, "What other schools are you looking at?"

After I finished my list, Salim looked at me and said, "Don't come here. Go to any of those other schools."

I did matriculate at Claremont five months later. One of the first people I saw as I was unloading my truck and moving into my apartment was Salim. He welcomed me to campus by asking, "Didn't I tell you not to come here?" Both of us laughed. I said, "You did, but they gave me money and a job, so I had to come and make the most of it."

He said, "Ain't nothing wrong with that, Black man."

I asked, "Where are Gary and Franklin? Do they live in this building too?"

"Nah. Franklin lives in East Housing. Gary, well, that's a longer story. He is no longer enrolled. Things are not going well for that brother, at all."

Salim told me of Gary's drug addiction and run-ins with law enforcement. He shared how he and others at the school were committed to supporting Gary and seeing him get back to health and back in school.

Near the end of my second year of the Master of Divinity program, we received word that a former student's home had burned. As it turned out, it was Gary's home. I was president of one of the student groups that collected funds to support Gary and his family. We did not have a current phone number for him, but we knew he was a lifelong member of Bowen Memorial United Methodist Church. I called the pastor of the church and was able to connect with Gary's wife to get her the funds.

A few weeks later, I was writing my final exams when I received a call. I answered, "Hello, Cedrick speaking."

"Good evening, Cedrick. I am Reverend Otis Fentry, the Los Angeles District Superintendent."

The district superintendent is the person in charge of all the churches and pastors in a specific geographic region. They report directly to the bishop and only call when things are serious. At least that is what I understood at the time.

He said, "You don't know me and I don't know you, but we have heard good things about you from the faculty and staff at the school. We know you are doing good work in Compton with Reverend Waters. The bishop wants to offer you an appointment to serve St. Paul United Methodist Church in Los Angeles."

I missed class the next morning and drove from Claremont to Los Angeles early so I could spend as much time as needed exploring St. Paul's and the surrounding community. I followed my MapQuest directions: "Exit 10 Freeway to Western Avenue. Turn right onto Western. Turn left onto Country Club Drive. Arrive 1200 South Manhattan Place."

As I turned onto Country Club Drive, I saw a large white building gleaming in the sun ahead of me. I slowed to a stop and sat in awe. I wondered why such a nice church would be open to a part-time pastor, a rookie who would only be there for one year? I began to pray, "Lord, I am not worthy. I am not sure what you are doing, but I trust you. If you think I can handle this, then you must know something I don't. I trust you."

When I stepped out of my truck to get a closer look, my keys fell onto the street. I bent down to pick them up and as I raised my eyes ever so slightly, to my immediate left was a worn wooden sign: "St. Paul United Methodist Church." The building behind that sign was equally as worn and in complete contrast to that sparkling specimen I thought was St. Paul's. The beautiful white building was the Mormon Church and they were not expecting me to be their pastor.

My joy and awe turned sour very quickly. My drive from Los Angeles back to Claremont gave me time to pray even more. "God, clearly I am not in tune with what you are trying to do. I am struggling to know if this is your will for my life. Am I trying to make your desire agree with mine or am I open to what you want?"

Later that evening, I received another call from Reverend Fentry. "There has been a change," he said. "St. Paul's decided they did not want a student as their pastor. They want someone full-time and with more experience. The bishop is now assigning you to Bowen Memorial United Methodist Church."

That meant I would be Gary's pastor. Three months later, George and Bessie Bell agreed to meet me on July 31, 1999, to hand over the keys to the church building. I was due to begin the next day. As I sat in my car waiting for them to arrive, I took note of the house next door to the church. It had extensive fire damage. I began to imagine the many ways the church could support that family in rebuilding their home and reestablishing their lives.

When the Bells arrived, I greeted them and asked, "When did those people's house burn?"

Mrs. Bell shrugged her shoulders and asked, "What people?"

I pointed toward the house a mere six feet from the church. "Those people. That house."

She said, "Reverend, we are those people."

"What do you mean? That's your house?"

"Naw. That house belongs to the church. It's the parsonage."

I was stunned for two reasons. First, when I met with the church and Reverend Fentry about my assignment, I asked if they had a parsonage and was told they did not. Second, almost four months had passed since it burned and no one had told me that I would be responsible for building a new parsonage upon my arrival.

I asked, "Who was living there when it burned?"

Mr. Bell finally responded. "Gary was over there doing anything and everything he was big enough and bad enough to do. It's just sad."

In my sixth month as pastor of Bowen Memorial, Gary's wife asked to speak with me. She said, "Gary appreciates that you keep asking me how he is doing."

I interrupted, "Of course I ask. I care about him and want to know that he is getting the help he needs."

She continued, "He wants to know if you will come visit him at the L.A. County Jail."

I had only ever seen jail visits on television and in movies. This was uncharted territory for me. But I recalled something my grandma told all of us when we were young. Her words guided me now. "Sure. I will visit him. Before I go, tell him I have adopted my grandmother's rule: I will only visit a person in jail or prison once. I will not come again. He needs to be sure this is the one visit he wants."

Three days later, I sat in front of a little rectangular window of triple-plated glass embedded with metal wire that separated the visitors from the inmates. There was a gray phone that did not have any numbers on it hanging to my left.

Gary sat on the other side of that glass and he picked up the phone on his side. We were so close to each other but we could not touch and we could not hear each other except through that primitive communications device. He told me about the food, the noise, the Bible study and Alcoholics Anonymous groups. He asked about the church and various members. We were alerted when our time was coming to an end.

Gary asked, "Will you pray for me?"

I said, "Yes. Of course. Let's pray right now." I began to pray through that phone. I could hear him murmur and groan as I prayed. Then, there was silence. I opened my eyes and could see Gary still with his head bowed and hand on the glass that separated us. I put my hand up to mirror his hand on the glass and although he could not hear me, I mouthed, "I love you. Stay strong. Stay out of trouble."

I did not know exactly what Gary did to end up in jail. I did not know what had caused the fire that destroyed the parsonage. I did not know the stories behind his addictions. I did not know how he had gone from seminary to jail in a matter of months. What I did know was that when a full story is not known, cannot or will not be fully disclosed or understood, the best I can do is to show up. It is what my grandparents and parents did for me. They showed up and by showing up they communicated their support for me. They may not have agreed with what I did, but they did not leave me alone. Gary needed me to show up for him in his dark hours. I needed my grandma to show up for me in my dark hours—she did, so I did.

Pay Your Debts

I hated working on Sundays at Sonic Drive-In. If I did not have such a need to be needed and suffer from a disease to please, I would have shucked that responsibility more often than I did. When I was not able to get up Sunday morning and drive my grandparents to church, it was painful. My heart was heavy and riddled with guilt.

All they wanted to do was to go to church and serve in their respective roles, granddaddy as chairman of the Deacon Board and grandma as head of the Communion Stewardesses. The two of them lived the better part of their lives in that community and had grown up and grown old with those people. They were in the twilight of their lives giving all they could to keep the church going and I was a hindrance to their ability to get there and to participate as often as they preferred.

Working on Sundays came with certain responsibilities. It was the only day of the week that I was responsible for opening the restaurant, which meant I was responsible for setting up the cash disbursements for the carhops, turning on all the equipment, setting up the kitchen, and prepping onion rings and fried pickles for the day. It was laborious work. The pickle juice would stain my fingers and the onions would cause tears to stream from my eyes. Sometimes I used the veil of the onions to mask my true hurt, anger, anguish, and disappointment. The job was not a bad job. I just hated the Sunday morning scheduling and yet it was what allowed me to be off on Friday nights during football season and on occasional Saturday nights so I could hang out with my friends.

Throughout my time in high school, I had a full experience. Everything I wanted to do, I did. I was yearbook editor for two years, played football and ran track for four years, joined the speech and debate team, helped organize a show choir class, and tried out for the cheerleading squad. My classmates elected me as class president and I loved every minute of it.

During my last semester of high school, we learned that the school board abruptly cancelled all baccalaureate services without any explanation. Our class was livid and we vowed to fight that decision. The baccalaureate service was a pre-graduation festivity as tried and true as Senior Skip Day and Senior Prom. We had waited our entire school career to have that experience.

Baccalaureate was usually more of a religious-themed event and less focused on the academics. The ones I had attended reminded me of a well-organized church service at one of the larger white Baptist churches in the area. It was nothing like the way we did church. They did not clap during the songs. They did not pray extemporaneously. They did not have various members of the congregation *raising hymns* from the pews and repeating the same lines for several rounds. There was a printed order of service with all the pertinent details included and there would be no deviation.

School officials were present to ensure a certain level of decorum and tradition.

After several weeks of protesting the administration's decision, we received an offer from the pastor of a local United Methodist Church who was willing to allow the service to take place at the church since the school was not supporting it. The class officers met with the pastor and quite honestly, he did not seem too much older than us and he showed great openness and understanding. He did not come across as a rebel but he did speak with conviction and a sense of justice that resonated with us.

We quickly agreed on the venue and set the date and time for the service. It would take place, as it customarily did, on the Sunday preceding the graduation ceremony. We did everything possible to ensure it would be well attended and it would be something we would remember as part of the culmination and rite of passage of our educational journey. When we shared the information with our class advisor and other school administrators, they commended our efforts and spoke with an air of support.

That Sunday began like many before it. My alarm rang much too early for any seventeen year old. I do not recall what I did the night before but it really didn't matter. I had to roll out of bed, shower, get dressed, and drive to Sonic. Everything had to be prepped before time to open to the public. That meant making several hundred battered pickles and onion rings. In case you have ever wondered if the onion rings were hand-battered on the premises, now you know. The onions were washed, sliced, battered, and layered on trays that went into the cooler. People loved eating them and I hated making them. This was a nondescript morning from what I recall and nothing special happened throughout the day, except what seemed a random call from my mom.

My shift always ended at four o'clock and that added to the strangeness when my mom called Sonic around three-thirty. She asked, "Are you able to come home early?"

I said, "I only have thirty more minutes to wrap up and I will be home right after." I wondered if she was excited about the event. After all, I was poised to be her first child to graduate high school. My own excitement had been percolating throughout the day as I worked the grill and fryer while going over my speech in my head.

She calmed her tone a bit and assured me there was no need for me to rush. She said, "I just wanted to be sure when you would be home. I already ironed your shirt."

I said, "Thank you. See you soon."

During the baccalaureate service, as the class president I was expected to offer an address, really a homily, in front of the class. By that point I had heard people suggest I might have a call to ministry but I had always brushed the idea off. My thoughts were on making my classmates, friends, and family proud when I stood before the audience and shared whatever wisdom I colluded within myself to share.

My shift at Sonic ended, I rushed home to shower, put on my suit, and get to the service. My mom had a different idea because my swift and purposeful entry into the house was met with a request for me to join her in the living room. That was a frightening proposition because people seldom sat in our living room. It was one of those showrooms that humans did not inhabit unless it was a major holiday or an overcrowded union organizer's meeting. I did not think of baccalaureate as a holiday that would warrant a living room encounter but then again, this was a big day.

I sat on the sofa and she sat across from me in a mauve-colored Queen Anne chair with an eggshell white pillow tucked tightly under her left elbow in a cast-like fashion. It appeared to offer support and restraint simultaneously. Though she leaned to the left, her right hand remained free to roam the air space between us as she began an inquiry about my spending habits.

I was only seventeen so lacking any experience with IRS audits or FBI sting operations, but what was transpiring in that living room brought forethought as to what those settings might entail. She asked a series of questions about how much I made per hour, average hours worked per week, and what recurring expenses I was responsible for. She already knew all that information. I was not sure why she was asking but I knew she had a reason because this was not my first time being asked to sit in the living room. I knew I could not short-circuit any portion of the conversation and I could not, under any circumstances, redirect or end the inquiry. My mom had us on a collision course with some version of some truth and we would arrive there on her terms.

After meandering through the past year of my financial woes and missteps, she finally let me in on what she knew. She asked, "Did you see a police car going down the hill as you drove up?"

I replied, "Yes. It was brown. Did something happen?"

She said, "Oh yeah! Something did happen, Cedrick."

I became woefully alarmed because she was too calm for the police to have just left our home. I did note the absence of my sister and I wondered if something happened to her. I asked, "Was it one of you? What happened?"

She said, "They came by here looking for you. They had a warrant to arrest you and it was issued for writing bad checks."

Her death-stare, coupled with a calm demeanor, was legendary and it lived up to its name that day. It was like what the weatherman described as "being in the eye of the storm." You knew there was something worse all around you but you were not experiencing the worst of it in that moment. Her lean was released and so was the pillow. As her volume escalated, her Queen Anne chair became a throne of judgment and a seat of rage.

My chair became a seat of shame and a pool of guilt and embarrassment. No one was ever supposed to learn of that $10 check I wrote for gas that bounced and was never honored. Instead of returning to the store to pay the fees associated with the check, I moved on to another gas station even though a friend of mine from school worked at that store. In fact, he was the one who received the check from me the morning I wrote it. In my mind, it was only $10 and it would eventually go away. The store called and left messages for me to call them or to come by, but I ignored those calls for months.

At the time I was living as though that $10 check never bounced, the newly elected Morgan County District Attorney had formed a Worthless Check Unit, to focus solely on folks who passed worthless checks and did not make good on them. I saw the local news stories about him and his efforts but somehow moved on as though that was about everyone except me. I was a high school student and it was only a $10 check at a little gas station in a town of approximately five thousand people. Why would my check matter to the District Attorney?

Be Ready to Speak

The Sunday afternoon they came to take me away for bouncing a $10 check and for not honoring the multiple and persistent requests of the gas station owner to make amends, my mom told them I was at work and that I was scheduled to be at my baccalaureate service that evening. She persuaded them to leave with the understanding and agreement that she would personally escort me to the police station the following morning to address the matter. When she told me what was waiting for me, I was scared. She encouraged me to pull myself together and to get ready for what I had to do that evening. That was probably the longest shower I have ever taken. The lathering soap was melting between my fingers and every bubble spoke a tale that pointed out my guilt and echoed my sin.

My mom drove me to the service and we did not exchange any words. We put on our game faces and entered the church ready to do what needed to be done. My classmates gathered and made the space ready and we welcomed others as they arrived. The details of the event are not quite clear to me but I do recall speaking to the crowd for a time. Applause and accolades followed. After the service and reception, my mom and I returned home in the same silence that delivered us to the church a few hours earlier.

The next morning, she came to my room and told me I needed to be ready to go within the next fifteen minutes because she did not want to be late for work. That seemed an odd concern to me given that this episode was probably going to derail my entire future. At this point I had already enlisted in the Air Force and was waiting until after my eighteenth birthday to report for basic training. There was no way I would be allowed to continue with that plan after my arrest and jail time. All of that was on my mind as we drove the twelve miles from our house to the Morgan County Courthouse and Jail.

I had been to that building before. It was where I had taken my driver's license exam. I had seen police cars enter and exit that parking lot as we passed by. I had never imagined I would be there under such dire circumstances, but here I was.

We walked in and I slowed my steps to allow my mom to approach the officer seated behind the small glass window across the lobby. She stopped, turned to me, and said, "Go on up there and tell them who you are." I did as she instructed. The officer asked for my identification and told me to have a seat. I sat and my mind churned memories of every bad and questionable thing I had ever done. I made commitments and promises to God that I would repeat many times over in future events. I swore if I got through this without having to go to jail, I would never do anything like this again.

Eventually, the officer pointed toward the green door to his left and said, "You can come in now through that door."

I heard a loud buzzing noise. I looked at the door and then at my mom.

She looked me directly in my eyes and said, "You did the crime. Go on!"

Inside the brightly lit room, another officer sat behind a dark gray metal desk covered with piles of folders and loose papers. He had a disheveled appearance that added to my discomfort. He asked, "Can you tell me what you did and why you did it?"

I said, "I didn't know the check was going to bounce. I didn't mean for that to happen."

He said, "But it did happen. It did bounce."

"I know. I am sorry. I was going to take care of it."

"If that were true, you would not be here right now."

"I am sorry."

"I don't believe that unless you mean you are sorry you got caught."

Before I could rebut or utter an excuse, he said, "Stand up and follow me."

He walked me across the hall, took my photo the same way they did on television when someone went to jail, and made impressions of my fingerprints. After that, I returned to the brightly lit room and waited. I used the time to make many deals with God until the officer returned to the room.

He said, "You are free to go as long as you pay $35 to the clerk's office."

I think I ran from that little room to the clerk's office on the second floor.

After paying the fine, I drove my mom to work, in silence. I did not even thank her for what she had done for me the day before. I did not thank her for going with me that morning. I did not thank her for the countless times she had covered my faults with and without my knowledge. She could have let the events of the prior evening play out entirely differently. She could have ensured that I learned a lifelong lesson by having the police come to my place of employment and haul me off to jail. She could have forbidden me from going to the baccalaureate service to teach me a lesson and not let me continue living as though everything was perfect in my world. I did not say a word to her and she did not say a word to me until she opened the door to get out. She said, "I hope you learn something from this. Go straight to school and come home afterward. Don't go anywhere else."

She closed the passenger door and began her trek into work. I drove away and made my way to school. After all of that, I was still there by second period.

Four years later, when I applied for a job with a security company, I was reminded of the saying, "You can have results or excuses, but you cannot have both." My grandma would always throw that one in around report card time. She was a strong proponent of education. She would ask, "How are those grades?"

My answer, "My grades are not as good as I am, grandma."

"You have to learn, son. You can't waste the opportunity you have to get a good education."

"I won't."

"That's right. No excuses for you."

Grandma also let us know that though things sometimes work out in your favor, there are no real secrets in the world. "What's done in the dark will come to the light." As part of the application process for the security job, I had a background check performed by the county sheriff's office. I was completely surprised when the clerk returned my form to me with the notation "PWC."

I asked, "What does PWC mean? Why is that on my form?"

She said, "Passing worthless checks. That shows on your record."

If I had known the word "mortified" then, I would have used it to describe how I felt. With my completed form in hand, I returned to the security office and submitted it to the hiring manager. She looked at it and asked, "What is PWC?" I explained about the bounced check and how I had caused and resolved the issue.

Her response was gratifying. "You were a minor when whatever that was took place. You should get that sealed because it should not come up on a background check like this." She thanked me for giving a real account of what happened instead of offering an excuse.

Third Night Is a Charm

During my last semester of senior year, I came in late for the third consecutive night. Although I had no curfew, there was an understanding of what was an appropriate time to come home.

That night, like the bombing of Pearl Harbor, is one "which will live in infamy." It changed the trajectory of my life and brought to the fore new questions of spirituality, family, and identity.

Up to that point in life I had been known as and had played the role of Cedrick Donyat Bridgeforth, my mother's middle son. I was an above-average student, socially active, spiritually inclined, and on my way to the Air Force. I kept my needs and disagreements to a minimum. My self-reliance and self-denial were the virtues that got me what I wanted and needed—martyrdom was mastered at an early age. But that fateful third night would prove to be one that had been in the making since the moment of my conception.

I came in with the ease and quietude any teenager would employ while entering his mother's home at an indecent hour. As the key clicked and each cylinder found its appropriate align-ment, my heart pounded as if I had competed against Usain Bolt in the race of a lifetime. With the door carefully closed behind me, I was shocked to hear a voice from the black cavern of our unlit living room.

This room was neatly adorned with a very large and ornate Victorian sofa and two matching chairs. A large gold leaf mirror hung over the sofa. The buffet by the front window held various floral arrangements and two blue and white lamps with teardrop ornaments dangling like icicles. Wall sconces with candles func-tioned as finely appointed accessories. In the center of the room sat an oval cherry coffee table upon which was placed an open Holy Bible. The Bible had a coffee cup stain that was nearly as old as me. Its center pages contained my family tree.

The left side of the tree traced George Darden Bridgeforth and his twelve, thirteen, or fourteen siblings to Darden Bridgeforth and Elizabeth White to their parents and their parents before them. George Darden's siblings were listed but some had been crossed out and rewritten to rearrange their birth orders, while others were recorded near the margins, just beyond the branches. With so many and an ever-changing decision of whether to count one or not, this tree was quite the undertaking for someone.

The right side of the tree traced Doris Voncelle Griffin to Clifton Griffin and Premina McDaniel. Clifton's branch only had his name and a couple others next to it but Premina's branches spread to include some of her known siblings, aunts, uncles, and cousins—many of whom I had met at some point in life. Three children were listed directly under George Darden and Doris Voncelle, but off to the side there were other names in parenthesis—Joe Lamont, Georgetta, and Pauletta.

When I would look at those pages and take note of the names and where they were placed in relation to mine, my mind would wonder and my heart would pound. I had a fear of someday and somehow being crossed out, parenthetically mentioned, or moved to one of those spaces just beyond the branches. With George Darden and Doris' siblings, their maternity, paternity, or marital status is what seemed to be the basis for which such locations were determined. But even with all those markings and listings, there were many more persons I knew as uncle, auntie, and cousin who were nowhere near the tree or not listed at all. I wondered about those folks and what they had done to be left off the tree or not thought of for years as these lists were constructed and renovated.

My own fear that my name would be relocated or removed was steeped in my deep abiding conviction that I did not look like, sound like, or act like anyone around me. No one ever told me, "You look like your dad," "We know you are a Bridgeforth" or "Look at those pretty green eyes." My skin was darker and my fingers were longer than those of my siblings. My feet did not have the same curvature as George Darden's and there was little he said that made me feel connected to him and the things he seemed to value most.

Hunting, fishing, chopping wood, and working on the farm did not appeal to me. I did not even enjoy riding bikes or playing baseball with my brother. Chasing women is what the Bridgeforth men did and having as many girlfriends as possible is what the boys did for sport and approval. My joy came through piano lessons and recitals. I liked playing alone in the backyard where I constructed model cities with roads, bridges, and buildings. The Hot Wheels racetrack we got for Christmas made the perfect bridge to my imagined suburban community with a modern school and a large church.

I suppose the church was the largest building in my self-constructed city because the church was the one place where I was encouraged to sing, play piano, read aloud, and share my opinion. It was the place where I did not feel I stood out from the rest but rather blended in to something others expressed as normalcy. It was a quiet but active space that allowed me to flourish. My skin tone, eye color, grades, oddly shaped toenails—none of those things mattered when I was at church. So, in my imagined perfect community with many Hot Wheels buzzing about, the church was always at the center and it was the largest structure.

I wondered if I would someday be able to live in a place like the ones I constructed of wood, mud, matchboxes, and popsicle sticks. But I would arrest my thoughts out of fear that someone might sense them and suddenly encompass my name by parentheses.

That night, I heard my mother's voice: "So, you think you are grown!"

I sheepishly replied: "No. I don't think I am grown."

"You must. You coming in here all time the night like you grown. Where have you been? Where are you going each night?"

"Work. Then hanging with my friends."

"That can't be true."

"It is."

"Nope. No, it ain't, buddy boy. You're gonna tell me where you've been and what you've been doing."

"I told you."

"Tell me what you've been doing."

"Nothing."

"Tell me."

"Nothing."

"You tell me now."

"I will tell you as soon as you tell me who my real father is."

Just like that, my deepest and darkest fear was out in the air. What I had spoken and thought brought light to why I feared being crossed out, moved to the margins, or found in parentheses.

The question was suspended above the room like the wide-blade ceiling fan with its spotlights that would illuminate us if someone had the will to flip a switch. Both of us were paralyzed and chose silence as the best option before us and before my deafening inquiry. After several moments the silence gave way to wailing and weeping, which was followed by silence. For what seemed hours, the great universe continued to press play, then rewind, then repeat, then rewind.

My consciousness cannot grasp the details of what transpired that night, but I do know it was heavy and it hurt. As dawn broke, my eyes rested upon that oval cherry coffee table and the open Holy Bible. Not only had I changed, but so had some of the details on the family tree.

Reimagine Routines

Later that day, my mom came home from work in a mood not much better than the one from the night before. We had crossed into territory that was uneasy for both of us. The difference between this moment and the last time we uttered words to each other was that this time there were words.

She said, "You said you wanted to know who he is. Do you want to meet him?"

Thinking she was bluffing or playing a cruel joke to get back at me for the pain I caused the night before, I said, "Yeah. I do."

She said, "Then let's go."

The familiar and routine path from our front door to the driveway seemed new and long this time, each step leading to a great beyond. We were already past the point of no return. My relationship with my mom would never be what it had once been. My belief in how I was related to my siblings had changed. Everything about my seventeen years of living had changed. Everything, including the cadence of my breath, the batting of my eyes, the curvature of my smile, the stride of my step, and the tenor of my voice, had changed. It did not matter if I opened the car door or not, the threshold of another opening had been crossed that far outweighed the fiberglass and metal of our Buick Century's passenger door. Now that door was ajar.

The drive from Hartselle to Decatur usually takes about twelve minutes, but this day, it seemed the sun stood still and all of eternity past and future passed through my mind's eye. This was a familiar and routine path from the hill atop Oakwood Street, down to Hillview Drive, left to Highway 31, and north toward Decatur. From there I was simply a passenger. I could not navigate because I did not know our destination.

When we made a left onto Beltline Road, I wondered if we were going to the Beltline Mall. Did he work in one of those fancy stores that sold suits no one I knew could afford? Did he know how to tie those neckties that no one at my church ever wore? If not the mall, did he own one of those large used car lots or insurance companies with offices on the second or third floor? When we passed the mall, I wondered if he lived in one of those two-story brick homes in one of those exclusive subdivisions.

What kind of car did he drive? Did he get good grades in school? Was he popular? Did his feet look like mine? Were his eyes brown, was his hair a bit coarse? I had fantasized about this day, even as I built my cities in the dirt. I dreamed of driving one of those Hot Wheels up to a fabulous home at the end of a cul-de-sac to say, "Hi dad! It sure is good to see you today." As a younger child such musings were common and comforting in my solitude.

This moment in the passenger seat of my mom's car was anything but solitary, except for the thoughts held in the recesses of my consciousness. Now that we had passed every place that seemed exotic and exclusive, I asked, "Where are we going?"

She responded, "Kentucky Fried."

I grunted, "Hmmm. Kentucky Fried Chicken?"

Both of us realized the absurdity of this reality as we smiled at each other for the first time in weeks.

As we pulled into the parking lot, in a tone barely more than a whisper, she said, "There he is."

I asked, "Where?"

She pointed into the distance and said, "The little red Corvette."

The moment was so pregnant with possibility and irony. I am certain my inner performer broke out into some Solid Gold dancer's rendition of Prince's hit about that same car and color. No one could see that my heart was twirling like His Royal Badness in heels.

I looked across the parking lot and saw the brightly colored, clean and shiny red Corvette with the silhouette of a man inside. I quickly withdrew my eyes from the car to peer down at my hands and feet. I was familiar with those appendages and I suspected that no matter what would transpire in the next scene of my life those things would remain unchanged. The dust and gravel on the floor mat would one day be vacuumed away and replaced by gum wrappers, French fry crumbs, and other people's shoe impressions. The deep, dark hue of the mat would one day give way to sunlight and lose its luster. My hands and my feet would eventually age but they would remain familiar and routine. As my mind spiraled to wonder if my hands and feet looked like his, I heard the rear car door open.

He said, "Hi y'all!"

She said, "Hi!"

I said absolutely nothing as she looked at me.

I suppose she was expecting me to utter something that would let this man know I could speak and that I had been raised to do so.

She continued, "Lawrence, this is Cedrick. Your son."

He said, "Hi. Nice to meet you, Cedrick."

I said, "Hi."

She said, "I am going to go get me a Coke."

We said, "Ok."

She exited the vehicle, leaving me in the front seat staring at my hands and feet, more mesmerized by the limestone gravel that was ground into the floor mat than I was with the fact that the missing portion of my being was seated behind me. The stranger sat in the rear behind the passenger seat with his breath full and rich enough that it warmed the interior of the car. The rapid pace of my heartbeat added to the cataclysmic energy of the moment. He broke the silence. "Your mom tells me you are going into the Air Force."

I said, "Yes. I am."

He asked, "When do you go?"

I responded, "September 21."

He said, "That's good. Are you excited?"

"Kinda."

"It should be a good experience for you."

"Yeah. I think so."

"I sure hope it is."

"Me too."

The silence returned and filled the crevices between the man who knew nothing of this being he had created almost eighteen years earlier and the boy who wished he knew how to talk to this man whom he had only imagined in dreams. In this moment we were at a loss for how to be relational, much less how to be related. There wasn't anything familiar or routine for either of us as we sat in the stifling and deafening silence.

My mom returned to the car with her drink.

He said, "OK. I have to get to work."

She said, "Alright."

He tapped the headrest and said, "Nice to meet you."

I said absolutely nothing as he exited the car.

I never looked at him and I never uttered more than four consecutive words in answer to the questions he posed. If only I had brought my report card, he would have known of my scholastic aptitude. If only I had brought my drawings and model of Mt. Vernon, he would have known of my dream to become an architect. If only I had brought my piano recital certificates, he would have known of my interest in music and the performing arts.

Later that evening I asked my mom a few questions about him. I learned he was a very good bass player and that when they met, he and his brother played in a band. Just knowing that one thing could have opened the conversation and made it more than a perfunctory exchange between strangers. Just that one fact could have been the missing link between the man who did not know he had a son and the son who did not know this man as his father. A chance meeting had robbed both of us of the chance for this introductory meeting to ever be familiar or routine.

Serve with Pride

During the Christmas break of my senior year, I went to the Military Entrance Processing Station in Nashville to complete my pre-enlistment. No one knew I was enlisting except my mom and the recruiter, Sergeant Thomas McRay. I kept my siblings, friends, and extended family members at bay in my decision-making process and did not include them in the pomp or circumstance surrounding my enlistment. I may have sensed some would try to convince me not to enlist and I did not want to hear it. Or I may have feared I might change my mind and I did not want them to know.

The decision to pre-enlist in December, while I was still seventeen, paid off in the long run. I was not aware that every male over eighteen at the time "owed" the government eight years of service, whether active or inactive. My clock began on my eight years in December of my senior year, even though I did not report to basic training until the following September.

So much about how I ended up enlisting in the Air Force remains a mystery to most. The truth of the matter is that I enlisted because I saw myself or what I imagined my future self to be the first time I saw Sergeant McRay. Each year a group of military personnel would descend upon my high school. They would host an assembly for juniors and seniors during which they would show videos and give speeches about all the exotic and hard-to-believe experiences of serving in the military. They carried themselves with a visible air of intentionality and purpose. It was all over their faces as they walked the halls to the school's under-resourced library where the presentation was held.

There isn't much that is memorable about the assembly except the man who helped me to see myself in a way I had not seen myself before that moment. He was seated on the left side of the podium and he stood out because he was the only African American, Whatever he said, his look, apparent character, and words convinced me to sign up to take the Armed Services Vocational

Aptitude Battery (ASVAB) Test. I knew enough to know that doing well on that ASVAB was my ticket to dressing, standing, speaking, and presenting as well as he had that day. I wanted to do and to be whatever he was. Throughout my school career, I had not had any Black teachers in any of my classes. Here I was in my senior year and this was the first time anyone I could truly imagine myself resembling in any way was standing before me.

The next day a few of us gathered in the library during our English Literature class to take the ASVAB. Sergeant McRay proctored the exam. He said, "This is not the most important test you will ever take. This is a test that will help you narrow your focus should you decide to enlist in the armed forces or not. The results of this test will qualify you for some branches and disqualify you from others. It will open a world of options for you and your family."

Sergeant McRay acknowledged those who had questions. The final question was asked by someone seated at the front table. "Sergeant, what happens if we fail the test? Can we take it again?"

He responded, "I don't see any of you gentlemen failing this test. A low score in certain areas will only narrow the job classifications that will be open to you in certain branches." He added, "The students with the highest scores will definitely receive a call from me."

That was all the motivation and information I needed. In fact, I was so motivated, there was only one other person who scored higher than me on that test. I know that because after I enlisted, Sergeant McRay asked me if I would volunteer at the recruitment office. So, after school on days when I was not scheduled to work at Sonic Drive-In, I would go to the Air Force recruitment office to answer phones and file paperwork. On one of those occasions, I was asked to file printouts of test scores. I had to look. I had to know how I did in relation to the others.

Being in that office gave me a sense of responsibility and it brought me in proximity with the man who had inspired me to enlist in the Air Force without any prior thought of such being an option for me. I had always been told I would go to college but when I saw men who were in college or who had gone to college, I did not feel inspired by them. When I saw Sergeant McRay, I suddenly saw myself in him and saw myself doing what he was doing.

By the time of my high school graduation, Sergeant McRay had received a transfer to the Huntsville office. Since no new recruiter would be assigned to the Decatur office anytime soon, he was still responsible for ensuring the mail and phone calls were managed. I took care of those things from the day he invited me to volunteer until it was time for me to leave for basic training. Being around him and in the space where he worked kept me engaged and it kept me open to greater possibilities. I was curious how I would turn out and I was curious if he would be proud of me and the work I was doing. It would not fully become clear for years but I was looking for a father figure and he offered me a glimpse of what I longed for. That is what drew me in. That is most likely why I mustered up enough courage to confront my mom that night and demand the truth.

The day my mom drove me to meet Lawrence at the Kentucky Fried Chicken was a day when I was probably supposed to be at the recruitment office. But, with Sergeant McRay barely coming in anymore, I was in charge of my own schedule. I had a key. I took care of what needed to be handled and forwarded him what he needed. I yearned for him to see what a great asset I was and for him to come back. Some of what kept my eyes facing forward and my mouth closed in sullen silence that evening at the KFC was rooted in what I had come to dislike about Sergeant McRay. He had abandoned me, and he had not asked me to come with him.

When confronted by the presence of Lawrence in the back seat, those two strangers were really one. Both of them needed to be punished.

Pack Your Lunch

The day in early 1988 when I first met Lawrence marked the beginning of a waiting game that has never ended. The days that followed our botched introduction exposed me to one of my life's regrets: not turning around to look that man in his eyes. Grandma told one of my cousins, "Regrets never lead to happy endings unless you change the regrets into actions." I wanted another chance to engage him and come to know him in some way.

After high school graduation the summer was long and tumultuous. I was reeling in the wake of my new and ungrounded identity. Everything was changing and stability seemed too distant to claim or to even place on a wish list. I was fired from Sonic at the beginning of the summer and fired from Olan Mills Photography's phone sales department at the end of the summer.

I knew his name. I knew where he worked. I knew I was his son. Although I knew those things, I also knew I never turned to look into his face. I did not know how he looked and that also meant I did not know how he viewed me. The moment rested within the swivel of my neck and the physical barrier of a headrest. All I had to do was turn around and look at the man, but my anger, anxiety, immaturity, and ego required more than the human equivalent of WD-40. I needed brute strength to turn around and I couldn't find it.

As I have looked back on that scene and played it over and over again, I have come to realize that he bore as much responsibility for how that moment unfolded as I did. I wasn't in that car alone. I had not called him to meet me. I had not coerced a meeting with him. I was driven to the spot and he got in the car and sat behind me. If only he had told me what to do or what he wanted, then I could have responded instead of reacting or not acting at all. Though we were both basically adults—I say "basically" because at seventeen, I barely qualified—he was the parent and I the child.

I did not have visions of playing catch in the front yard because I was not ever good at baseball. Football was only on my roster of activities because it was a way to be with my friends and escape being accused of being gay. I did not have any expectation that he would teach me anything in particular about life because my mom, grandma, Miss Betty and Uncle JuJu, Auntie Eunice, and others had already done a pretty good job in that regard. I did want to know about him. What did he think? How did he live? What was he like as a younger man? Was he married? Did he have other children and what was his relationship with them? I also wanted to apologize for how I behaved when we met because my reaction was not indicative of how I was raised to treat people.

Whenever I faced tough issues, I would often discuss them with Auntie Eunice. She lived two streets over from us and she was always willing to listen and offer advice without telling me what to do. I told her how things went the night at the Kentucky Fried Chicken. She said, "That was the first problem. Who arranges that kind of intro at that place and especially when everyone has time limits?"

"Well, he was on his break, so that was probably the only time he had available."

"Ced, he is a grown man. He knew the reason for the meeting. He had to know it would take more time than his lunch break would allow."

I felt I needed to defend him from what seemed like an attack. I said, "He was very nice and stayed as long as he could."

"Baby, all I'm saying is this is not your fault. There were two grown folks who were responsible for setting up the meeting and making sure it went the way it needed to go. You were not and are not responsible."

Her words of assurance helped a little, but I wanted to fix it. Even if I was not to blame for messing it up, I wanted to make it right for all our sakes.

She told me to do whatever I felt was best and made the most sense for me without putting myself in position to be hurt.

I reached out to my friend Lynn, who had been my best friend since sixth grade. He helped me concoct a plan for how to meet up with Lawrence again. Lynn called the plant where Lawrence worked for five consecutive days at different times throughout the day until we finally figured out the shift he worked. Based on that, we worked out what time he would take his dinner break. I was impressed with how knowledgeable this former Boy Scout was about figuring out these details.

With this newfound information, I made a plan and what I believed was a full-proof method to connect with Lawrence. Throughout the spring and summer, I spent as many days as possible on stakeout, either near the access road that led to the plant or at the Kentucky Fried Chicken. I would sit at the entrance to the frontage road looking for a little red Corvette. I would sit in the parking lot at Kentucky Fried Chicken praying for him to eat dinner there that night.

Lynn and I reasoned that if he came to that restaurant the day we met, then he would definitely come again. I know for certain he did not have chicken the six nights I sat in the parking lot in June, the eight nights I sat in the parking lot in July, the eleven nights I sat in the parking lot in August, including the day of my birth, and the seven nights I sat in that parking lot in September.

He did not even have chicken the night before I was to leave for basic training.

The day I left for basic training, I vowed to leave behind any notions I had of ever getting to know Lawrence, but I couldn't hold that promise for long. He was ever present on my mind and I kept wondering what I could do to connect with him. While in basic training, I finally made a call to the plant where he worked. I knew he would be there because Lynn and I had sketched out his schedule on the blank page in the back of my little Bible: three days on and three days off. As long as I had that Bible and a calendar, I could track when he was at work and I had a way to reach him. When I called, he answered, "Engineering. This is Lawrence."

"Hello, Lawrence. This is Cedrick. Remember me?"

"Cedrick?" He seemed lost or as if he was searching for words as he said, "Yes, I remember you. You are Doris's son. How are you? Shouldn't you be in training by now?"

"Yes. I am in training but I had time to make a call, so I decided to try to reach you."

"How is it going?"

"It is going well so far. I think many of the guys are struggling, but my grandma didn't play when it came to making beds, folding clothes, cleaning, and doing as you were told, so I am fine."

"I guess knowing all of that before you get there is a good thing."

"Yes sir. It is."

"Well, thank you for calling, but I have to get back to work."

"OK. I understand. I just wanted to check in and see how you were doing."

"Alright, Cedrick. Good-bye."

He hung up and I felt as unfulfilled as I had before he answered the phone. The conversation seemed incomplete and disconnected and no matter what Auntie Eunice said, I believed it was my fault. I made the call and I could have set a different tone for the conversation.

Whenever I would come home on leave from the Air Force, there were some routines and activities that remained constant. I would visit Miss Betty and Uncle JuJu, Auntie Eunice, and my grandfather. I would hang out with my high school friends who were still in the area and I would try to fashion a scheme that would get me an audience with Lawrence. The conversations we would have when I called to let him know I was home on leave all ended with him promising to find a way for us to meet. When I did not receive the return call, I would resort to the surveillance activities that carried me through the summer before basic training. The difference now was that the Air Force had taught me more stealth forms of observation.

Stand Your Ground

Several weeks prior to my high school graduation my manager at Sonic Drive-In asked, "Are you planning to go sin at Panama City Beach after graduation?"

I said, "I don't think I should go."

He laughed and said, "I don't think anyone should go to that place, but they do and they will. I just need to know if I can put you on the schedule or not. That's all."

I confidently responded, "You can put me on the schedule. I am not going."

He said, "OK. Just let me know if you change your mind. I need to know before I post the schedule."

The week of graduation was filled with excitement. Most of my friends made plans to spend the days following graduation at Panama City Beach, Florida, a party destination that seemed like the perfect endcap to our high school years. At first I wanted to go too, but after I heard about the wild hijinks that were expected as a rite of passage, my comfort level lessened. Another drawback was that although I worked at Sonic and had maintained that job throughout high school, I did not have any savings to pay for a trip.

I was keeping up many façades by maintaining a very public four-year relationship with Rosemary, while constantly opening myself to encounters and relations with boys. I struggled with it. Rosemary appreciated my willingness to not pressure her to engage in sexual activity. She did not know that often I would drop her off at home, then spend the night with a boy I was having sex with. I also had regular encounters with Veronica, a much older woman who lived in our town. That is not to say that Rosemary and I never did anything, because we did and it was scary enough to convince me not to do it again—the condom broke. I figured there was no need to go down that road and have my mom half-kill me for impregnating someone. I left the notion of sex with Rosemary on the shelf. I had many other outlets and distractions that allowed me to be the perfect gentleman with her.

All of that was going on and things were not anywhere near settled at home. But I felt I was experiencing a spiritual awakening of sorts as I studied the Bible, prayed more, and attended youth events with friends. I was deeply conflicted, if not convicted, by the contradictions that existed in my life. I was always uneasy. When I was with my friends, I felt I did not fit in because of my burgeoning spiritual pursuits. I felt dirty and guilty about my sexual activities because I knew I was not supposed to be engaging in that behavior. I felt alone but I was always with someone. I felt I had so much to prove and even more to live up to. I felt I was the one who had to make everyone proud. I felt I was the one who had to "make it," but I did not even grasp what that meant in the context of my life.

At one of the youth events I attended, the counselor asked me, "What do you believe is keeping you from surrendering everything to God?"

I said, "Probably telling him all my secrets."

He said, "God already knows all about you. God made you. So, what are you trying to hide or what do you think you are hiding from God?"

I wanted to tell him everything. I wanted to tell him about being scared when I thought Rosemary might be pregnant. I wanted to tell him about my affair with Veronica. I wanted to tell him about all the boys I liked who also liked me. I wanted to tell him about my drinking. I wanted to tell him I was scared I would grow up and be unhappy like my parents. I wanted to tell him my whole life story. Instead, I began to weep uncontrollably and somehow said, "I am afraid because I don't know what will come of my life."

The counselor held me and he wept with me. He said, "All you need to know right now is that God knows your future because God made your future. You have to follow and God will lead you into it."

Although I was not sure I fully understood, I did feel heard, affirmed, and loved. That counselor's care, support, and affirmation was what really solidified my decision about Panama City Beach. I knew nothing would happen there that would draw me closer to God or give me answers I needed about my future. As the week of graduation approached, my manager posted our work schedule. I saw that I was scheduled to work the weekend after graduation.

I approached the manager, "You mean I graduate and you expect me to work the entire weekend?"

He said, "You told me to put you on the schedule because you were not going to the beach. Do you remember that?"

"I remember that, but I thought I would at least get one week-end night off."

"You do have one—Friday. You don't have to be in on Saturday until six in the evening. That is two hours later than your normal Saturday shift. Besides, I had to schedule my wife to cover for you being out on Friday. She won't work two nights in a row, so you have to be here."

I was upset but I let it go. Up to that moment, I had not been at odds with the manager at all. He trusted me to run the store when he was not there. I had keys and functioned more like an assistant manager than anyone else other than him, his wife, and a woman who had worked there for almost ten years.

When one of my older cousins started her first job, grandma told her, "Don't ever let them know they can get along without you, because they will." I heard that more than once and I followed it in my roles at Sonic, as high school yearbook editor, and as class pres-ident. With all the affirmation I received as a result of my commit-ment and contributions, I slipped into believing I was irreplaceable and valuable.

Shortly after that conversation, a friend invited me to attend a Christian concert with him that Saturday night. I told him I was scheduled to work. He asked, "Do they really expect you to flip burgers on the biggest weekend of your life?"

I said, "I told my manager I would work but now I will tell him I want to be off."

When I went in for my next shift, I told the manager that I would need to be off on Saturday to go to a concert to celebrate graduation. He reminded me that I was scheduled and told me there were no other options and he was not open to discuss it any-more. I tried bargaining with him again and again. I told him I was going to the concert. He said, "If you fail to show up on Saturday, there will be dire consequences."

He sounded serious but many employees had missed shifts throughout my three years working there. People had quit and been rehired several times. The only thing that I knew he would never overlook was theft and that was not what I was doing. I had given him fair warning of my intentions. We were clearly locked in a classic game of "chicken" and we were determined to see who would flinch first.

CHAPTER 3

MANAGE
YOUR LOSSES

Be Aware of Your Emotions

My high school graduation was emotional because of all that was swarming around for me personally, but even the actual service held a tension that I was not prepared to handle. We were the first class to hold graduation in the new gymnasium. We were the largest graduating class in history with seventy-nine graduates. I was one of three leads on our class song and I made it through my announcement without crying.

After we all tossed our caps in the air and hugged each other, my friend Anna tugged at my purple graduation gown. It was time for us to give Jason the custom wood storage chest we had made for him to carry with him to Art & Design School. He absolutely loved the gift and thanked us as he gave us framed paintings he had made of us. We hugged and cried for a few minutes. Then, the unthinkable happened. Jason addressed the two of us: "I have really enjoyed being friends with you. Both of you are talented and you make me laugh. But, when we walk out of here tonight, I never want to see either of you again."

He was always a little dramatic, so while I heard and felt his words as he walked away, I still half-expected to see him later that night and throughout the summer before he went off to art school in August and I left for basic training in September. But that did not happen. His abrupt dismissal of who and what we had been to each other was another relational rupture that I did not expect and could not explain. I wanted him to tell me the reasons for his decision. I wanted him to change his mind. But one of the qualities I admired most about him, beyond his artistic talent and passion for life, was his ability to be decisive.

As I watched him disappear into the crowd, I stood motion-less in that large room filled with friends and classmates, none of whom mattered more than Jason in that moment. Anna eventually shrugged and moved on. She felt confused, but encouraged me to trust that he would get over himself and everything would be fine. She was so wrong. It would be twenty-one years before I would be in close proximity to Jason again and be courageous enough to explain my feelings.

I attended a few parties that night, but mainly spent the evening riding around the dark country roads with a friend. The next day was Saturday. I had told the manager at Sonic every day that week that I would not be at work. I went to the concert at Von Braun Civic Center featuring Carmen, a Christian recording artist. The following day I went in for my scheduled Sunday morning shift.

The timeclock was located just to the right of the milkshake machine and was in plain view of the manager's desk. It was odd for him to be there when I arrived. He usually took off on Sunday mornings so he could go to church with his family. I would open the restaurant, set up the registers, cut onions and make onion rings, and batter pickles. That was my Sunday routine for the three years I worked there unless I put in a special request to be off on Sunday for something my grandparents needed me to do.

I walked over to the timeclock and when I did not see my timecard in the third slot from the top, I asked, "Do you have my timecard?"

He responded, "Yes. I have it."

"I need it so I can clock in."

Without looking up from the mound of papers he had in front of him, he said, "No, you don't."

"What do you mean?"

"I mean, you will never need this timecard again."

I looked at him with nothing but puzzlement on my face. He looked up and as our eyes met, he raised up what appeared to be my timecard in one hand and an envelope in the other. He continued, "I told you if you failed to show up last night, there would be dire consequences. Didn't I tell you that?"

"Didn't I tell you I would not be here? It's just like when these other people call in, but they call in last-minute. I told you every day this week that I would not be here."

"And I told you . . ."

I interrupted, "That is not fair. I have sacrificed a lot for you. Other people get many chances. I only wanted to be off one night to celebrate my graduation."

"It impacted all of us. We got slammed last night. I had to call my wife to come in. We had our little girls sitting here at this desk for three hours because we were both so busy."

"But that is not my fault."

"You may be right, but you were wrong not to show up last night. I have your timecard for you to sign and I have your final check."

I signed the timecard, tossed the keys on the counter, and snatched my check out of his hand. I expected him to call me later that day or at least within the week as he had done when other employees quit or were fired. That call never came. I was disappointed because I felt I deserved another chance. I learned a lesson. No matter how loyal I proved myself to be, his loyalty to his wife was greater than his loyalty to me. I moved on to Olan Mills Photography and worked as a phone sales representative until the end of August, when they fired me for low sales and for taking long lunch breaks. I carried great pain with me throughout the summer regarding my identity, sexuality, loss of Jason, and uncertainty about the Air Force and life beyond.

Wear the White Cape

In 2009, over twenty years after high school graduation, I had a serendipitous encounter with Jason at a church in Los Angeles. That Sunday was not unlike every other Sunday since I had begun my role as district superintendent a year earlier. I was responsible for overseeing approximately eighty clergy and staff, forty-eight churches, two campus ministries, and a host of community service programs. One of the churches in my district was Crescent Heights United Methodist Church in West Hollywood. It was a congregation that catered to the gay, lesbian, and trans communities and hosted several cannabis support groups. The pastor was one of the lead activists responsible for getting medical marijuana approved in California. That church had been a headquarters and rally-point for the movement to legalize recreational marijuana. The building was a true gathering place for the community and for groups with a mission to serve the needs of residents in West Hollywood. A decade or more before I became district superintendent, the church was featured in local and national news for its worship experiences that featured Broadway show tunes. The congregation was also very active in the fight against discrimination during the AIDS epidemic in the 1980s and 1990s.

By 2009, the church building and congregation were in deep decline by every metric. Multiple interventions and strategies to turn things around had failed. I scheduled a meeting with the church leaders to discuss the probability that the church would close within ninety days.

The meeting was scheduled for Palm Sunday and the pastor asked me to preach that Sunday. He said, "The people here don't really know you. If you preach, that will give them some connection with you before you have to address them in the meeting."

"OK. That makes sense."

When I left my home that Sunday morning, I knew my route to the church. I planned to arrive about twenty minutes before the service was scheduled to begin. As I approached Slauson Avenue, I realized I forgot to bring my robe. I made an abrupt U-turn to go get it. I still had time to arrive about ten minutes before the service was scheduled to begin. That was closer than I care to cut it but that was the best I could do at the time.

On my second attempt to get to the church, as I approached Florence Avenue, there was a detour due to road construction. I followed the orange signs to the alternate route. That added more time to my travels and so did the accident at Adams and 28th. By the time I reached the intersection of Fairfax and Fountain where the church was located, I was almost ten minutes late. There wasn't a spot available in the church's small parking lot or anywhere on the street near the building. I drove around the neighborhood until I found a space about three blocks away.

I jumped out of my little silver Chevy Cruze, threw on my long white robe, and started jogging toward my destination. When I reached the corner, I thought it a good idea to at least look at the opening line of my sermon before I walked in. It was then that I made a mad dash back to my car to retrieve my Bible and sermon from the back seat.

This time I struck out in a full-on sprint, robe flowing in the wind and Bible in tow. I must have looked like a superhero with a white cape, attempting a takeoff. I stopped outside the entry to catch my breath and to gain some sense of composure. I could hear singing, which meant the service had already started. That made sense given that it was scheduled to begin twenty minutes before that moment. I walked in, picked up a copy of the worship agenda, and scanned for the title of the song they were singing. It immediately preceded my sermon.

The congregation concluded the song, the pastor named his gratitude for my safe arrival and presence with them, and I was invited to come forward. He knew something was not right because I was always a stickler about time.

When we were told what time to be somewhere, we were there before the clock struck whatever the appointed time was. My grandparents were responsible for opening the church for worship on Sundays, choir rehearsal on Tuesdays, Bible study on Wednesdays, and meetings and cleaning on Saturdays. I was their helper when I was younger and their driver during my teenage years. Longtime churchgoers often say, "We were at church every time the doors opened." Thanks to my grandparents, I ask, "Who do you think unlocked and opened those doors?" I learned the art and necessity of punctuality at a very young age. The military reinforced what was already ingrained and it carried over into my personal and professional spaces.

Showing up late for a church service when I was scheduled to preach was bad enough. It was even worse given that I was there to inform the congregation that the church would be closing within

MANAGE YOUR LOSSES ∿ 89

the next few months. I needed to appear professional, compassionate, and resolute. I walked to the podium which was situated in the southwest corner of the sanctuary. There were colorful throw pillows around the altar area that caught my eye.

I addressed the congregation. "Good morning, Crescent Heights. It is a pleasure to finally be here in your midst."

As I scanned the crowd, it was odd that there were more than thirty people seated in the sanctuary. Recent services had had no more than ten in attendance. The congregation sat with stoic expressions as I attempted to rouse them into some semblance of a call-and-response experience common in the Black church tradition. They offered no noticeable reaction to anything I said. At the conclusion of the service, I stood near the front and offered greetings to folks as they filed by.

There was one woman that I knew and she introduced me to her cousin. The two of them engaged me for a few minutes and while they were talking, I noticed a man standing off to the side. It seemed as though he was waiting for me. Given that these two women gave no hint that their conversation would end anytime soon, I excused myself and stepped toward the man, extending my hand to shake his. "Hello, sir. So glad you are here today."

"Thank you for saying that. I am glad I came too. So weird."

"Do you attend here often?"

"Oh no. I come here for holidays and when I just want to check off the box for my mom."

"I understand how that works. Well, I am glad you came today." He was fidgeting with the worship outline he had in his hand and pivoting his left foot in what seemed the beginning of a ballet move. "So, was today about checking off the box?"

"Yes and no. My friend Lee," he said, pointing to a tall gentleman with a long ponytail standing near the coffee cart, "told me to come today because a mean homophobic church official was coming to shut down the church. He said we needed to have a show of force and make sure people were here so he would change his mind."

"I'm the church official but I am not homophobic." Both of us began to laugh and his laughter held a familiar cadence that I had not heard since high school graduation.

"Jason!"

He said, "You just realized who I am?"

"Yes. Oh my goodness!" We hugged and laughed with repetition and synchronicity that only two people who know the deepest mechanics of the other can master. Our laughter caught the attention of the pastor, who came over to where we were standing. The pastor said, "You boys are laughing like two old friends. Let me in on the joke."

I said, "Well, we are more than old friends. He was my boyfriend in high school."

The pastor gasped and then he joined the laughter. He asked Jason, "Did you know he was going to be here today?"

Jason replied, "No. I came at Lee's invitation. I almost didn't come but I was told it was important to have as many people here today as possible for some meeting." The pastor tried to quiet Jason midsentence but Jason was never one to be silenced in any way.

By that time, most of the crowd had dispersed. I was so taken aback by this encounter with a lost love I had thought of often but never sought out that I told the pastor we would reschedule the meeting for a later date. Jason and I made arrangements to meet that following Friday night. As for the church, it remained open for almost three years before I got around to closing it. It was saved by Jason's presence that Palm Sunday and so was I. We were able to rekindle a connection that seemed to have been on more of a pause than a stop for over two decades.

Choose a Comfortable Seat

September 20, 1988, marked a shift in my life. My mom drove me that morning to the Air Force recruitment office in Decatur. All I had with me were the clothes I was wearing, a change of clothes in my recently purchased trumpet case, which doubled as my suitcase, and an old, pocket-sized King James version of the Bible.

I was eighteen and had made the decision almost a year earlier to enlist in the Air Force. Some people have asked why and if it was to gain funds for college. I did not see the Air Force as my route to college. I knew I would go to college—I had to if I was ever going to become the great architect I longed to become— but I did not know how to get there. I knew my mom did not have the money nor the pathway plotted for me to go. The Air Force was something to do. It was my way to be like the professional, confident, and competent man I saw in Sergeant McRay.

Sergeant McRay redeemed himself to me that day because he showed up in Decatur to be with me. I was elated. This was the first time I had seen him in weeks. This was also the first time I had seen him in Levi jeans and a t-shirt. He shook my hand and hugged me. He said, "Thank you for keeping the operations going and for making me look good to these other guys around here."

My mom was within earshot of his words. I could see that she was becoming emotional. He comforted her by saying, "Mom, you have raised a strong man. He is prepared to go out into the world and make something even greater of himself."

He returned his attention to me as he encouraged me to give my best and to stay open to opportunities as they came to me. I had my best stoic mask on my face and showed little, if any, emotion as he spoke to me. Some of the Navy recruiters who manned the office next door arrived while we were talking. One of them laughingly said to Sergeant McRay, "I guess you will have to come back here and do your own job now."

Sergeant McRay said, "Yes, but I won't ever work as hard as Bridgeforth did." He put his hand on my shoulder and pulled me into his side. It was an embrace that was so much more than the muscle and sinew that held us together. It was a spiritual superglue experience where I felt some part of him joined me and would be with me forever.

The big blue and tan bus was waiting. My mom hugged me and cried. She handed me a handwritten note and told me how proud she was of me. As the bus pulled out of the recruitment office parking lot, I waved good-bye to my mom and Sergeant McRay. I was unaware of what was to come. I had enlisted for four years. I was leaving everything and everyone I knew. Even though my life was often uncomfortable, it was familiar.

The bus headed north on Highway 31. As we crossed the Tennessee River, I looked out the window at the Keller Memorial Bridge. It was my favorite bridge as a child because it was a drawbridge and when we drove over it there was an eerie sound that would reverberate through the car. We crossed that bridge on our way to go shopping, to visit my grandparents, to go to church, and just about everything else of significance. It was the bridge to everywhere—including my new life in the Air Force.

As I read my mom's note, my tears flowed in streams of uncertainty about the future and certainty of an unrelenting love between a mother and a son. We had a very close-knit bond. It had been tested greatly in the preceding months, but it did not break under pressure. I left home knowing I was loved and she let me go knowing that when all else failed, our love would succeed.

Several individuals boarded the bus in Huntsville and one of them, Kevin Waldrop, introduced himself to me. We needed to connect because Sergeant McRay told me Kevin had all my enlistment paperwork. I put my mom's note away out of fear I would cry in front of Kevin and the other recruits. My tears had dug ruts in my cheeks throughout the summer, so the path down which they were flowing now was well worn. We rode in relative silence to Nashville, Tennessee, where we would complete the formal enlistment process.

I did not know what to expect when we got off that bus in Nashville. I had not even thought about how we would get from the Military Entrance Processing Station in Nashville to Lackland Air Force Base in San Antonio, Texas. Thankfully Kevin was in charge of getting me and one other person through the airport and to our designated meeting areas.

Two days later, we touched down at San Antonio International Airport. It was hotter and muggier than anything I'd experienced. As soon as we arrived at Lackland, they had us file off the bus and stand next to our luggage. There seemed to be seven drill instructors for each one of us. As soon as one asked a question, another would ask another question. This went on and on for hours. It was disorienting. I kept trying to listen for Kevin's voice in the mix but I could not hear him. He told me he would be with me every step of the way, but his commitment was in question as all these men and one woman yelled and screamed at us.

When we finally got settled into our dorm, I was in a bunk between Kevin and a guy from Oklahoma named Joe Davis. Over the next two days we would all get haircuts, select our uniforms, and be assigned jobs in the dorm. As our drill instructor, Sergeant Filmore, began making assignments, I remembered Sergeant McRay telling me about the various jobs and which ones to avoid.

He said, "If they ask if you know how to paint, sing, or walk in a straight line with your eyes closed, say no."

I asked, "Why? What do those things mean?"

He said, "If you can paint, you can polish, and that will get you on the cleaning crew. If you can sing, you will be assigned to call cadence for the marches. If you can walk in a straight line with your eyes closed, you will be the guidon—the flag bearer. But no matter what job you get, don't be the dorm chief. It is the absolute worst and you have to answer for everything anyone in your flight does."

Sergeant Filmore asked those questions and I had my own internal comedy chuckle as the others raised their hands and were assigned various tasks, just as Sergeant McRay described. There was one question that Sergeant McRay had not mentioned. Filmore asked, "Who wants to be a politician or preacher at some point?" I raised my hand. He said, "Stand up, Airman. What's your name?"

"I am Airman Cedrick Bridgeforth, sir."

"Sir? Do you see anything on my shoulders, Airman?"

"No sir!"

"Sir? There it is again. Let me help you. It is 'Sergeant,' not sir. Save sir for someone else."

"Yes Sergeant."

"What are you saying yes to?"

"Sergeant, I am saying yes to wanting to be a politician or a preacher."

"Airman Bridgeforth, I am going to take you at your word that you want to be a politician or a preacher. I think politicians and preachers make good dorm chiefs."

I could hear Sergeant McRay's words playing in my mind. It was too late now. My assignment made it necessary for me to move bunks to the front of the dorm, which meant I left Kevin and Joe behind. The airman next to me was now Ron Hill from South Carolina.

Our "sister flight" was a group of forty-four men who also began basic training the same day we did. Throughout our six-week training we did most activities with or in competition with them. Their first dorm chief was Airman Malden. He was a tall, dark-skinned brother from somewhere in Louisiana. His voice had a James Earl Jones quality to it and I tried to match his commanding volume and tone as much as my high-pitched alto voice would allow. He only lasted one week as dorm chief, but that was longer than any of the others they had. It became a game for us to bet each morning as to whether their dorm chief would make it through the night. They were astonished at how our flight was able to maintain the same leadership the entire six weeks.

As dorm chief, I was responsible for getting everyone up and out of bed and back to bed at night. I had to take charge of the flight whenever Sergeant Filmore was not with us. I had to know where all forty-three other airmen were at all times. Whenever one of them had an emergency, I was responsible for advocating for them or getting them where they needed to be. The administrative and managerial side of it seemed natural to me. I knew some of the lingo from working in the recruiter's office and from watching training videos Sergeant McRay recommended. I was prepared for most of it except for when someone would find out they had a sick child or a spouse was expressing deep loneliness.

All I knew to do was to grant them extra phone privileges, release them from some chores, or pray with them. Those tactics worked until the day in week four when Airman Kelly's grandmother died. He did not find out directly from his family. The sergeant came to tell him in the presence of all of us. In one sense Kelly knew he was not alone, but in another sense he was really put on the spot to hide or show his deepest emotions among virtual strangers. All too soon, I would revisit that moment and how it was handled.

Manage Your Expectations

At the end of week five, we were granted town pass because we had passed our exams and inspections with honors. This was one of those times that being dorm chief showed its sacrificial nature. I had to be the last person to leave the dorm and the first to return so I could check everyone out and back in at the end of the day. That meant my time exploring San Antonio would be limited.

In anticipation of my abbreviated timeline and limited knowledge of the city, I settled on one destination and that was the Alamo. I read about it in school and figured since I was so close, it would only be right to take in a historical site instead of frolicking in a brothel, getting a tattoo, or any of the things I heard others name on their itineraries.

It was eerie walking from the dorm to the bus depot alone. I didn't realize I was marching and making 90-degree turns at street corners until some guys yelled "It is ok to walk!" out their car window. I had only moved in a formation since my arrival at Lackland. I had not been alone since the night before I left home. Even then, I was not completely alone because I spent it with my friend Lynn reminiscing about all the craziness we had experienced. I was shipping out to the Air Force the next day and he was preparing to report to Army basic training the following week. We laughed at how each of us had made our decision to go into the military and how we chose our respective branches. My decision was based on the image and character embodied in Sergeant McRay. Lynn chose the Army because he wanted to wear a beret and jump out of airplanes. There was something about the rush he felt when watching the video of men parachuting out of perfectly good airplanes that captured his imagination and got him to sign up.

I took a bus to the USO reception center. I expected to see balloons, ticker-tape, confetti, crowds, and at least a recording of Bob Hope. The bus pulled up in front of a nondescript gray building and the driver announced, "Your one and only stop—the USO. Y'all have a wonderful day in San Antonio!"

It was for the best as I would not have had time to see a concert, dance, listen to big band music, and tour the Alamo before my curfew. I got off the bus, went in, grabbed a cold drink, and asked for directions to the Alamo.

The lady who helped me took out a map, circled where we were, and drew a straight line to the Alamo. I asked, "What bus do I take to get there?"

She looked confused, "Bus? There isn't a bus."

I figured it must be so remote that buses didn't go that far. I asked, "Do I just tell any taxi driver to take me to the Alamo?"

She said, "If you follow this map, you don't need transportation."

I said, "I have to be back on base before four o'clock. I don't have a lot of time to waste. What's the quickest way to get to the Alamo?"

She grabbed my hand and led me out the large double doors. She stood over my right shoulder, gently shifted me to the right and said, "Allow your eyes to follow along my arm and beyond the tip of my finger. Do you see a large white sign with black letters on it?"

"Yes. I see it."

"Walk to that and you will see the Alamo."

Now I felt we were finally on the same page. I would walk to that sign and from there I would get on whatever transportation was needed to get out to the Alamo. My journey from the tip of her finger to the large white sign was a short five-minute walk.

When I reached the sign, I looked to the right and I saw another sign: "Welcome to the Alamo." It was apparent that what

I envisioned, based on pictures in my old high school textbooks, must have been how San Antonio looked before the mall and the Olive Garden restaurant were constructed. I did not expect one of the most famous forts in American history to be surrounded by a mall, but it was. I was sorely disappointed. The tour of the Alamo consumed all of twenty minutes, including time spent reading pamphlets about other tourist sites around San Antonio.

There were two other airmen leaving the Alamo as I was walking out. They invited me to join them for lunch with two ladies they met earlier. I agreed since I was not going to be out in the wilderness for hours. We found a little restaurant a couple of blocks away. It was a tiny place on a nondescript side street that served pre-mixed margaritas from what looked like a slurpee machine. They were over twenty-one so they ordered drinks for the table as the two ladies joined us.

The taller of the two was wearing a blue and yellow dress with a split up the left side. It was high enough that when she crossed her legs and allowed her foot to rest on my shin, I could see her entire leg and it was heavy. The other lady spoke rapidly in Spanish to the waiter and bartender but kept her interactions with us to a minimum until she asked me, "Why are you here?"

One of the guys said, "Hey! He is cool. We invited him to join us."

"Yeah, but we did not know there would be three of you." She pointed to the lady with her foot on my shin and continued, "Tell him we didn't know."

My leg felt much lighter as the lady uncrossed her legs, leaned back in her chair, readjusted the straw in her slushy margarita, and said, "It's ok. It will cost extra for him."

I almost choked on a tortilla chip. I said, "I'm sorry. I did not know what was happening until right now."

I pulled some money from my wallet, tossed it on the table, and ran outside as quickly as possible. Since the one thing that stood out to me when I looked around was a familiar sign, I received it as an invitation. I had lunch at the Olive Garden, strolled along the river walk, and went back to base a few hours early. Being there was almost as unsettling as walking alone because the dorm was home to forty-four men and now I had the space alone for almost two hours—no chanting, taunting, cleaning, folding, or studying.

My time in San Antonio, along with basic training in general, taught me to manage my expectations and not allow my limitations from the past to dictate what I could accomplish in the future.

I managed to serve as dorm chief the entire six weeks without caving to pressures from the drill sergeants or the other airmen. Other instructors complimented how well our leadership held together and questioned the secret to our success.

Once, when our family singing group had not connected well with the audience, my grandma told my uncle, "You have to learn how to read a room."

He asked, "What does that mean?"

I learned that it meant listening to those who are speaking, honoring those who are not, and paying attention to what both are communicating. I was in charge of forty-three men ranging in age from eighteen to twenty-seven. Some were fresh out of high school, like me, and others had gone to college or had wives and children. I had to get to know what they needed, what they could offer, and how they could satisfy what we were asked to do.

My experience of volunteering for grown-up jobs during big events at church, my role at Sonic, and my leadership among my peers at high school served me well. When it came to selecting squad leaders who would speak for me or lead the group when I was not around, I selected a diverse group so that together we would have someone everyone could connect with in some way. That was how I assembled my friend group in high school—I was friends with folks in every clique and that allowed me opportunities to move in and out of multiple settings with relative ease. I learned how to read the room.

I gave my best each day. When I became aware that twelve of the airmen in my basic training flight would also be with me in security police training school, I knew I would have their friendship and support for the next leg of the journey. When we arrived at our next training assignment, I was chosen to serve as the leader of our class. I had the opportunity to select others who would be members of my team. I selected from the twelve I knew from basic training.

When I bumped into two of my squad leaders stumbling along the river walk after imbibing too much liquor, I almost questioned the choice I made in selecting them to lead. I thought about my own glass house and figured it best to be mindful of my stones. They were young men out in a town they had never visited before and this was their first engagement with the outside world in five weeks. The locals and the military expected a little carousing and rule-breaking during town pass weekends.

Stars do Shine

I was on a plane from Lackland to Fort Dix, New Jersey, for a six-week Air Base Ground Defense course before I knew I would have to participate in two bivouacs. This was only my second air flight in my life so the last thing I needed was more information to process while being concerned about flight safety and wondering how planes actually fly. My first flight had been the one from Nashville to San Antonio a few months earlier when I had flown off into the wild blue yonder to begin my six weeks of basic training.

This time I was on a commercial airplane with several other airmen on our way to Fort Dix to complete the second half of our technical training as missile security officers. On the flight, I was informed that our training included a two-day and a five-day bivouac. If you are not aware of what a bivouac is, do not feel bad—I didn't know, either. Upon further inquiry I learned that a bivouac was a stay in temporary camps. We were to set up makeshift tents and dig and fortify temporary foxholes as part of a military training exercise to prepare us for the unlikely event of our participation in wartime activities within or on the borders of enemy territories.

The Air Force is the branch of the United States military that does not have an infantry unit, so I was confused and concerned about the reason for such training. It was the dead of winter, we were on our way to one of the coldest regions of the country, and there was no expectation that the United States would go to war with anyone in the foreseeable future.

Two years earlier President Reagan had stood at the Brandenburg Gate and chided the Soviet Leader: "Mr. Gorbachev, tear down this wall!" That day on the plane, I had no idea that in less than a year, the Cold War would come to an end. Even so, there was no hint of the U.S. entering any conflict that would lead to war. So why would men and women who enlisted in the non-infantry branch of the military be required to learn how to set up makeshift camps and command posts, dig foxholes, navigate using self-made topographical maps, and patrol fence perimeters at night? Most importantly, why would we need to learn these things in New Jersey in the winter? There were military bases located in warmer and more exotic climates. Why didn't we train at some of those?

Every day at Fort Dix was a struggle for me. I hated the icy cold weather. I hated the way the Army instructors yelled at us for

no reason. It was the polar opposite of my experience at Lackland.
I felt like I was back at my mom's house with a thousand extra rules
to follow that had no rhyme or reason to them. There were three
episodes at Fort Dix that stick with me and cause me to question
what good came out of my presence there.

I did not meet Airman Jill Rogers at Fort Dix, but we parted
ways there. Our ambiguous entanglement began during the six-
week missile security training at Lackland. She was a few years
older and had worked as a kindergarten teacher before enlisting in
the Air Force. We hit it off right away when we met.

I first noticed her the day we moved into our dorm. It was the
first time since basic training began almost seven weeks earlier that
I heard an entire song on the radio. Al B. Sure's "Night and Day"
was filling the corridors as folks flowed through the narrow pas-
sageways with boxes and suitcases. Some were moving out as we
were moving in. As I made my way through for my last trip, someone on the quad turned their music to full volume as Rob Base &
DJ EZ Rock's rendition of "It Takes Two" nearly exploded those
speakers. Boxes and suitcases were tossed to the side as we created
our own version of a Soul Train line in the quad. That was when
I came face-to-face with Jill for the first time. We boogied our way
down the line together and doubled over with laughter as we made
it to the end. I introduced myself. She replied, "Pleased to meet
you. I am Airman First Class Jill Rogers." She smiled after she said
it, so I repeated it every time I could.

We weren't intimate while at Lackland, although there was an
understanding that we were probably moving toward something.
During our third week of training, Jill injured her leg during a
training drill and was placed on medical leave. That meant she got
to go home to complete her physical therapy while the rest of us
completed security training and then moved on to Fort Dix, which

was only two hours away from Jill's hometown where she was recuperating. We kept up with each other's lives via phone.

After each of the bivouacs we were granted extended time off. Jill decided to surprise me after the first bivouac by coming to visit for the weekend. When she called to tell me she was in town and wanted to see me, I panicked. All of a sudden, I experienced a sense of dread and obligation. I felt bad that she had driven two hours to see me and I had no desire to see her. She stayed at a motel near the base and left messages for me at my dorm. I eventually called her. I said, "I really wish you had told me you were planning to come. I would have made sure to be available."

"Why aren't you available?"

"I made plans with the guys in the dorm."

"Since you see them every day, can't you change those plans?"

"I don't want to be rude."

"Too late. I drove two hours to see you and you are telling me you are not going to be available at all for nearly three days. That is rude."

As much as I felt fond of Jill while we were at Lackland, I realized that the phone romance we had moved into was not one I was really committed to or interested in. The next time I heard Jill's voice was almost three years later at the peak of the troop buildup for Desert Storm.

Many persons from my base in Wyoming volunteered to deploy to Iraq and the Air Force brought temporary transfers from Vandenberg Air Force Base in California to fill in for them. My roommate, Mike, was one who volunteered for deployment and that freed his bed for one of the temps from Vandenberg.

I welcomed the guy and tried to make him feel at home in his temporary quarters. I allowed him to use my phone, television, and even toiletries. He shared with me that he was engaged to someone who was also stationed at Vandenberg but he was not sure if he would actually go through with the marriage. He said, "She is beautiful and smart. I think she would be a great mother if we had children. But she's too damn bossy. She had to be in charge of everything." I wondered why he had asked this woman to marry him if he felt that way. I wondered if she knew how he felt about her forceful and aggressive nature.

One weekend he decided to fly back to Vandenberg for a few days. When he returned, he seemed extremely happy. I asked, "Did you soak up enough of that California sunshine or did that sunshine soak you up?"

"Nah. It's nothing like that."

"What has you smiling so much?"

"My girl."

"Really? The one who is too bossy? Did she cave and let you decide what y'all would have for dinner?"

"She's pregnant, dude. She is pregnant."

"Congratulations! That is a reason to smile."

He went on to tell me that they made the decision to get married within the next few weeks so they would be married before the baby was born. Also, there was a good chance that he might be deployed to Iraq soon. He wanted to have things in order since he was going to be a father.

As we were reveling in the moment, the phone rang. I answered, "Hello, Cedrick speaking."

The person on the other end said, "Cedrick! Cedrick Bridge-forth?"

"Yes. The one and only. Who is this?"

"Believe it or not, it is Airman, I mean Senior Airman, Jill Rogers." She could barely get her own name out without laughing.

"Jill Rogers!" I could not believe it was her.

My excitement from the news about the baby had spilled over into this interaction with Jill in ways that numbed me to the last phone encounter we had while at Fort Dix. I continued, "Not to be rude, but why are you calling me?"

"I'm not calling you."

"You just happened to dial the wrong number and got my room?"

"No. I'm calling to speak with my fiancée."

The second memory of Fort Dix was shaped by one of the Army training instructors who told us he was Lisa Lisa's cousin. She was in my pantheon of female pop stars at the time, which included Tina Turner, Tracy Chapman, Janet Jackson, Debbie Gibson, and the ladies of Exposé. He told us their families lived in the same building in New York. I did not believe he was her cousin. I thought that if he had such a rich and famous cousin, he would not be in the Army—he would have everything he wanted.

The notion that all people who are famous are also rich would change after I moved to California and began to see celebrities at the same restaurants, stores, gas stations, and concerts I attended. My first celebrity sighting was in the summer of 1999, the night I attended Ruby Dee's one-woman show, "My One Good Nerve." A classmate invited me to attend and he warned me that our seats were not together. He sat near the front of the theater and I was seated in the middle orchestra section, three seats from the aisle.

We arrived just in time to take our seats before the curtains opened. That was due to my insistence that I remembered a route that would get us there faster than the route he intended. I was wrong. At the intermission, the lady to my left moved her long blonde mane from my left arm and said to the gentleman to her left, "Q, I have to go to the ladies' room. Do you want to come?"

He said, "I don't think they will let me in there." The two of them laughed as she kissed him and then rose from her seat.

At the end of the show, Ruby Dee stood as poised as ever at center stage and thanked several individuals who were there to support her on the final night of her performance. She named Debbie Allen, Phylicia Rashad, and others, then said, "My friend, the one and only Quincy Jones. Please stand, friend. I am so grateful." The man two seats to my left, who had joked about not being allowed in the ladies' room, was Quincy Jones.

Around 2005, I was asked to give an invocation at an awards banquet hosted by the Los Angeles alumnae chapter of the Delta Sigma Theta sorority, and I was seated between Ruby Dee and Lela Rochon. That gave me an opportunity to tell Ruby Dee how much I enjoyed her show and to tell her my story of sitting next to Quincy Jones without knowing who he was and standing in line for the men's room with Samuel L. Jackson after the show. Seeing people I idolized at the same events and venues I frequented shed a different light on the possibility that the Army training instructor may have been Lisa Lisa's cousin.

When he would share stories or show us pictures, I dismissed him and treated him as though he was fantasizing and lying. The deepest appreciation I had for his mention of her was that it took me back to the night I drove with my friend Buck to see her in concert. The warmth of the innocently sensuous encounter we had on that drive came to mind every time I heard Lisa Lisa. The only thing that almost topped my memory of the drive was the pictures the training instructor eventually showed us of the two of them together in Atlantic City. I don't know if she was really his cousin or if he happened upon her while they were gambling. I do know his lie or his truth kept an effervescence of Buck in my psyche.

Death Is Really a Thing

The details of my time at Fort Dix have never been clear to me because of what happened while I was there. The morning of February 15, 1989, changed my center of gravity and brought me to a point of reckoning with my own mortality. It was a cold, dark, quiet morning as I came to life from within a large tent with several others on my team. It was day three of the five-day bivouac and we were ready to do whatever needed to be done to get over the hump and to reach the end of this experience. The only things between us and graduation from Air Base Ground Defense School and a trip to our first duty stations was completion of this second bivouac and a final fitness exam.

Our teams finished breakfast and began the day's assignments. We moved slowly throughout the morning. It was inevitable that we would have to complete at least one night maneuver, so we allocated our time wisely to ensure success for our team. The team was in sync and finding proactive and efficient means of leaning on each other's strengths. While gathered around a series of abandoned foxholes, we retrieved our food rations, formed a defensive circle, and began to eat lunch. Just as I traded a disgusting pouch of chicken ala king for a slightly more scrumptious chili with beans, the sergeant drove up in his jeep and asked me to join him on a ride back to basecamp.

When we arrived at basecamp I dismounted from the vehicle and awaited instruction or reprimand. It had to be one of the two. I was directed to the large green tent that served as the command post. It had been deemed off limits to us on the first bivouac just as it had been for the first three days of this one.

It was obviously for a higher ranking populous than the one I was a part of. There were heaters with multi-directional blowers, coffee makers, and water dispensers. I saw a comfy-looking sofa, leather desk chairs, and desks dotted with stress balls and family photos. I was so consumed by the opulence and warmth in this tent that I was losing track of my list of possible reasons I was hauled into this space. It never occurred to me that I was being promoted but it would have been a nice place to work, if you have to work in a remote station in the dead of winter in New Jersey. The other reason a promotion would have been nice is because what came next nearly knocked me to my knees.

The officer who delivered the news was someone I had only seen in passing one day in the commissary. I remembered him because he'd been pushing his two sons in the shopping cart and singing to them. I paused as I saw them pass me on the cereal aisle. I always pause when I see a dad engaging his children in loving and compassionate ways because there is something so otherworldly about it to me. It captivates my gaze and my emotions every single time and I stand in awe of the dad and in envy of his children.

So, here I was in this tent with a stranger. He said to me: "Airman Bridgeforth, we have received word from your mother that your grandmother has died."

The stillness of the day became a heaviness in the moment. The opulence of the tent became a tomb for so much I could not name or contain. He asked, "Airman Bridgeforth, do you need to sit? Would you like some water?"

I just looked at him. I wanted to be whisked into a shopping cart and I wanted him to sing to me as he had sung to his children in the commissary. Why wouldn't he just do that for me? It was about the only thing that would have secured me in that moment. He continued, "Airman Bridgeforth, would you like to be transported back to base so you can make arrangements to go home to be with your family?"

He explained to me that it was my choice to stay or to go. Did he really think there was a chance that I would not go to be with my family at a time like this? All I was thinking was "get me on the first thing smoking between here and Alabama." There was no question in my mind about going until he explained that since I had not completed the bivouac, I would have to return after the funeral and repeat the entire five-day bivouac and the final fitness exam. There had been absolutely no equivocation on my part. However, when faced with the requirement of returning to Fort Dix, I had to pray and ask God for guidance.

My grandmother had been the guiding and foundational spiritual figure in my life. I am not sure I even realized how important she had been up to that point. Envisioning a life that did not include her humming spirituals while cleaning house or cooking a meal or dog-earing a Bible passage that Reverend Willie Walter had quoted the previous Sunday, I became as still and as heavy as the air outside the tent earlier that morning. So many questions began to well up in my mind as tears gathered in my eyes.

Where would I seek wise counsel or glean unsolicited life lessons? Who would make a whole pan of cornbread just so I could crumble it up in buttermilk as a snack? Who would sprinkle sugar on white toast and convince me it was better than the toast they served at school? Who would drop knowledge and truth on me in ways that allowed me to hear it without being judged or damned? Who would show me how to remove and replace purse linings to hide money? Who would make hot toddies to fight a cold that no one who is not a certified wino should drink—much less a ten year old? Would anyone ever again allow me to break the saltines on the Communion plates every First Sunday? Who would read the Sunday School lesson to granddaddy to include him despite his illiteracy?

I thought about Airman Kelly and how he must have felt when he found out during basic training that his grandmother had died. The sergeant had called him to the front where all of us could see him, and said, "Your grandmother died sometime between last night and this morning. You need to decide if you want to go be with your family or if you want to stay here and complete your training."

Airman Kelly stood still and quiet. The sergeant addressed all forty-three of us: "Airmen, what I hope you learn here today and never forget is that every day you move closer and closer to death. The longer you live, the closer death comes to you. That is just a part of life. Death is a fact of life."

One by One They Die

The sergeant's words were as prophetic as they were true. I was living in California in 2003 when Auntie Eunice died. I was pastoring a church in Los Angeles, completing my doctoral coursework, and working at the seminary. My mom called to let me know Auntie Eunice's cancer had returned and the treatments were not working. Her voice was darker than that of a thousand midnights. "Eunice is not doing good with this cancer."

"Who actually does good with cancer? She is a fighter. You know that."

"Yeah, but her body is giving out on her. She can't continue struggling like this."

My mom began to sob, which was not something she did easily or often. The two sisters were extremely close and their bond had only grown deeper and tighter as the years progressed. My mom's pain was so palpable that I could not even consider my own sorrow and grief. I made arrangements to fly to Alabama for a few days to say my farewell to Auntie Eunice and offer my deepest gratitude for how she never judged me harshly. Her interventions were the ones that kept me and my mom engaged during those turbulent high school days.

Auntie Eunice was a daddy's girl and I believe that helped her have a deeper understanding about my disgust and anger about Lawrence's unwillingness to connect and my inability to accept the love and presence my dad George eventually tried to offer me. I was so torn. I wanted love from a father who would never come around and rebuffed affection from the one who gave me his name. It was as though if I could not have the one I wanted, then nothing and no one else would suffice.

Auntie Eunice was my confidant and protector. She encouraged me to go after my dreams and to dare to be and do more than I ever saw anyone else in our family be and do. She had the "birds and bees" talk with me, she knew I was gay, and she trusted me with her secrets, too.

The last conversation I had with Auntie Eunice was at her bedside at Decatur General Hospital—the hospital where I was born and had worked as a security guard. I asked if I could have alone time with her and everyone left the room. I sat at her bedside for what seemed an eternity. I said, "You showed me how to be a good person and to love myself. You helped shape me into the man that I am. Thank you." I was aware of the ticking of the heart monitor and the drip of morphine. I dredged the depths of my heart in hopes that she would receive what I offered. "You have done your best for me, my mom, Mario, Elon, Derrick, and all of us. We can get it from here. You can rest now. Thank you for everything."

I walked out of that room certain I had said what I could. I stayed in Alabama two more days before I flew back to California. My mom did not leave the hospital much while I was in town. She quarantined herself to her sister's bedside and sat watch over her. As I drove the three hours to Atlanta, I wondered how my mom would handle this death. They had always had each other to lean on. When I stopped to fill the rental car with gas, I called the hospital to let them know I made it to Atlanta safely and to check on everyone. My mom cleared her throat. She said, "She is gone, Ced. She is gone. Eunice is gone."

The last time I remembered crying so intensely was fourteen years earlier when grandma died. Cutting short my bivouac was the beginning of a fraught journey. I had to book my first solo flight, I took the wrong bus and ended up in New York City instead of Newark, and I ran through an airport and still missed my flight to Huntsville.

When I boarded the bus at Fort Dix, I told the driver, "I am going to Newark. How will I know when I get there?"

He said, "It's the last stop. You can't miss it."

I took him at his word, took my seat in the area Rosa Parks never would have accepted, and went to sleep. My eyes had not closed since the sergeant's words ripped my heart out of my chest, so this long ride was the lullaby my body craved. My slobber and dreamscape were interrupted by clapping and cheers. I sat up in my seat and looked out the window to see a tall banner that covered almost the entire side of a building. It had an image of a New York Yankees player and read "Welcome to New York!"

My knowledge of geography wasn't the sharpest, but I was certain we would have to bypass all of northern New Jersey to get to New York City. I tried to remain calm until the bus came to a stop and the driver yelled, "Last stop. Everyone must get off here."

I was the last passenger on the bus. I asked, "Are we at the Newark Airport?"

He said, "No. We are in New York. Our last stop. Isn't this where you said you needed to go?"

"No! I asked how I would know when we got to Newark?"

"Son, I am sorry. I guess it's your accent. It sounded like you said New York. Get your bags and come with me. I will take you to the bus that only goes to the Newark Airport."

By the time I reached the airport I only had fifteen minutes to get to my gate. This was my third flight ever and my first on my own. I ran as fast I could but I did not make my flight. The lesson was to enunciate and be sure my southern drawl did not send me forty-five minutes past where I intended to go.

Another notable thing about that time was that I moved up to the second row at the funeral. Prior to my grandma's funeral, I was always a "cousin" or "extended family member" at anyone's funeral, which meant I was far back in the family procession and several rows from the front. At grandma's funeral I escorted my mom so I ended up on the second row. My placement in the procession and seating order was significant to me. My parents were divorced and my older brother was not present. I had to step into a role reserved for the senior man in my mom's life, and at that moment, it was me.

Her body was in a casket almost as an "x" marking the spot where she told me "Boy, one day you're gonna preach!" long before I ever did, the spot where I professed Christianity and gave Easter speeches as a young child, the spot where I would stand five years later and hug my grandfather after delivering my first sermon in that church. I could hear her voice in my mind, recapping Sunday School lessons, encouraging someone to raise a particular hymn, naming the special ingredients in a famed recipe, describing the healing effect of a particular herb, divulging the cause of death of a loved one that no one knew except her, and misquoting Bible verses. She was gone but she felt so present.

As I wavered between fetching tissues for my mom and tucking my own tear-soaked tissues in my jacket pocket, I heard sergeant's words, "The longer you live, the closer death comes to you."

Don't Ask and Barely Tell

In March 1989, barely a month after my grandma's death and my arrival at Francis E. Warren Air Force Base in Cheyenne, Wyoming, I went to a local park where the gay, bisexual, and sexually curious men in Cheyenne would gather, troll, and meet others of like propensities. There wasn't a bar, lounge, or any other indoor establishment that catered specifically to gay clientele. This was long before cell phones, online dating, or hookup apps. The only way to meet another gay person was to know where they gathered and find an entry point into that sphere.

The entry point was usually someone in-the-know who trusted you enough to tell you. Other times you could stumble upon information about places to meet scribbled in public restrooms. There was also a book, *The Damron Gay Men's Travel Guide*, which listed hotels, restaurants, stores, travel agencies, cruise lines, gyms, bathhouses, and public spaces that gay people might frequent or patronize. The first time I saw one of those guides I was overwhelmed by the vast amount of information. The first place I looked up was my home state of Alabama, then my home city of Decatur. I thought I knew all of the closeted, curious, and gay persons in my high school and locale, but I did not know there were places in that southern riverboat and industrial town where they gathered in public. I found it all in the Damron Guide.

I don't know if I was more surprised, disappointed, or frightened by what I discovered in that book. Imagine learning that the site where my grandparents took us fishing along the Tennessee

River was a place frequented by gay and bisexual men looking to connect. According to the guide, this was also a local hotspot for the police to stage sting operations and arrest persons for engaging in lewd behaviors in the nearby woods. How was it possible that I had sat on that little plastic bucket next to my grandfather on the riverbank and not noticed men wandering past me to rendezvous nearby? Were we so focused on fishing that it never occurred to us to question why folks would drive to that remote wooded area to take a stroll in the middle of the day without a hunting rifle, fishing pole, or anything to engage the natural elements? The mall where my friends and I would hang out on weekends was another place that had made its way onto the Damron list, as did the pavilion at Rhodes Ferry Park.

In Cheyenne, the park with the tennis courts and dog playground was the place to be. It was listed in Damron and the description was as precise as possible, with directions to the exact area where cars would be parked, a key to what the count of flashing headlights or taillights signaled, and a warning about police harassment if you were in the park past ten o'clock at night.

That's how I found myself sitting in my car in the park, looking around and wondering if I was in the right place, because there were no other cars nearby. Suddenly, a car passed me, continued to the end of the lane, and turned around. As it passed me the second time, the driver slowed to catch a glimpse of my face. He proceeded to the end of the lane again. This time he stopped and flashed his brake lights two times. I remembered from the guide that two taps meant the person was interested in connecting. If I were interested, I then had to respond with two taps of my brake lights.

I had not done this before. I tapped my brakes to show my interest and the other car looped around a third time and proceeded to park four spaces from me. I was now terrified because the guide did not have instructions as to what to do next. Was this a set-up by someone trying to trap me and have me charged for being homosexual?

Nestled in the cab of my little red Chevy S-10 pickup, I remembered sage advice I heard a few months earlier from one of the training instructors at Fort Dix. He said, as we were holding live grenades preparing to throw them over a wall, "Until or unless you know what to do, do absolutely nothing."

This moment felt like that moment. I was sweating and aware of every heartbeat. I felt the presence of a proverbial hand grenade, but I wasn't sure if I was holding it or if it was about to be lobbed from four spaces away.

As I sat there, wondering and waiting, the person in the car four spaces away tapped his brakes one time. I was not exactly sure what one tap meant versus two taps. I played along. I tapped my brake light so he could see it as well. This little game of tap, wait, tap, wait, went on for quite some time. While that was happening, there were other cars that drove through the park slowly, looked, and continued on their way. Eventually the car started its engine. As I saw the reverse lights flash, I realized something was about to change. It seemed our tap, wait, tap, wait game would end.

In a panic, I did what any person on the verge of entering an abyss would do—I turned on my headlights. Again, there was not any notation in the guide about headlights, but I felt desperate to capture the attention of the person who had held my gaze across a darkened parking lot. When I flashed my headlights, the car stopped, changed directions, and proceeded toward me. The four spaces were now reduced to none as he parked in the space directly beside me.

Now, the game shifted from tap, wait, tap, to look, look away, look, look away. It was easier to imagine a person staring at me from across a dark parking lot than it was to have them right next to me and know it was happening. If the hand grenade scenario was driving my narrative, then so was the terror I felt at my freshman homecoming dance.

I wanted to dance or be asked to dance but I was afraid. I knew dancing required movement and acquiring a partner required openness and at least an ounce of vulnerability. Just as back then, I wondered if I would be left this night in possession of my dance card. The difference was that this time I wasn't frozen, paralyzed, or reacting out of fear. I was really unsure of what to do and simultaneously keenly aware of what could happen and how it could change or alter the course of my life. That deep sense of knowing the gravity of the moment could have been weighted because I felt like a familiar stranger in this new space even though I was clearly a stranger in a strange land.

Ask Curious Questions

If that encounter had happened a couple months later, I would have known exactly what to do. I know that to be true because it was about two months later when I would meet Andy in this same park. But I was not supposed to be at the park that night, playing tap, wait, tap or look, look away, look. I was not supposed to be using the Damron Guide to plan outings. My supervisor at Warren Air Force Base, Jim Lentz, had given it to me to review.

It all started with a conversation on one of those nights when we were on a three-day deployment in the missile field. A herd of wild horses, an antelope, a rabbit, or the wind could set off one of the missile alarms. Whenever that happened, we would have to go out to the missile site, which could be upwards of fifty miles away, and find a way to reset the alarm.

This was the second consecutive night that Jim and I found ourselves sitting at Tango 10 missile site. To a plane flying above or a civilian driving past it or any of the other nine missile sites in the area, it would appear to be a four hundred square foot fenced-in area covered by a mass of concrete maintained by the electric or phone company. But a hundred feet below that concrete slab was a Peacekeeper missile with at least ten nuclear warheads attached. The alarm sensors were set to detect even the slightest intrusion on or near the fencing.

The first night we sat at Tango 10 for approximately three hours before the alarm reset. The second night, which ended up being a night to end all nights, we were there nearly six hours. Jim was my training supervisor and he outranked me. That meant I was responsible for getting out of the vehicle and walking the perimeter of the missile site in total darkness while he sat in the comfort of the Chevy Suburban. We did have radios that allowed us to communicate with each other and with our base. After walking the perimeter several times, to no avail, we were instructed to wait onsite while the missile officers tried to clear the alarm.

While we sat there again as we had the night before, I noticed that Jim was writing profusely in a spiral bound notebook. The night before, he wrote the entire time too. I took note of his tension in the deliberate strokes of the pen as it hit each page and curved each letter. I finally mustered up enough courage to ask him a question.

I asked, "What are you writing?"

He responded," A letter, dumbass."

I wasn't prepared for him to speak to me that way and had he not laughed after he said it, that would have been the end of that conversation. But his chuckle left the gate open for me to journey into a conversation.

I asked, "Who are you writing the letter to?"

He replied, "Mary."

"Your wife?"

"Yes!"

"Why are you writing a letter to your wife?" I asked because I knew he lived with his wife and her ten-year-old son, Ben. "Is she out of town?"

He said, "Nope. She has her ass at home where she is supposed to be."

That time I laughed. I was confused. He then asked me, "Do you have any other questions?"

"Yes. I do have one question, but I am not sure if it is appropriate to ask you."

"Well, you little shit, you are already in my business so go ahead."

"Are you writing to her about something you already talked about?"

"Yes. I told her I want a divorce."

"How did she take that news?"

"She was not happy, but she realizes we have not been happy for a long time."

"Wow! That must be hard to write and to share your deepest thoughts with her."

"That's not what I'm doing with this letter. I already told her I want a divorce, so there is nothing else to discuss about that. I am listing everything I want in the divorce."

"You mean like custody of Ben?"

"No. He's her son. He would not want to come with me anyway."

"So, what are you asking for?"

"I want to make sure I say exactly what I mean. I want her to have a full understanding of what I want out of the house."

I remember when my parents divorced, there were fights about property and assets. The funny thing is, I don't remember us having very much. As for custody, we were asked if we wanted to live with my dad or my mom. At age eleven, that was a big deal. It seemed a no-brainer that my younger sister and I would definitely go with my mom but my brother was a wildcard. Ultimately, he decided to remain with my dad. That was a decision I appreciated at the time, but looking back, it may not have been the best choice for him or for us.

As Jim continued scribbling, I yet again interrupted his flow to ask a question.

"What are you asking her for?"

He said, "I only want four things out of the house: the china in the dining room, the oil painting hanging in our foyer, the pewter collection, and I want her gone."

These seemed like odd requests for a thirty-something-year-old man.

"Those must be very nice, expensive, and special items."

He said, "I like nice things." He turned and looked at me across the darkened cab of that Chevy Suburban. "Let me guess, you have another question."

I said, "Yes. But I do not want to offend you or get into trouble, so I can let my question fade and you can finish your letter."

His eyes rested on me as I sheepishly looked away from him and out into the distant darkness toward Tango 10, wondering why I was wondering what I was wondering about my supervisor. His voice rang out with a twang of a Kentucky accent: "Spit it out!"

"No, it is OK. I do not want to offend you."

He said, "You will not offend me with anything you ask or say. So, say it."

While I continued to gaze across the landscape beyond the fence line of Tango 10, words welled up from my belly and landed in the darkened vehicle as though from another passenger who had been there the whole time.

"Based solely on what you have asked for in your divorce, I am curious."

His dark green eyes pierced mine. In that millisecond between his gaze and my words that followed, I felt I could leap a tall building with a single bound or stop a locomotive with my bare hands. Just as I had sat on the steps of that dorm during Boys State and disclosed my sexuality to Chris Granberry, I found the bravery or abandonment necessary to ask Jim, my supervisor: "Are you gay?"

Once the words were out, I held my breath and could not exhale. Then the same laugh that he belted after referring to me as a "dumbass" filled the cab of the vehicle. As he laughed his neck swiveled away from my direction. Maybe he was charting a pathway into which he might run and escape the question that was hanging in the still night air. Out of his bellows of laughter came a simple response. "Yes, I am. Are you?"

"Yes, I am."

"No shit? I never would have guessed."

I was now breathing. I joined his laughter and said, "I would not have guessed that about you either, except that your choice items in your divorce were a dead giveaway."

We spent the balance of that time at Tango 10 sharing stories of how we came to realize we were attracted to men, until the alarm was cleared and we could return to base. As we drove back, he told me there were a great number of people like us stationed at our base and he would like for me to meet them. As intrigued as I was by this notion of meeting other gay people in the Air Force, I was afraid. I lived undercover as far as my sexuality was concerned. I was a devout Christian, a leader in my church, and popular among my classmates, and I always had a girlfriend. What was not widely known was that I always had a boyfriend too. My family, my religion, my need for self-preservation, and my conviction that somehow and someday I would change led me to believe if I just never gave public voice to my reality, everything would eventually work itself out. When I entered the Air Force, I had no intention of acting on my sexual attractions within the military sphere.

Learn How to Park

Jim offered to introduce me to his group of gay friends who were also in the Air Force. He assured me they would take care of me. He said, "We'll show you what you need to know and do so you won't be caught off guard or get caught into situations that are not good for you." That meant a lot to me even though I had no point of reference or context upon which to weigh his promises or commitments. He inquired if I had a Damron Guide. I didn't because I had never heard of it. Up to that point I had never been more than seventy miles from my hometown and the only "gay" anything I knew anything about was Steven Carrington, a character on *Dynasty*, and the boys from my high school that I had chance encounters with. Now Jim was telling me there was a guide for being gay.

A few days after our return to base, he invited me to pick him up at his home so we could go to a nearby park. I wondered why my supervisor wanted to go to a park, but I had probably asked a sufficient number of questions and thought it best not to push my luck.

Jim and Mary lived in one of the homes along the train tracks that ran through the middle of Frances E. Warren Air Force Base. That particular section of housing was once reserved for commissioned officers, but since the base had built newer and larger homes for officers, it was made available for enlisted families. The red brick two-story homes with white trim and wooden shutters made it seem as though time stopped as you strolled or drove past them. They were from a long-ago era but housed contemporary families, electronics, and secrets that their architects most likely never intended.

It was awkward making idle chitchat with Mary for a few moments while I waited for Jim to get ready. Did she know that I knew about the pending divorce? Did she know that I knew Jim was not Ben's biological father? Why would any of that matter if I knew the biggest secret of all?

As we departed the base en route to a local park, Jim reached into his green backpack and pulled out a small book that was as dog-eared as my grandmother's faux leather Scofield Study Bible. The title on the worn cover was *Damron Men's Travel Guide*. He said, "This is standard for all us gays. I will loan it to you and show you how to order one for yourself. For now, just look at it and familiarize yourself with it so that on our next six-day break, I can take you to some places in this book."

We drove to the park and it looked like a normal park except for a circle of cars at the far end of the parking lot. I could see men standing in the center of the circle created by the cars. We parked nearby and got out. As we walked toward the circle, Jim began naming the different men there. I noted something peculiar about his language: he used the feminine pronoun "she" in reference to each of these men. I was not familiar with such a concept, but I figured I had already reached my quota of questions so I simply listened.

Jim introduced me to the cast of characters in that circle. Some of them were locals and others were members of the Air Force. Although they were all white, I felt an immediate sense of ease with them. Ken, Bill, Jay, and Chuck were enlisted in the Air Force. Jason was a long-haired blond who had recently moved to Cheyenne from

Grand Island, Nebraska. Alongside Jason was Phil, an ex-Mormon who escaped a small town in the southern corner of Utah to make a new home in Cheyenne as a cook at a local diner. The two older men in the group were longtime lovers who claimed to be married, although this was nearly thirty years before same-gender marriage was legal in the United States. They owned the local adult book-store and wouldn't charge people they knew personally—basically, gay men—for most items in their store.

These men were from different places around the country and they had found kinship with each other. I hadn't felt this since my high school years, when Lynn, Jamie, and Jason had offered me solace and comfort as I discovered my preference for and magne-tism toward men.

During this encounter at the park, I learned that these men represented just a small portion of the gay members of the Air Force. They were naming names, telling me what types of cars the men drove and their various proclivities. I was a tad embarrassed. I was amazed that they were so comfortable sharing about them-selves out in the open with other men listening. That was my first real public gay conversation.

We did not stay at the park very long, but Jim did tell me on our way back to the base that this park was where men would go at night to meet other men—locals as well as other Air Force men. I dropped Jim off at his home and hurried to my dorm to crack open the Damron Guide. I missed my standing racquetball game and dinner to read as much as humanly possible.

That was when I discovered all of the haunts where gay men and men who enjoy encounters with other men would meet in my hometown. Jim told me the park we had gone to was *the* park in Cheyenne. I verified this in the guide and as soon as the sun set that evening, I drove as quickly as I could back to that same park.

Is it a Crime?

This is how I found myself sitting in my truck, in the park, in the dark, with a man I did not know sitting in his car parked next to mine, wondering what would happen next as we played a game of look, look away. I would look in his direction until I sensed he might look in mine. I would look away just before his head would turn in my direction. As we did this dance, I heard music coming from his car. The song was "Is It A Crime?" by Sade.

The irony was too much to handle. Here we were on this clandestine venture and the soundtrack asked whether loving someone was like criminal behavior. I assumed that adding music was another step and in response, I rolled down my window as an equal step. Would this end the game that began with brake light taps and waiting, followed by look, don't look?

I sat there listening to the hallowed melody of Sade as I heard him singing along with her. It was then that I realized he was not looking at me at all. Had I longed for it or imagined it? It was I who was staring at him as though he were center stage at Carnegie Hall in front of a sold-out audience. He was performing that song and I was his fan. When the song ended, I said, "Wow." It must have come out like that line in the film *When Harry Met Sally*: "I'll have what she's having!"

I thought I was speaking to myself, but I quickly realized that because my window was down, he heard me. Out of embarrassment, I began to chuckle the way Jim had chuckled a few nights before during our awkward conversation at Tango 10. He laughed. I saw the whiteness of his teeth in the dark. Then he rolled down his window, looked at me, and said, "I hope you were not raised to believe it's polite to laugh at people."

I said, "No. I was not raised to laugh in people's faces. Is that your favorite song?"

"It used to be. I've lived a little while past this song's life on the charts."

"Scorned by love?"

"No. I am the one who does the scorning around here. Don't you forget that!"

"What's your name?"

"Frank. Yours?"

"Don."

One of the early lessons Jim had taught me was never use your real name. However, as I used an assumed name and introduced myself to Frank, I wondered if that was indeed his real name. I also wondered if the men I met earlier that day in that same park had used pseudonyms. I knew Jim's real name because he was my supervisor. His name was on all of my paperwork and he wore a uniform with his last name sewn on the chest. The reason Jim gave for using pseudonyms was so it would be harder for people to find you or to exploit you in any way. It did not take me long to realize that this practice was common beyond military circles and was a staple within the gay community.

Frank and I sat in the park until closing time. I had lost track of time but the police car sitting at the entrance to the park was a clear sign that it was time for us to go.

Frank said, "Give me your number and I will call you tomorrow."

I gave him my number, and we departed the park.

On my way home, I replayed the events of that day and the days leading up to it. I was not sure what my next steps would be, but I knew I had turned a corner and entered a cave or space that seemed to have no end.

Frank did not wait until the next day to call me. By the time I reached my dorm room, I had two messages on my answering machine. The first one was from my sister, telling me to give her a call as soon as possible. The second message was from Frank. "Great meeting you tonight. I look forward to seeing you tomorrow evening for dinner. I will call you tomorrow with details. Oh yeah! Get your story straight by 7 p.m.!" What was he talking about? What dinner? What story? He continued, "Good night, Cedrick, Joe, or whatever your name is."

Oh. The outgoing message on the answering machine was clear: "Sorry we're not available right now. To leave a message for Joe, press one. To leave a message for Cedrick, press two."

I was embarrassed that I lied and he knew it. But my curiosity was piqued. He left the message in the correct voice mailbox. But how did he know to press 2?

Use Your ID and IQ

By the time I met Andy at that park two months later, I was well-schooled in the art of meeting other gay men, concealing my identity, and making conversation in groups where I remained a fun and relatively unknowable entity. Jim and his friends delivered on the promise to teach me what I needed to know about living this life while hiding in plain sight. They introduced me to the Denver gay club scene, bath houses, sex parties, porn shops, adult theaters, and the proper etiquette for cruising men in the local parks and malls. Jim repeated, "I never want you to be surprised or caught off guard because being gay can be dangerous."

He told me that with every new experience. Those men shepherded me as though I were a sheep to be domesticated, not one to be slaughtered. They showed me what looked dangerous and persons who did not have a savory agenda. Although I was barely eighteen, I was immersed in the wiles and culture of gaydom in the late eighties. All I had to do was flash my military identification to the doorman or bouncer and the doors would open. I mentioned Jim's name to any bartender and the booze would flow freely. I never used my real name and I always lied about where I was stationed and what my specialty was.

It was easy to tell versions of truths and portions of stories because the assumption was that everyone else was creating their reality on the fly just as I was. We were all afraid that everything could be taken away from us if our truth was known. That is why when I showed up at the Twin Dragon Chinese Restaurant on Pershing Boulevard to meet Frank for that 7 p.m. dinner, I was resolute in my belief that he might be the one who would destroy me. I was prepared to sit across from him and dine on a cuisine that I had never tasted before and hold to every lie and untruth that I could. That felt more powerful to me than telling him my name, where I worked, or where I lived. There was the problem of him knowing my name was not Don, however, and we had to address that first. When Frank called me the morning after that fateful meeting in the park and I attempted to tell another lie to cover my original lie, he said, "Save the truth of who you are and whatever you wish to share until you are comfortable with me."

Who was this man? I walked into the Twin Dragon promptly at 7 p.m. The hostess greeted me and asked if I had a reservation. I told her I was meeting someone. She bowed slightly and smiled. She said "The gentleman you are waiting for has already been seated over there."

She pointed across the restaurant to a corner booth and there he was, with that smile that I had seen through the window of his car. That smile was attached to a man much taller and more stunning than I had gathered some twenty hours earlier.

As I approached the table, he stood. We shook hands and I sat across from him. After a few moments of small talk—and yes, he did poke fun at my name—he motioned for the waitress. He asked me if I had any allergies or any favorite Chinese dishes. I said, "No. I'm good with all of it." I had lied about that, too. The truth of the matter was that I had never eaten Chinese food before. I was praying he would order something I would like or he would tell me what was preferred on the menu.

I asked, "What do you usually order?"

He said, "I like the dumplings and sweet-and-sour pork."

I thought to myself, I have had chicken and dumplings before, so I like dumplings too. I also thought I like pork, and if it is sweet, that is even better, and I will figure out what makes it sour later.

Frank really liked to hear himself talk and I enjoyed the show he provided. All the while, I questioned whether he was telling the truth or making up the stories as he went along. About halfway through dinner, a nearby couple stood up to leave. As the man put on his jacket, he turned and saw the two of us seated at the corner booth.

When he recognized Frank, he shouted across the restaurant: "Hello, Lieutenant Parker!"

I thought, Lieutenant Parker? Was that Frank's real name? How had I missed a Department of Defense officer sticker on his car?

Frank looked at me and apologized for what had just happened. I had no idea why he felt the need to apologize. All the man did was refer to him by his title and last name. I knew neither of those prior to that moment. I also did not know if Frank was his true first name. In fact, it did not matter if Frank was his first name because I had lied about mine. I reasoned that any untruth he offered had to be acceptable. At least, that is what I told myself in that moment.

I tried to move us back to lighter banter, but Frank was clearly rattled by what had happened. In an effort to ease some of the tension and level the playing field, I told Frank my full name, where I worked, and my hometown. He asked, "Why did you do that?"

I said, "I am comfortable with you."

That was not entirely true but it seemed the right thing to say in the moment so that we could move forward in our conversation and complete our meal. I went out with Frank a few more times and hung out with him at his apartment but it was clear we were both too afraid to let down our guards with each other.

One night I called Frank to see if he wanted to go to a movie. He told me he had other plans but would be open during the weekend. I was due to go to the missile field over the weekend so there was no way we would be able to connect. I was disappointed that he was not available. I was bored and free. I decided to go to the park to see if anyone was there that night. When I arrived, there were several cars lined up at the back of the lot in the same area where Jim had introduced me to his friends.

I had been there enough now to recognize some of the local's cars and I knew enough to scan very quickly for military decals on vehicles. As I parked at the end of the long line of cars, Jason ran over to my truck. He said, "Girl, you're not the newbie anymore. We have a new one tonight."

There I was, as male as I knew to be, but being referred to by the feminine pronoun. That is how Jim spoke of those guys when he introduced me to them. I felt as though I had arrived. I was one of the guys—or one of the girls, take your pick.

I walked over to the group with Jason holding me by my arm. There was one unfamiliar face in the crowd. Jason introduced me to the newcomer. His name at the beginning of that night was Robert. I spent that night hanging on Robert's every word. He was different from all the others. His diction was perfect. His hair was perfect. His smile was perfect. At the end of the night we left the park together, and I noticed the interior of his car was perfect. There was something about this man, Robert, that captured my full attention. By the time the sun rose the following morning, I had moaned and groaned enough through the night that I knew without a doubt that Robert was really Andy.

Come Out

During my second year in the Air Force, I was in love. Nothing could have convinced me that this love would not last a lifetime. Of course, that is the certainty that only a nineteen-year-old could have. I was serving my country, feeling grown, and madly in love with Lieutenant Andrew "Andy" Roberts, and I was convinced I would spend the rest of my life with him.

Late one night while Andy was away visiting his family in Pennsylvania, I found myself missing him madly. I was so lonely, and so convinced of my love and my commitment to the relationship, that I put pen to paper and I wrote my mom a long letter.

The letter went back to early childhood memories and adolescent curiosities. It told of feelings and desires that a son should probably not share with his mother, but I did. I even included a clause about how I understood how this news might render our relationship null and void and how I would find a way to move forward without her and without my family. I wrote:

> You raised us to always tell the truth, but there has been so much about my life that has not been on the up-and-up. I did not feel safe telling you that I was gay because of some of the things I heard you say about people who were gay or you suspected might be. I loved how you told people you were proud of me. Sometimes I felt like a trophy you had won and

that brought me joy. At other times I just wanted to be placed on the shelf to collect dust like Dad's two bowling trophies that used to sit in the living room. I never wanted you to look away from me or to look at me in disgust or to feel disgraced by me. I did not want you to be ashamed of me or to stop loving me. I have taken pride in being your son even in those most recent times when I have put you through hell . . . I am not sure that I still believe God will damn me to Hell for living my truth. Because of that, I am willing to hold the truth of what I do know of God more than I am willing to rely on what others have told me about God . . . Now I know what it feels like to be loved unconditionally—to be loved for who I am. I suppose that is what you have sought in your own life and relationships. I'm sure I got it from somewhere because it is a strong and never-ending desire—to be loved unconditionally . . . Given what I have found in my current love with someone who truly puts my needs above his own and looks at me with as much pride as you do, I have what I need to write this letter to you and let it land however it does and know that I have done my part to be honest, compassionate, and open with you. I love you and that will never change . . . With that knowledge and assurance, I have come to realize that if you turn your back on me because I have shared my truth with you, then that raises far more questions about your integrity than it does about mine.

I was so convinced of my love and my commitment that I filled every page with words that made it abundantly clear that I was gay and I was not open to debate that fact. I neatly folded those pages, placed them in an envelope, affixed a stamp, marched downstairs and over to the post office box, and dropped the letter into the box.

As that little blue door slammed shut, so did my throat. I gasped, "What have I done?" I stood next to the post box wondering how I might retrieve that letter and destroy it. Suddenly I was not as convinced or as committed as I thought I was.

I ran back upstairs and called my good friend Bill. I told him what I had done and he assured me I would be fine. Time passed more slowly that night than it had the day I was sitting in that little room at the County Courthouse. I questioned if I had done the right thing. I wondered if my mom would ever embrace me again. In fact, I wondered if she would disown me and curse the day I was born. Before I scripted that letter, I was so convinced of my love for Andy that I was willing to forgo ever seeing or interacting with my family again. If they disowned me, I knew I had the love of my life to make a new life with and my absence from their lives would be their loss.

The next morning, as the sun rose, I called my mom at work so I could have one more conversation with her before she received the letter. I wanted to hear her tell me how proud she was of me for serving my country and for staying true to my faith. I wanted her to say how much she believed in me and how she realized my struggles over the past year were not the sum total of my character, but came from a place of pain and confusion. I wanted to end that conversation just as we had ended all the others—convinced of our love and commitment to support each other, even when we were on each other's nerves.

A few days went by and I did not hear anything from her. I was worried she had received my letter and this time she would go silent and never speak to me again. In the days since I mailed the letter, I rehearsed what it would be like to walk into the house at some ungodly hour now that she knew my truth. I imagined the foul labels and insults that would be hurled at me. After all, for me this was not new, but for her and for others it would be news. The scenario constructs proved too taxing for me to handle alone so I drove to Denver to visit Bill. He had lived most of his life as an out gay man.

He had been discharged from the Air Force a few months earlier and he made being gay seem so easy and natural. His family loved him and included him in their lives the way I was convinced mine would before I mailed that letter. I shared with him my anguish and concerns. This was the longest stretch of time I had gone without speaking to my mom. When he heard far too much from me, he disappeared into the kitchen and I heard him talking to someone on the phone. Eventually he emerged from the kitchen and handed me the phone. He said, "Here! It's your mother. Talk to her."

I sat there as confused as I was that evening at Kentucky Fried Chicken when my mom introduced me to Lawrence. I was not prepared or equipped to have the conversation. The weight I felt with Lawrence as we sat in that car in silence had journeyed to Denver for this very moment. It took its rest upon my shoulders and I nearly collapsed underneath it before I finally took the receiver and said: "Hey!"

She replied, "Are you alright?"

I said, "I am alright. How are you?"

She said, "Just finished cooking dinner and don't think I really want to eat now that I'm done. I am ok. How are you?"

"Oh ok. What did you cook?"

"Salmon patties, corn with butter beans, and some cornbread. I think I burned the bread a bit but it will do for now. Your sister is at a basketball tournament, so it's just me. You know I have some questions about that letter."

"I know. I did write a lot. Where did she go for the game?"

"I think they went somewhere near Montgomery. She been gone two days and be back late tomorrow if they win all their games."

"Are they expected to do well?"

"She seemed to think they would do alright. I want to know if you blame me for this."

"No! I don't blame you for anything. I didn't say that in my letter."

"I know, but maybe I didn't do something right. Is that why this has happened?"

"There isn't anything to blame you for. This is not about you. Nothing has happened, except that I was born and now I can tell you I know I am gay."

"How can you be sure? You know what the Bible says about this."

"That's probably why it took so long for me to be honest. But I have heard and read what the Bible says about a lot that does not make sense to me. I also know how I feel and what I have always felt. I cannot lie about it or deny it."

The conversation went on for a while. Bill sat next to me and held my hand tightly as I spoke boldly and courageously with my mom. She asked questions about friends, classmates, and people I worked with. She asked who else knew and how they knew. Some of these questions I was prepared to answer. For some, I was more circumspect; I did not think it appropriate to out other people or discuss my intimate relationships with my mom.

After much discussion, she said, "I am hurting, but that is not the most important thing. The most important thing is that you are my son and I love you and that will never change. OK?"

I responded, "OK. Thank you. I love you, too."

I was so convinced of my love and my commitment to Andy that I failed to consider that my mom's love and commitment to me was stronger than any other love that may ever come my way. It was a love that had stood the test of time. No truth or any lie would dispel her love for me. Her commitment to care for me was guaranteed.

PART TWO

LIVING OUT LOUD

CHAPTER 4

LISTEN WELL

The Buck Stops Here

It had been several months since the letter to my mother and our conversation over the phone. She and I had created a new rhythm of conversing. Prior to the letter, we spoke every week, usually on Sundays when I had free time and could talk longer. Of course, back then a long long-distance call was probably no more than about fifteen minutes because of the expense. No telephone company offered free or unlimited long-distance calls on landlines.

We would laugh and talk about some of the struggles we had lived through in our earlier years. If she encountered one of my high school friends or their parents, she would tell me about their happenings. Our conversations covered so much ground that when I would go home on leave, I felt as though I had not been gone. I knew what people were doing, where they lived and worked. I knew of births, agonizing deaths, bankruptcies, plant openings, promotions, new restaurants, and the best flea-market finds and yard sales.

While we were planning one of those visits home, my mom had this wild idea that instead of me buying a ticket and flying home, she and Auntie Eunice would drive from Alabama to Wyoming to pick me up. We would all drive back to Alabama together. I wasn't sure why she thought this was the best idea but I did not want to be resistant. We were finding our way back in the relationship, so it seemed reasonable to accept the offer and make the most of it. I was due for a trip home but the primary reason I needed to get to Alabama was that a warrant had been issued for my arrest for failure to appear in court.

The summons had arrived at my mom's address and she was as alarmed as she was surprised to receive it. Before even telling me about the warrant, she did a little *Murder She Wrote* and *Matlock* detective work. My mom believed the warrant to be erroneous and she wanted to settle the matter without my involvement. After doing some digging, she found that the offenses were in connection with some unpaid traffic tickets. When she got that information, she assumed this was not a big deal and she could tell me without it upsetting me. She was wrong.

I received the call from my mom in the middle of the week. That alone was odd but not cause for great alarm. In a somber tone, she said, "You got some mail a few days ago."

I said, "OK. What was it? Did you open it?"

"Yes. I opened it because it was from Madison County and it looked important because it was thick."

"What was it?"

"I found out it was just about some tickets you didn't pay."

"Tickets? I haven't gotten any tickets. You sure it was for me?"

"Well, I think all you have to do is pay the tickets and some other fines and it will be alright. It's not a big deal unless you don't have the money. I could see what I could do to help you pay them."

"I understand, but I have not gotten any tickets in Madison County."

I had never received a ticket, but I had been stopped a few times by the police. The first time was on the way back from a Lisa Lisa & Cult Jam with Full Force and Exposé concert at the University of North Alabama. I had only had my driver's license a few months at the time and my mom let me drive that sixty-mile-each-way trip on a school night.

I carefully planned how to address any and all concerns she would present. Before asking if I could drive to the concert, I told her Fred wanted me to come and he would pay for my ticket. She loved Fred and claimed him as one of her adopted sons, as I claimed him as a brother.

My mom knew how much he looked out for me and she did all she could to encourage him in his quest to further his education. While he was away at college, since he was orphaned and did not know his birth family, our home became his home and our family became his family. It was just what it was. So, for Fred to ask me to come see him and do something on his campus was not out of the ordinary. What was different this time was that it would be a weeknight excursion.

To mitigate her concern about my driving alone, I told her that Buck was also going. That made her even more likely to say yes. Buck was a few years older than Fred, which meant he was at least four years older than me. Both of them had grown up at the Boys Ranch, which was a modern-day orphanage and group home for boys. Boys lived there until they turned eighteen, and then they had to move out into the world of adulthood.

When Buck graduated high school, he moved to Decatur, started taking classes at the local community college, and got a job. He met a young woman and moved in with her to make a life together. They stayed together a few years and eventually parted ways. When he left her, he rented a house about a mile from our house. When Fred would come home from college, he would divide his time between our house and Buck's.

My mom trusted both Fred and Buck, so my plan seemed foolproof. I had affirmation on going to the concert on a school night as long as Buck went with me and Fred had our tickets. The last and final barrier was transportation. Buck was a working man, but his car was not the best and not to be trusted to get us to and from Florence in one day and in one piece. I had acquired use of my mom's old Eldorado Cadillac as my primary vehicle. It was never given to me, nor was it ever referred to as mine, but I was the only person who drove it and took care of the maintenance. It was assumed by most people at my school and in our town that it was mine.

My mom eventually agreed to my request to drive Buck and me to the concert. It took some convincing, but we got to a good understanding about speed limits, alcohol, additional passengers, call upon arrival and departure, and a reasonable time to be back home. After the concert, which started about an hour later than scheduled, we walked Fred back to his dorm and hung out a few minutes before getting on the road to make the agreed-upon curfew. Fred called my mom to let her know the concert went late and that Buck and I were on our way home. I drove as Buck manned the radio and gave directions. Once we were on Highway 20, I knew where I was, and I knew the way home.

While Buck reclined in the passenger seat, I turned up the volume on the music. During the ride, Buck and I allowed our hands to slowly drift closer and closer toward each other. At a point our pinky fingers interlocked for a few seconds. I did not take my eyes off the road. Up to this point, I had no inkling that anything like this would ever occur with Buck.

After releasing and reconnecting our pinkies a few times, my right hand and his left hand became intertwined. I remember my heart pounding profusely as I kept my eyes on the road. Either he pulled my hand from the console onto his thigh or I put it there. We caressed palms and fingers and his thigh. Then I saw flashing blue lights appear behind me. He said in a very soothing voice, "Don't panic."

He shifted from caressing my hand to holding it as one would when guiding a blindfolded person through a darkened room. He added comfort in that moment. He talked me through enough for me to slow down, pull over to the side of the road, roll down the windows, and turn off the engine. I turned and looked into his eyes. He smiled and said, "It will be fine."

After the police officer saw that my license was still new and he heard we were coming from a concert at his alma mater, he warned me to slow down and not to run any more red lights. I had been so engrossed in what my hands were doing that my eyes were not aware of the speedometer or the two red lights I had zipped through on Highway 67.

Mom Comes Out

This business of missing court for overdue tickets was upsetting because along with that came a suspension of my driver's license and the only way to address the warrant was to present myself in Madison County Court before a judge.

About the same time this was unfolding, Auntie Eunice told my mom that she would love to get out of Alabama for a few days. She wanted to see something she had never seen before or do something she had never done before. Upon hearing that, my mom had the bright idea of the two of them taking a road trip from Alabama to Wyoming and back. They could pick me up and we would drive back together so I could clear up the warrant confusion in Alabama.

I agreed to the plan because I was scared of what all that meant for me and my Air Force career if I did not get this taken care of. There was also concern about the impact it might have on my relationship with my mom if I refused her offer to help. Factored into that were Auntie Eunice's wishes. Auntie Eunice was everyone's favorite auntie. She was older than my mom but she always remained young at heart. She drove a black Trans Am like the one Burt Reynolds drove in *Smokey and the Bandit*. She did not create or enforce a lot of rules like the other grown-ups. Auntie Eunice would go skating with us, let us drink beer, and hold all of our secrets. Since this quickly concocted plan involved her and what she wanted, my response was in the affirmative.

They were due to arrive on a Saturday evening around 5 p.m. I planned everything around their projected arrival time. My work schedule was set for me to end my shift at 4 p.m. That would give me enough time to check them into the room I secured for them in the on-base hotel, and be waiting for them at the main gate to sign them onto base.

At approximately 9 a.m., I received a call from the front gate officer informing me that someone claiming to be my mother was there with three other family members, requesting entry onto the base. This could not be true. They were not due for nearly eight more hours and there should only be two people—my mom and my aunt. Who were these other two people? Why were they there so early? I worked in the Armory, which was a below-ground secured facility that I could not simply leave. I asked to speak with my mom.

"Hey! We made good time so we are here early. It looks nice here."

"I see. Well, I don't get off until four and I don't know when you can check into your room."

"OK. We will try to find a motel nearby. We just wanted to let you know we made it."

"Wait! Let me see if your room on base might be ready earlier so you don't have to spend extra money."

At this point I was nervous and concerned. I was nervous about seeing my mom and I figured she had told my Auntie Eunice about my letter. I told her to give me five minutes and I would call back to the gate to let them know what to do. She gave the phone back to the guard and I explained that the visitors were my mom and aunt and I would call base housing to see what my options were.

After making a few calls, I learned their room would not be available for occupancy until at least two o'clock. I panicked. I called Andy to share with him what had happened and how frustrated I was that they had arrived so early and that apparently there were two other people with them that I was not expecting. He calmly said, "Hold on, big guy! This is not a problem. I will go sign them onto the base and they can hang out here at my place until you get off."

That option had never crossed my mind—because if it were to do so that would mean I would have dismissed the brevity and weight of the total situation. Not only would this mean that my family would be walking into the home of my partner, but he would have to go on an official log as the one responsible for signing them onto base. That may not seem like a major issue now, but it was.

Andy was a lieutenant, a commissioned officer, and I was an airman, a noncommissioned serviceman. There were rules against officers and noncommissioned airmen fraternizing in any way. Even though he was not in my chain of command and we did not serve in the same unit, the rules still applied. Not only were we breaking the fraternization rule, we were in a relationship and that was forbidden by military law.

So here was my own "personal lieutenant" making his way to the front gate of Warren Air Force Base to vouch for my family to come onto the base. Not only did he sign them onto the base, he escorted them to his apartment in the officers' quarters and told them to make themselves at home. I was still at work in a secured facility and could only allow my feeble mind to generate narratives of all varieties except good ones. After a few hours, Andy called my office phone and reported, in a whisper, "They are here."

I asked, "What are they doing?"

He said, "Well, they said they were hungry, and I offered to make breakfast, but they weren't having it." He described the scene for me: my aunt cracking eggs into a cast iron skillet, lining a pan with bacon, and squeezing all ten Pillsbury Grands into a round cake pan; my mom sitting on the bar stool next to the kitchen waiting for the coffee water to boil.

Neither of them were fans of percolated nor brewed coffee. Andy was amazed that of all the things for them to travel with, Maxwell House instant coffee was their product of choice. He was tucked away in his bedroom giving me the play-by-play recap. To a point he was taking all of this in stride. But as he was describing my mom and my aunt's reactions when they went on his balcony to smoke, he burst into laughter. The altitude in Cheyenne made the air quite thin and their Alabama lungs could not handle smoking at that altitude.

Then he said, "Your cousin and his wife are very nice."

"My cousin and his wife?"

With all of the commotion about their early arrival, the gate guard calling, and my nervousness about how they might interact with Andy, I had forgotten about the other passengers. They turned out to be my aunt's youngest son, Derek, and his wife, Mallory.

In some ways I was relieved that they were there. That meant I would not be alone with my mom and aunt should they decide to double-team me. I knew my cousin and Mallory's tumultuous relationship would demand the spotlight at least once per day and all eyes and energies would be focused intensely upon them. I wondered what questions they might ask Andy, but knew he was tough enough to handle that crowd.

About an hour or so later, I was able to sneak an unauthorized break as I convinced my coworkers to unlock our secured facility and allow me to leave for about twenty minutes. Andy's apartment was in the building behind the parking lot where I parked for work. That made it ultra-convenient for my truck to be parked in that lot at any time without suspicion or question.

We were nearly inseparable except when one of us was out in the field. When we began dating, he was a missile launch officer and I worked missile security. It would have only been more coincidental or completely orchestrated by fate if we had also been assigned to the same area, but we were not. He served in the 89th Missile Field and I was in the 90th. That meant he was in western Nebraska, approximately one hundred feet below ground, monitoring alarms and prepared to launch nuclear missiles if the command ever came.

I was in southeastern Wyoming responding to alarms set off by antelopes, rabbits, an occasional bison, but most often by wind or lightning. Andy worked for twenty-four hours straight and returned to base, while I worked three days at a time before returning to base. When our off days would sync or overlap, we would head south on Interstate 25 to Fort Collins, Denver, or Colorado Springs.

We had a good time together and we were prepared for any questions that might threaten our standing in the Air Force. I recall asking, "What do we tell people when they ask how we met?"

He said, "We met while taking a walk in the park."

"Well, that has some truth to it. But what about why we continue to spend time together?"

"Yeah. We will need a bigger story than a walk for that."

I said, "I got it. You went to college with my older brother and he asked you to look out for me since we were both stationed at the same base."

"That works. Who would say no to helping out someone's little brother?"

We didn't need that story with the folks at the park. They knew we were lovers and they celebrated it. We were an "It couple" at Cheesman Park on Sundays in Denver. We would go there to play volleyball, followed by dinner at Racines and dancing at Charlie's. Everywhere we went, people knew we were military, gay, and in love. The bouncers knew I was a protégé of Jim's, so the fact that I was underage did not matter.

Our cover worked well. We even added a layer to it by joining the variety group that performed on base once per month. Andy worked costumes and props and I helped the technical team with lights and sound. Eventually we came up with our own act that was incorporated into the show. The most infamous routine was a naughty reindeer skit set to Nancy Sinatra's hit, "These Boots Are Made for Walkin.'" It was a big hit with the fifty people who saw it.

The director of the variety group had served several seasons as the host for Tops in Blue, the Air Force's touring entertainment company, and when Tops in Blue's technical director reached out to him to get recommendations for someone who could join the current tour, he offered my name. The director called and asked if I would be interested and I told him I was not in position to leave Cheyenne at that time. They called two more times within the next year and each time I said no.

I said no the first time as a way of demonstrating my commitment to Andy. I said no the second time because of my own insecurities about my abilities, even though I was more advanced than the persons they already had on the team. My third and final no was due to my commitment to my church and my process of discerning if I was called to pastoral ministry. By that time, Andy and I had gone our separate ways. My focus was on religious pursuits and his presence was no longer welcomed. I did not know how to balance my love for him and my love for God. Little did I know had I said yes, I would have inevitably met someone who would change my life when we did finally meet over a decade later.

Failure to Appear

My mom, Auntie Eunice, my cousin and his wife, and I drove 1,300 miles from Wyoming to Alabama. It was an uncomfortable ride since there were five adults crammed into a midsize Pontiac Grand Am. There were bribes every 100 to 150 miles involving who would ride the hump in the middle back seat. I chose to do most of the driving so I would not have to ride that hump and so I could avoid serious conversations about my letter, Andy, or anything controversial. I wanted to get to Alabama, clear my name, and return to Cheyenne as soon as possible.

Auntie Eunice, my cousin, and my mom had to give up smoking the whole time they were in Wyoming and were eager to leave the thin air. Each time we would stop for gas, food, or a stretch break, one of them would ask, "How high are we now?" It's a good thing there weren't any police around when they asked that question.

I knew the pain they felt from the thinner air. When I first arrived in Cheyenne, my roommate challenged me to race him from our dorm to the gym which was less than a quarter mile down the street. He grew up in Oklahoma and I grew up in Alabama—two of the flattest states in the country. We barely made it across the street before we found ourselves gasping for air and something to lean on.

The antics between the smoking and avoiding the hump in the back seat provided just enough comic relief to get us from Wyoming to Alabama. Growing up, I didn't experience a road trip like this. My mom and I had only ever driven about forty miles alone together in any one direction. Before my parents divorced, we did take one driving trip to Decatur, Georgia, to visit one of my dad's sisters who had relocated there. She and her family lived off Cherry Street. The house was big enough that both of our families could stay there and I enjoyed a multi-day slumber party with my cousins.

The drive from Wyoming took us just over twenty hours and I still had energy when we arrived at my mom's house. That energy seeped out like a leaky balloon as soon as I walked into her kitchen and saw the mail on the table. My mom never owned a letter opener so the letters from the court were ripped open the way an excited child would attack a large box on Christmas morning. I read each of the three letters that bore my name and driver's license number. I saw the dates in question and was confused as to how they wrote tickets to me when I was not even in Alabama. Due to my ongoing romance with Andy and limited vacation time, I did not make frequent visits home.

My mom walked through the two swinging café doors that separated the kitchen from the family room. As the hinges creaked, she said, "We will go in the morning to get all this straightened out."

"I know. It just doesn't make sense."

"Well, you have documents from the Air Force showing where you were on all those dates that they say you were here. That should be all they need to see."

The next morning, we drove down to the Madison County Courthouse and found the courtroom of Judge Stanley. His clerk informed us that the judge would not be available until after lunch, but she would be willing to look over what we had and tell us if she thought he could help. I showed her the warrant letter, my driver's license, my military identification, and a notarized letter from my First Sergeant that outlined my whereabouts on the dates in question.

She looked over the paperwork, then she got up from her desk and said, "Don't go anywhere. I will be right back. We have a problem." It took her about ten minutes to return, but when waiting in a courthouse in a judge's chambers with a warrant for your arrest, ten minutes is like an eternity.

When the clerk returned, she told us this matter was something that would require a hearing before the judge. I said, "I understand. Can we do that this afternoon?"

"You could, but you have to get things cleared up with Limestone County first since your first violation was with them."

"But I have everything right here that shows none of this could have been me."

In the most southern and motherly accent imaginable, she said, "Hun, I hear you. Matter of fact, I believe this was not you, but there isn't anything I can do to help you until you clear things with Limestone."

I held back the tears that had the force of Niagara behind them. I thanked her and received the piece of paper with her number on it before we exited her office.

We drove from Madison along Highway 72 West to Athens. When I was younger, before my parents divorced, we would drive past this courthouse most weekends on our way to the grocery store or to Bonanza Steakhouse. It was a large stately building that sat in the middle of town and was surrounded by four blocks of locally owned shops and diners. My mom had told us how they used to hang Black people in front of that courthouse.

This day I was holding a warrant for my arrest as I ascended those eighteen steps up to the large glass doors that opened to a marble-lined corridor with dark wood-framed doors. As we passed each door, I read the nameplates and all of the inhabitants shared the first name: "Judge." The one at the end of the hall was the one I had to see: "Judge Lindsey."

Although the hallways in the Madison and Limestone County Courthouses were twin in appearance, the judge's chambers were in stark contrast to one another. While Judge Stanley's office was modern and brightly colored, with fresh flowers on the table, this one was small and cramped, with one small window that held an air conditioner. The clerks in each office resembled the respective décor in how they addressed me. The clerk in this office was cold and on edge. She barely looked at my paperwork before telling me that I needed to get cleared by the Morgan County Courthouse before Judge Lindsey could do anything. I tried to plead with her. I wanted her to know I did not do what I had been accused of and I had proof. Her dismissive tone and gestures turned me around and I exited disheartened. Although no one had taken me to jail, no one had taken me seriously either. I was being passed around from courthouse to courthouse without any resolution. I believed if anyone would take five minutes to hear my side of the story, they would dismiss the warrants and I could get on with my life.

By the time we reached the Morgan County Courthouse, the clerk was on lunch break. My mom said, "If they are on lunch break, we should take lunch too. Let me buy you a hamburger." I said, "OK. That will work."

Penn's and Piano Lessons

A few blocks from the courthouse was a little hole-in-the-wall hamburger stand that the locals loved. Penn Hamburgers served the greasiest burgers in the tri-county region. I loved it because every Saturday morning when I was little and taking piano lessons, my mom would give me two dollars that I could spend after my lessons. I would rush through those piano lessons so I could hurry across the street to Penn's. My order was the same every week: a hamburger with grilled onions, French fries, and an orange drink. That is what I ordered that day too. We sat at the counter and reminisced about those Saturday mornings so many years ago. My mom asked, "Do you miss playing the piano?"

"Sometimes I do. Especially when I am at church and the musicians seem to have full command of the congregation. I wonder how I would handle that."

"You would have to be humble with it. That's the only way."

"Well, maybe that's why I wasn't able to keep it up. My humility was not in check."

We laughed and toasted our bottles of orange soda as though we were sipping brews on the dock of the bay.

"Why did you give up playing, for real? You were very good at all of your recitals."

"Yeah. I really liked playing."

"When you quit, you said it was because you didn't think we could afford the lessons."

"That was true, right?"

"It was a struggle but I never missed a payment on the lessons or on that piano."

"I know, but I felt guilty about you paying for that when sometimes our lights or phone would get cut off. Piano lessons seemed like a luxury we could not afford."

"But I told you I would always take care of it and you said you believed that was true. So, what made you quit?"

"Remember when I signed up to be in the band at school?"

"Yes. You wanted to play the trombone or trumpet, I think."

"It was the trombone. You asked why I wouldn't choose the saxophone."

"I liked the saxophone. I didn't know how those other ones sounded."

"Your response that you did not have money for me to be picking up and putting down all these instruments discouraged me from joining the band."

"I didn't mean for that to happen. I just . . ."

I interrupted her. "It wasn't just that. The taunting by other boys is what did it."

"Who taunted you?"

The grease from the burger had run down my arm during this conversation. I had not put it down. I confessed, "Some of the older boys at school saw me in the hall one day and when I turned to the doors that led to the band room . . ." I choked up as I told her this, just as I had that day when it happened. I continued, "One of them said that's where all the fags go to play. All of them started laughing."

"Oh no. I am so sorry. I didn't know."

"I told Mr. Minor, the band director, that day that it would be my last day in the band. He tried to convince me to stay but there wasn't anything he could say that would change my mind. The next day I changed my extracurricular activity to football and I never looked back."

"I wish you had told me back then."

"I couldn't tell you. I figured I would kill two birds with one stone. No more money going for music lessons and no more accusations about my sexuality."

As we finished our burgers, I found myself staring across the street at the little side door that still had "E.E. Forbes & Sons Piano Company" embossed on it. I imagined what could have been as we drove the two blocks back to the courthouse. When we arrived at the second floor, I trembled as I remembered when I stood at that same little window to pay my fine for bouncing a $10 check. Would they be inclined to believe my story since they had a record of my lawbreaking activity a few years earlier? I had to take my chances. In so many ways, I was back at the beginning of my story.

The clerk took a look at my paperwork and directed us to a nearby waiting room. We sat there until she called for us to go into the judge's chambers. My mom asked, "Which judge are we seeing?"

The clerk said, "Judge Bryant."

My mom moved in close to the clerk's little window and said, "I just saw Judge Breland walk by. Is there any way we could see him instead of Bryant?"

"Well, let me see."

She made a call and seemed to be disgusted with whoever was on the other end, but when she hung up the phone, she said, "He has an opening right now. Go to Room 215 and I will let them know you are on your way."

When we entered Judge Breland's office, he said, "Doris, it is good to see you again."

She said, "Thank you. Good to see you too."

"What can I do for you? I don't have much time before I have to get back into court."

My mom knew Judge Breland from when she divorced my dad. They had a bitter battle over assets and child support. Judge Breland was very supportive of my mom and he made sure she got what he believed was fair. She trusted him. Through the years I had heard her tell people that he was an honest and fair judge. As I shook his hand, I accepted that he would do the right thing.

My mom said, "This is Cedrick, my middle child. You probably don't remember him because the kids were so young when we were here."

He said, "You had two boys and a girl. Are you the oldest, son?"

"No sir. I am the younger of the boys. I'm the well-adjusted middle child."

He laughed as my mom looked at me with the side-eye of a puma about to strike. She passed my paperwork to him.

I interjected, "Judge Breland, my mom got these warrants in the mail stating I missed court for some tickets issued to me. I was in Wyoming at the time these tickets were written. I have documentation to prove it."

He sat down behind his large wooden desk and rustled around for his reading glasses. He gazed over the documents we gave him. He said, "Son, you are still in the Air Force?"

"Yessir."

"Are you going to stay in for a career?"

"No. I want to be an architect when I get out."

"I think you would make a fine architect or anything you set your mind to. I will write a release of judgment and dismiss the warrant for Morgan County."

"Thank you, but what about Limestone and Madison? I already went to those courthouses and they sent me here since Morgan County was the oldest warrant."

"Hold on, son. Let me finish. It's obvious it wasn't you who got these tickets. You don't seem to know who did this. I will write the dismissal here and ask the other two courts to write concurrent dismissals." He took off the glasses and tossed the paperwork on the desk. "Let me see if this old judge still has any clout in these parts."

He picked up the phone and asked his assistant to call the Limestone and Madison Courts to request dismissal of their cases against me. It only took about ten minutes for all three cases to be dismissed. My mom and I were elated. As we stood to leave Judge

Breland's office, he said, "Everything's taken care of and you can get back to serving this great country of ours. Cedrick, keep making your mama and me proud."

Again, I fought back tears. "Yessir. Thank you so much."

I was grateful to Judge Breland for standing up for me. I was grateful my mom made the request for us to speak with him. I was grateful to God for intervening. I was mad at whoever used my driver's license number and got me into that mess.

My mom and I shared a conversation the night before I was due to fly back to Cheyenne. I expressed gratitude for how she supported me and never doubted my innocence. We created a short list of men in our family who would have been crafty enough to use my information instead of taking responsibility for their own crimes. At that time in Madison, Limestone, and Morgan counties an officer did not need an actual license to write a citation. That was my experience of identity theft long before the term was coined.

Then she asked me how I felt God viewed my choice to love men. I told her, "I believe God knows me better than anyone on earth ever will. I believe God knows my struggle. I believe if God wants me to love women, men, or no one, God already knows how that will come to be known by me."

She said, "You know I don't approve of your lifestyle, but I love you. I will never stop loving you and I will never stop praying that you always live a life that is pleasing to God."

I assured her my greatest desire was to please God and to find my way to happiness. On my way to happiness, I wanted to find out who impersonated and incriminated me without any tangible proof that they were me. Although he never confessed, my brother never denied using my name, birthdate, and social security number when he was stopped by police.

New Revelation

The story of how I found or was led to New Kingdom is akin to much of my life happenings where I set out for one thing or with one purpose and others were revealed. Since I was a church boy, one of the first things I did upon arriving in Cheyenne was to look for a church to attend. For several months I ventured into church after church, trying to find something like what I knew back home. The Baptist church services were lively like ours but they lasted more than two hours. I was accustomed to that in my youth and at the behest of my family but as an adult exercising religious freedom, I was not giving that much time to church all in one day. The Methodist churches—African Methodist, Christian Methodist, Free Methodist, and United Methodist—were too quiet and there were only old people in them.

There was a service on base at 8 a.m. that would allow me to get church out of the way before breakfast. I went to the base service for a few weeks but I did not understand much of what they were doing or saying. It was vastly different from the base services I attended at Lackland Air Force Base during my training and it was nothing like my church back in Alabama. Our pastors were known to strut back and forth across the pulpit and to wave the Bible in the air but they never made any repetitive motions tracing from their forehead to their chest and from side to side.

I had done some drinking the night before I attended the first service so I slipped out the back door before time for Communion. Imagine my surprise when I showed up the second week and they were doing Communion again. That was not supposed to happen. In my home church, and every other church I ever attended, we only took Communion on the first Sunday of the month—no exceptions. I saw one of the guys from my unit in line for Communion that second week. The next time I ran into him, I asked, "Do you attend chapel every week?"

He said, "Yes. I go to Mass as often as possible."

"Mass?"

"That's what Catholics call the service. Obviously you are not Catholic."

"Oh my!"

"What?"

"That's why it was so different. It is not a Christian service."

He looked offended. He said, "Wait! Catholics are Christians. It is just a different expression of Christianity, like Baptist or Methodist. You really should not say that again."

"I'm sorry. I didn't know."

"Yeah! A lot of people say stuff like that because they don't know."

I told him about my experiences at the Catholic Mass the two weeks I went. He helped me understand the kneeling, the liturgies, and the motions the priest was making. When he did it in front of me of course I could see it was the sign of the cross.

I left that conversation enlightened, embarrassed, and hungry. I walked over to the base dining hall to have some lunch. It was a cafeteria-style setup like a Piccadilly, Morrison's, Furr's, or Luby's, where you get an oversized brightly colored tray made of Formica and place single servings of an assortment of foods on it. I liked cafeteria-style dining as an adult because I could choose what I wanted. As children, when we would go to one of these restaurants, my mom would select what she wanted us to have. She might ask, "Do you want this?" No matter what we answered, she would add it to the tray or not based on her mood or her belief of whether or not we would eat it.

I completed my food selections, paid for my meal, and found a booth in the corner to sit in. I have since learned that what I deem

an obvious sign that I don't wish to be bothered is not always inter-
preted as such by others. On this particular day, while sitting in the
corner enjoying my Salisbury steak, mashed potatoes, French-style
green beans, sourdough roll, and red Jell-O, I was interrupted by
another patron. He was wearing a dress blue Air Force uniform, as
were about half of the people in the building.

I saw him as he approached. There were a few empty tables
between us and I thought he would sit at one of those. He didn't.
He walked right over to my table and asked, "Mind if I join you?"

Given that I had been raised with some manners and my
Southern good nature and charm had not yet dissipated, I said,
"Of course. Have a seat." I looked at his name tag and I included his
name, "Sergeant Grumbault."

He smiled and laughed, "You pronounced it perfectly. Thank
you, Airman Bridgeforth."

We exchanged genial banter while I consumed my high fat and
high calorie lunch and he devoured his Caesar salad and vegetable
soup. I learned that he grew up in Ohio. He had only been stationed
in Cheyenne for a few months and he was a dining hall supervisor. In
the midst of the conversation, I realized he was flirting with me and
I was returning the favor. We were interrupted several times during
our conversation by others in the dining hall and we would quickly
return to the chatter that held us at that table for almost two hours.

As the dining hall finally began to clear of the lunch crowd,
Grumbault announced that he needed to get back to work. I said,
"You have been working."

He blushed. "Yes. I have been working."

"If anyone asks, tell them you were surveying patrons to see
how good the service was."

"Well, so I have data to report: How was your meal?"

"I will let you know after I finish eating it. I can say the company was great, Sergeant." I must admit I added a little wink as I said "Sergeant."

Somewhere along the way in our conversation I must have disclosed or intimated that I was a religious-inclined person because as he stood to leave the table, he said, "Thank you for blessing me with your time, Cedrick."

Now I was the one blushing as I expressed gratitude for his time and the sentiments he offered. We exchanged phone numbers and he disappeared into the kitchen.

Throughout that week and into the next, Sergeant Grumbault and I played a game of phone tag. I heard the outgoing message on his answering machine so many times, I could recite it word for word and match the tone of his voice as it played. I imagine he had the same folly with mine. I tried timing my meals so I could run into him at the dining hall but that proved fruitless each day. Eventually I gave up and called the number for the dining hall. I asked to speak with him. It was a risk that I would come on too strong, but I wanted to talk to him. I also wanted to know if he wanted to talk to me. I rationalized that the worst-case scenario would be his admission that he did not wish to speak with me.

When he came to the phone, he said, "Hello! Sergeant Grumbault speaking. How may I help you?"

I said, "You can help me by being home the next time I call, Sergeant."

He laughed as though his favorite comedian or his ridiculously drunk uncle had told his favorite joke.

He replied, "Yes sir! It is great to finally hear from you."

"It is good to hear your voice live and not on my answering machine. How have you been?"

"I've been alright. These dining hall renovations have really taken over my life. I can't even think about anything else right now."

I did not know if that was his way of letting me know his work overwhelmed him or if he was letting me know to back off and leave him alone.

I said, "Oh my! That sounds like a lot."

"It is but I think I am getting a handle on it. I met this guy who offered me some great insight. He took time to listen to me and he encouraged me."

I was growing a little misty as he said such endearing words about me. After all, we had only spoken for two hours and that was more than a week earlier. I could not believe I had that much of an impact on him. He continued, "He invited me to his church too."

I thought, "Wait! Church? He is not talking about me at all." Trying to hide my embarrassment, I said, "That is awesome! Are you going to go to his church?"

He said, "Yes! You should come with me so I don't have to go alone."

I agreed to go but noted I would need to meet him at the church because I had plans to drive to Denver later that night and to spend the weekend there. My plans were now twofold. I would go to this church service which should not last more than about an hour since it was a Friday night and then make the ninety-minute drive to Denver. I would get in my time with this handsome man, go to church, and then carouse in Denver for the weekend. I copied down the address and directions to the church and looked forward to the service and my weekend.

When I arrived at the address I was confused. It was a little white house on a corner in a residential neighborhood. I drove around the block to see if maybe I had transposed the street address or written "turn left" when it should have been a right turn. After circling at least two times, I saw people wearing traditional church attire walking toward the house. Eventually, I spotted Grumbault exit his car. He looked around as though he had an intended target. I figured I was the target, so I jumped out of my truck and waved to him.

New Kingdom

We entered the little house together, not realizing that not only would we be in the main worship area upon entry, but that there was a prayer service already in progress. All of the persons I saw enter that house ahead of us were kneeling in front of their respective folding chairs. All of them were praying aloud at the same time. I had never heard or seen anything like it and I had been to churches of all brands and sizes. Grumbault grabbed my hand and pulled me down to kneel at the two chairs nearest the door. I thought that was smart because when we finished our prayers, I could slip right out the door and head to Denver.

Someone failed to alert the preacher of my plans. Someone failed to alert the architect who designed the building of my plans. We had arrived at 7 p.m. for the preliminary prayer service. The main service, which was coined "Joy Night," began around 7:45 p.m. Throughout the service I began to look for opportune times to make my escape. The music was exceptional. The testimonies were deeply personal and heartfelt. The offering was lengthy. When it came time for the preaching portion of the service, Grumbault tapped my leg and said, "He is the one who invited me. He is the minister tonight."

The pastor's wife introduced him as Minister Hanes. He was, she boldly proclaimed, "...a man after God's own heart who preaches and teaches the uncompromising word of God."

I did not see him until he stood to speak because my view was blocked by the podium. He was over six feet in height and was obviously a military person. I could observe that. What I would come to know was that he was devout in his study of the Bible and an avid student and teacher of scripture. After Minister Hanes began to explicate the scriptures, I became mesmerized and enthralled by the depth of knowledge, relevant language, and direct application to my life. I had never heard anything like that before.

We did not emerge from that building until approximately 10:30 p.m. I still had time to get to Denver, but I did not have the drive or desire to go. After hearing how much God had in store for me and how much responsibility I had as a recipient of God's love, I felt overwhelmed, loved, and for the first time, responsible for something. I felt responsible for sharing the love of God with others.

That night, Minister Hanes opened my understanding that the love of God is not just something that comes and goes; I have a part to play with moving it on to others. I had to rethink my priorities. I remembered my grandma or one of my mom's sisters saying, "The Holy Ghost will either draw you or drive you." That night, I had been drawn in. I found a place where I felt I could belong. I heard truths from familiar passages of scripture that ultimately played a role in my decision to alter my plans for that Friday night and many that would follow for the next few years.

My lunchtime rendezvous with Grumbault ushered me into a faith community that became my spiritual home. He also became very active in the church. Both of us attended Tuesday night Bible study, Wednesday night midweek service, Thursday night choir rehearsal, Saturday teachers and ministers meeting, Sunday morning Sunday School and worship, and Sunday evening Young People Willing Workers services. With Joy Night on Fridays, we only had Mondays to do other things. We were deeply committed to that church and what it stood for in that city. It was a holiness church—not as dogmatic as others but it taught us to look to the Bible for guidance.

While attending New Kingdom, my sense was that homosexuality and intimate love one man might have for another was not acceptable—it was an abomination. There it was again. That teaching and revelation showed up in my home church and at the Baptist church I visited in Cheyenne. I think the priest at Mass may have said it. The military had rules about it, and New Kingdom showed us scriptures and church laws to back it up. All of that became even more complicated as I learned I was not the only man, single or married, in that congregation who loved other men.

Grumbault eventually confided in me that he had an ongoing fling with Minister Hanes. That explained why they would often disappear together after evening services—until Grumbault's wife eventually joined him in Cheyenne. Yes! Grumbault was married and none of us knew it until his wife moved from Germany to Cheyenne almost six months after we first met. Her presence curtailed Grumbault's relationship and set me on a course to take his place in Minister Hanes's lineup.

It all began quite innocently. I was enamored of his gift of teaching the Bible. Each time I met with him to study together or just to talk, I was reminded of how Grumbault described his initial encounter with Hanes. I felt encouraged and heard. I wanted to do better.

Both of us lived on base and only three buildings apart. One night we were in Hanes's room, studying and talking. It had gotten late. He said, "You should rest your eyes, sir."

I said, "I guess I am tired. It's been a long day. I should go back to my dorm."

"You should do that after you rest your eyes here first."

He had a way of insisting and conniving all at the same time. That made it difficult to resist him. I said, "OK. I will lay down for fifteen minutes before I go."

I stretched out atop his bed which was a makeshift double bed formed by pushing the room's two twin beds together. He did not have a roommate because of his rank. I had a roommate at different times because of my rank. He had a quilt his grandmother had made from his old band uniforms and clothes he had outgrown thrown across his bed. That quilt had traveled with him to Germany, Japan, England, and Korea, and was now in Cheyenne, Wyoming. That was the first of many nights that I wrapped myself in the comfort of that quilt and in the warmth of the embrace he provided.

New Man

Hanes and I would have late-night study sessions that would end with me slipping out the side door of his dorm to get back to my dorm undetected. When I had a roommate, it was awkward to be out most nights yet have my truck parked in our parking lot. That made me keep relational distance between me and roommates. It also was the cause of some internal conflict. We heard one gospel and knew one teaching at church and in many ways affirmed it, but in private, we made our own rules that allowed us to be together and to be intimate with each other. We became nearly inseparable until the fateful day that I learned he had plans to get married.

I seldom missed Sunday worship unless I was out of town or working. One Sunday I was at work on base and I received a phone call from one of my female friends. When I answered, she spoke with an air of suspicion and contempt. She said, "Why didn't you think you could tell me? I am hurt."

"What are you talking about? Why are you hurt?"

"Don't act like you don't know. I thought we were all closer than that."

At this point, Hanes and I were very close with this woman. He had known her since junior high school. She was married to a man in the Air Force who was stationed at Warren Air Force Base with us and they also attended New Kingdom. We often talked about how ostracized we felt because we were not as dogmatic and traditional as most members of the church. We studied together and spent a lot of time at their home cooking dinners and praying about whatever was going on in our lives. Of course, we did not include her in the full scope of our relationship, but she was privy to all those parts that were public. I grew concerned very quickly during this conversation because I did not know why she was bothered and I did not know why she had brought this frustration and accusation to me.

I calmly stated, "Please tell me what you are talking about. If I know more than I have told you in the past, I promise I will come clean and I will tell you everything."

She said, "I can't believe you didn't tell me your friend was getting married."

"What friend? Who's getting married? What are you talking about?"

"He announced it to the whole congregation today during worship, so you don't have to keep his secret anymore."

"Who are you talking about?"

"Hanes! He told the whole church he had found a wife. He proposed to her and she said yes. He invited all of us to the wedding. You know you could have told me."

"Really, I couldn't have told you because I did not know."

She realized by the somber tone in my voice that I did not know. She began to apologize for accusing me. I told her it was fine and everything would work out.

Everything was not fine and I questioned how and if things would work out. I did not know how I would confront him. I did not know if I had a right to say anything. I did not know why he would keep something so important from me. I did not know if this was some ploy to keep people from knowing about us. I had so many thoughts. I was angry. I felt betrayed. I wondered if this was another case of me getting involved with someone who did not have as much as me to lose. I wondered if I was being punished for falling for a devout minister of God. I wondered if this would be the catalyst to save us from homosexuality. I wondered if this would be my ticket to some sense of freedom that I even found difficult to imagine. As good as it felt to be with this dynamic and powerful person, there was also a weight of guilt and shame that accompanied the relationship. Sometimes I would pray and ask God, "Don't let me be a stumbling block for him. I want him to be everything you want him to be. If I am in the way of that, move me out of the way."

I would repeat that prayer every time I felt as though I could not imagine a life without him. I did not want what I wanted to interfere with or supersede what God wanted for him. I did have that much conviction about my faith and belief in what God would and could do in my life and in the lives of those who commit themselves wholeheartedly to the things of God. I had been taught that from an early age and it was a foundation of my faith.

When Hanes and I spoke later that evening, he was slow to tell me about his announcement. I sought to be the bigger person. I sought to be supportive. I wanted him to believe that my love and commitment would not be altered by anything he felt he had to do to be faithful to God.

He said, "I want to see you tonight."

I wondered how those words could come out of his mouth at that moment.

"Hanes, why would you want to see me tonight?"

"I want to see. That's the only way I will know you are really alright."

"I'm fine. I promise."

He was not one who ever received a negative response with favorability. I don't know why I thought tonight would be different. He insisted, "I'm hanging up and will be there in a few minutes."

Very little time passed between the dial tone that followed our call disconnecting and the knock at my door. He had the combination to the lock, so as he knocked, he entered. I looked up from the desk where I had taken his call. He came over, stood in front of me, and took both my hands. He gently guided me to my feet as though he were escorting me at a cotillion. I stood and stared directly at his gold cross on its tarnished gold herringbone chain, considering what it would now mean to bear my own.

He spoke softly, "Let me see your eyes."

I looked up but I could not look into his eyes.

He said, "I believe you. You are alright. Thank you for being you."

I pulled away and motioned for him to take the seat I had surrendered. Hanes sat down in the chair and I sat on the edge of what would have been my roommate's bed. We engaged in lighthearted conversation until he mustered up the courage to ask, "Will you be my best man at the wedding?"

"What? Why would you ask me that?"

"You are my best friend. I know I can't do this without you right by my side."

That was a true dark night of the soul. I wanted to honor his wishes. I wanted to be a good friend. I wanted to show my public support for him. I wanted him to be happy.

I did not know what happiness would look like for me with him and his wife. Not only would he now have a wife, but she already had children from a previous marriage. He would be a father. Of course, I agreed to be his best man and eventually grew to love and appreciate his wife and her children. In fact, after their marriage, I grew distant from him and developed a great friendship with her. He and I never engaged intimately again. He went on with his marriage and I set out to frame a different future for myself.

I followed what I believed was a call from God for me to go back home to Alabama. There was some consideration and hesitation in my response to God's call because I wanted and needed to be sure I was not abandoning my plans—to enroll in Colorado State University, an hour away from Cheyenne, Hanes, and New Kingdom—because of my ruptured relationship. I had to be sure it was not another flash of insecurity like what surfaced when I said no to joining Tops in Blue. I had to know that it was not my bruised ego overpowering me. Ultimately, through prayer and good counsel, I reached a point of comfort that allowed me to lean into the directive to return to Alabama. I trusted that everything would work out.

CHAPTER 5

LEARN HOW TO LET GO

Domino's in Decatur

I completed my four-year Air Force enlistment and made that fateful decision to forgo matriculation into Colorado State University's occupational therapy program. I moved from Cheyenne, Wyoming, back to my mother's home in Hartselle, Alabama. That was the house I had lived in throughout high school and never imagined returning to except for routine visits throughout the years. However, once the voice of God came unto me and beckoned me to return to Alabama, I had to figure out a new plan and a new life for myself.

Since I had moved away to serve my country, my mom had opened a flower shop called Precious Moments. It had become a passion project and she struggled to manage the shop while also working at her forty-hour per week job. As soon as I returned, she asked if I would be interested in managing the shop. Since I did not have any other job prospects, I accepted. She was aware I would be looking for other employment but in the interim I would take care of ordering and picking up supplies, scheduling deliveries, tracking finances and inventory, and coordinating events. This meant I needed to know more about floral design and wedding planning if I was really going to take this business to the next level.

About six months into my role as manager of the flower shop, I began working as a security guard at the hospital where I was born. I would work at the shop during the day, sleep evenings, and report for duty at the hospital at 11 p.m., five nights per week. That schedule was my norm for several months before I began to experience a rekindling of my desire to become an architect. That had been my dream since as far back as I could remember. Maybe arranging flowers, setting up weddings, and reconfiguring the flower shop had reawakened my dream.

Even with two jobs, tuition would be a far stretch on my budget. I calculated what I would need to take a few drafting classes and prerequisites at Calhoun Community College and still was short of what I would need to pay tuition and cover my living expenses. Late one night while sitting in the guard shack, I saw an ad in the Decatur Daily classified section for delivery drivers at Domino's Pizza at an hourly rate. I did the math and figured out that I could work there for two months, earn what I needed for the semester, and quit. This was a short-term solution for a long-term plan.

I called Domino's the next day and spoke with a manager named Beth. She told me all the perks of the job and asked if I could come by between two and four o'clock to interview for a position. When I arrived at the Glen Street location for my interview, Beth was the only person at the site. I asked, "Where is everybody?"

She said, "There is only one driver right now and he is out on a delivery. This is our slow time."

"How do you make sure you meet the thirty-minute guarantee with only one driver?"

She returned to folding pizza boxes as I asked a few more questions. Then she said, "I thought I was going to interview you today. Why does it feel like I'm the one being interviewed?

"My bad. I apologize. I guess I'm just excited."

"No problem. I think it is great. So, why do you want to be a delivery driver?"

"How honest of an answer do you want?"

"Very honest, Cedrick."

"Well, I really don't want to be a delivery driver. I want to be an architect."

I joined in the pizza box folding task as we continued the interview.

"Now I am intrigued. Why would someone who wants to be an architect be here interviewing to become a pizza delivery driver?"

"Good question. I need money to pay for some classes at Calhoun. I can make the money I need in a short amount of time by delivering pizza."

She looked past my left shoulder and into the parking lot.

"Is that your truck?"

"Yes. It seldom sees a car wash. We call it dirty red."

"You can tell me about that later. Is that what you will deliver pizza in?"

"It's the only vehicle I own. Would that be acceptable?"

"That really depends on whether or not you have insurance."

"I do have insurance on the truck."

"What size shirt do you wear?"

"Medium."

The phone rang and she answered on the second ring. She shared some numbers with the person on the phone as she did a visual inventory of cans, boxes, and bags. I continued folding boxes and overheard her say, "Just wrapping up with our newest driver.

I will call you back." She hung up, looked at me, and asked, "Can you be at an orientation tonight? I know it is short notice but if you can make it tonight, I can put you on the schedule as soon as tomorrow."

I was elated.

I attended the orientation that evening and began training as a driver the next day. When I told my mom that I had gotten another job she said she was happy for me, but I could hear concern in her voice. I asked, "What's wrong. What are you not saying?"

"You already have two jobs and I see how hard you are working."

"Yeah, but one of those jobs is really taking money from you that you don't have. It's helping me pay rent on my apartment but it is not helping you build your business."

"It will get better at the shop. I can handle it for now."

"I know you can, but you don't have to. This way, I can still work the same hours and you can give me less money and invest more back into the business."

Within two or three days, I was making deliveries on my own and loving it. The tips were great and the job was not hard.

During my second week as a driver, I saw an order to be delivered to the plant where Lawrence worked and his last name was on the label. I froze as I thought of the irony and the possibility. He would have to come get the pizza. If I were the one to deliver it, I would get to see him and say all the things I wanted to say so many years before.

My coworker, Gordan, was rearranging pizza sauce cans on the tall metal rack. I asked, "Do you mind if I take the next order? I think I know the person it's going to."

"Is the person a family member or friend?"

"Family and we are not friendly, at all."

He laughed, "Doesn't sound like they would be a good tipper either."

"Probably not."

"That being the case, you can take it. Save me the hassle."

The pizzas ran through the oven on a conveyor rack that moved them from start to finish in six minutes, but that pizza seemed to make a couple of U-turns or something to prolong its process. I retrieved that medium pepperoni-and-sausage-with-light-cheese from the oven, cut it, bagged it, and was out the door as if my life depended on it.

I sped off, only slowing as I turned onto State Docks Road and realized I was potentially less than five minutes from coming face to face with Lawrence. I gathered myself and proceeded to the main gate.

The security guard asked, "How can I help you?"

"I have a pizza delivery."

"OK. Park next to that white building. The lady inside can help you."

No More Chicken

The lady inside was cordial and firm. She handed me a wrinkled white envelope that had the money for the pizza and tip enclosed, and told me to leave the pizza on the table next to her desk. As I was walking away, I heard her tell a person on the phone that their pizza had arrived. Thinking quickly, I spun around and asked, "Do you have a restroom I can use?" She pointed to a blue door across the lobby. I exhaled a sigh of relief mixed with dread as I paced back and forth in the stall.

When I heard the murmur of voices, I exited the restroom. But I immediately realized that the man who was carrying the pizza was not Lawrence. My disappointment turned to surprise when he stopped and said, "Wait. Aren't you Quanza's brother?"

"Yes, I am." As soon as I answered his question, I focused on him and realized he used to live across the street from us until he divorced his wife. His two younger daughters were my sister's very close friends and his oldest daughter dated one of my cousins.

"Didn't you go into the service?"

"I served in the Air Force for four years."

"How about that? Now you are delivering pizzas."

I heard his question and statement as judgment on the state of my life. I could have said something indignant but he had only given voice to what I had been thinking.

"It's something to do while I figure out my plan for school."

"Doesn't the Air Force pay for you to go to school?"

"No, sir. That is not how that works."

"Well, good luck with all that. Good running into you."

"That's not your name on the pizza. Is it for you?"

"Yes. My coworker bought it for me since he lost a bet."

"Oh. That makes sense."

"You know that is true. Well, tell your mama I said hello when you talk to her."

"I will. Thanks."

From that day forward I would commandeer every order that was going to the plant where Lawrence worked in hopes of seeing him. Eventually I worked up the courage to call him at work. I did finally get him on the phone. This time I was determined to be more direct than I had been when I called from basic training. When he answered the phone, he said, "This is Lawrence, engineering."

"Hello, Lawrence. This is Cedrick."

Again, I did not know how to introduce myself to him. Was I supposed to say, "This is Cedrick, your bastard seed"? I was a bastard but not a classic bastard. My parents were married when I was conceived but they were not married to each other.

Nothing that crossed my mind sounded like anything that would resonate with both of our realities. He said, "Hello, Cedrick. How are you? Are you in Alabama?"

"I am fine and I am in Alabama. In fact, I live in Decatur now."

"How long have you been back?"

"A while now." I wanted him to believe that he was not a priority.

"What are you doing now? Are you working?"

"Yessir. I am working at Decatur General Hospital as a security guard and I recently started at Domino's Pizza."

"We order from them a lot out here. Maybe you will deliver to us sometime."

"I deliver there all the time, but I have never seen you."

"Usually when our department orders, somebody else goes to get it because our office is all the way at the back of the plant and I don't want to walk to the front."

"I saw your name on the first order I delivered here."

"Really? I guess if I had known you were bringing it, I would have walked to the front."

"Well, next time I see your name pop up and I am the driver, I will call you ahead of time to let you know."

"That would be great. Look, I have to get back to work. I look forward to you bringing my next pizza delivery."

We hung up and I did call him every time I was the driver delivering a pizza with his name on it. Every time we would have a similar surface-level conversation about the last pizza I delivered. Since it was obvious to me that he was never going to advance the conversation beyond where I had started it, during one of our pre-delivery conversations I interjected, "When can we schedule a time to sit and talk?"

"It may be easiest if we just meet one day after my shift. That way I won't be in a rush."

"OK. What day works best for you?"

"Next Tuesday or Wednesday would be good for me."

"When will you know which day and how will you confirm?"

"I will call you this weekend to confirm the day and time that will work for me."

"That is good."

"Alright. I have to get back to work."

I disrupted his statement, "You don't have my number, so let me give it to you."

"I have a pen right here. Go ahead."

I shared my phone number with him and ended the call with hope that this was a new beginning and a connection that would grow with time. This would be the redemption I sought. This would be the do-over that I longed for. I felt this was my second chance to make a good impression on him. It was as though the universe orchestrated a few pizza orders at Lawrence's place of work so that I could whet my appetite for a relationship with him. My optimism soon turned into a season of questioning what was wrong with me and what I had said that would cause him not to respond. I wondered if I had come on too strong with him. He did not call me and the pizza orders slowly dwindled to nothing. Every shift I would check the order history to see if I missed any deliveries to that address.

When I was not at work, I was volunteering at Progressive Christian Outreach. It was no match for New Kingdom but it did allow me to continue my spiritual quest to serve and to figure out which parts of church work spoke most deeply to me. It did not take me long to fully enmesh myself into Progressive's leadership and become a trusted participant and supporter of the ministry. Although I volunteered my time, it was like having yet another job that I had to factor into my calendar.

I tried several iterations of a schedule that would allow me to work at the shop during the day, deliver pizza in the evening, be present at church regularly, and work as security guard at night. It was a grueling schedule, but I was committed to do what I needed to do to make the money I needed to take those classes at the local community college. My plan was still to quit the delivery job when I started classes.

After almost six weeks of driving for Domino's and helping as shift leader on occasion, Beth asked me to become her assistant manager. I agreed to take on the role without any hesitation. The promotion would definitely improve my financial situation. However, as an assistant manager, I would have to be more flexible and available more hours. That meant that I would have to reconsider one of my other jobs.

I decided the best thing to do was to reduce my responsibilities at the flower shop. That way my mom could hire someone with design experience to be there during the day when I was not available. I would also have enough money that she would not have to pay me anything. In fact, I would be able to contribute some funds to the shop. My mom refused to accept any money from me but she did agree to hire someone.

Decatur General

The security job at the hospital was never in jeopardy of being eliminated. That job did not interfere with any other responsibilities and it gave me direct and frequent access to Nurse Shelly. She was also a member of the church I attended. When I first encountered her at the hospital, I did not recognize her as the chocolate drop in the second row of the alto section of the choir.

She had caught my eye a couple Sundays but all of the trauma and drama from my days in Cheyenne with Andy, Grumbault,

Hanes, and others had me skittish when it came to intimacy, romance, and commitment. I did not want to complicate any part of my life with a relationship. But I thought that maybe God brought me back to Alabama so I could live a life that was not defined by my attraction to men. In Decatur, I could conform to life in a familiar place while I grew into a different expression of myself.

Each night that Shelly and I were both working the late shift, we would talk on the phone when we weren't busy, eat together in the cafeteria, and find just about any excuse to meet up. It did not take long before the sparks were flying between us and we became very serious. One night I felt compelled to share something with her.

We were in her apartment together, watching some movie we had rented from Blockbuster. I picked up the remote, clicked the pause button, lifted her head off my shoulder, and said, "I have to tell you something." She adjusted her hair so it all fell behind her right shoulder. She did not turn to look at me in the same way I did not turn to look at Lawrence in the Kentucky Fried Chicken parking lot. She kept her eyes toward the television. She asked, "Are you about to break my heart? If so, please don't."

"I am not about to break your heart. In fact, I never want to break your heart. That is why I have to tell you something about me."

"Is it about your past?"

"Yes. It is."

"Is it still in your past?"

"What does that mean?"

"Is whatever you think you have to tell me something that you believe will be a problem for us now or in the future?"

"No, but I don't want to have secrets."

"We have both lived lives that involved other people. We have made choices and decisions that we would not make today, but we made them then and we learned from them. So, if it happened before us and it will not impact us, then I don't feel I have to know."

"I want you to know. I feel like I have been keeping a secret from you."

"If that is what you feel, then that may be what you are doing. So, just know, breaking my heart tonight is not an option."

"Shelly, I have been in relationships with men before."

She turned to look at me and when she did, I began to cry. She wiped the tears away. She asked, "Are you crying because you feel a weight has lifted now that you told me that?"

I nodded in affirmation. She said, "Thank you, Cedrick."

"Why are you thanking me?"

"Because you honored my request. You did not break my heart. Instead, you answered a prayer."

As I began to dry my own tears and nudge her up and away from me a bit, I asked, "What prayer?"

"That God would do something to lighten your load. You always seem like you are carrying too much. I see how hard and how much you work. I see how much you love being around people, but you also seem distant and reserved sometimes. I want you to be free to be the best you possible." She clapped her hands as though her favorite performer had granted her a double encore. She kissed me and vowed not to bring up that conversation again.

The next time I cried in her presence outside of a church service was the Valentine's Day I proposed to her. The ring I purchased was sold to me by the older sister of one of my football teammates in high school. She worked at one of the jewelry stores in the mall and she gave me a discount. When she asked me if I was marrying

Rosemary, I laughed and asked, "How do you remember who I dated in high school?"

"Everybody at school was sure the two of you would be the couple to get married."

"Sorry to disappoint but it is not her. She is happily married with two children. I'm marrying a woman I work with at the hospital."

"Whoa! Aren't there supposed to be rules against coworkers dating each other?"

"I know they say 'don't get your honey where you make your money,' but I don't work for the hospital. I work there for a security company."

She wrapped the little black box with a silver bow and wished me luck with my proposal.

Shelly and I had exchanged some gifts before we spent time at our pastor's home, went to dinner, and walked around the pond near her apartment. I was nervous when I asked her to marry me and presented her with the ring. I wondered if I had moved too quickly or misread where we were in our relationship. When she looked down at me on bended knee and said, "I will marry you," the waterworks broke free.

Everyone who knew us at the hospital was elated for us. The people at our church were very encouraging and almost pushy about forcing us to set a date for the wedding. Neither of us were in a hurry to get married but we were committed to marrying each other when we felt the time was right.

The job at Domino's was even more crucial to my financial stability because I was now engaged to a registered nurse. I had to raise my game if I was going to be able to provide and contribute at the same level that she did. While attending a training for assistant managers, the district manager asked me what I wanted for my future. I said, "Rick, I want to be an architect. I may eventually go to Bible college or seminary, but for now, I know I want to be an architect. Why do you ask?"

He said, "You know the word 'architect' can be used to describe many things, don't you think?"

"I don't know what you are getting at, Rick."

"As I understand it, architects help build things. They add finesse and flair to things to make them look better than they would without their input."

"You seem to have given this some thought."

"My dad is an architect and he can't see what I do as measuring up to him and his success. I think what I do touches just as many people as what he does and I don't think the results are all that different when you think about it."

This was by far the longest conversation I had ever had with Rick and I understood why. Just before my eyes rolled back in my head, he tugged my arm to prevent me from walking away. He pulled in close enough to my left ear that I felt his hair on my neck.

In a whisper as though he were sharing a secret, he asked, "If you were offered an opportunity to manage one of our stores, would you take it? Would you design schedules, pizzas, and food orders?" He created a slight distance between us. "See, that's being a pizza architect."

"I could do that, but I can't leave Decatur. I just got engaged."

"I know. Congratulations. I can make you a manager in Decatur, if you give me the right answer."

"If you can guarantee me Decatur, then you have the answer and the answer is yes."

In a matter of minutes, I went from dreaming about how I could make more money and get ahead to having an opportunity handed to me. As excited as I was about the possibility, I did not assume it would happen right away.

No Guarantees

Within a week I was the manager of one of the three Domino's in Decatur. In December 1993, shortly after I settled in as manager, we received word that the company was eliminating its thirty-minute guarantee on all deliveries. That was necessary because of the $79 million dollar judgment against them that came as the result of a finding that the guarantee contributed to negligent driving habits.

That change of policy impacted driver morale in positive ways and upset customers who had grown accustomed to setting their stopwatches to time the delivery in hopes of getting a discount and to complain about a pizza that may not have been extra hot when it arrived. There was no way to win that game except by being kind and reiterating the new policy every time an order was placed.

As a manager of my own store, I could not continue to work five nights a week at the hospital, so I gave my resignation to my supervisor before I discussed it with Shelly. When I told her about it, she understood the decision but did not understand why it was not a discussion. I said, "The decision was clear and talking about it with you was not going to change the outcome." She was upset by my response. She reminded me that open and clear communication were requirements for a healthy relationship. I apologized for how I handled the situation and we moved on.

Shelly and I spent less time together after I quit the security job. Some of that was due to the loss of time together at work and the longer hours I put in at Domino's. When we were not working, we were usually engaged in some function at our church. She was involved with the youth group and I volunteered as a Bible teacher and as the church administrator. During that time, I was instrumental in helping the church secure a new facility and launch several new initiatives.

One of the annual highlights on Progressive's calendar was a trip to Anderson, Indiana, to celebrate the anniversary of our pastor's spiritual mentors. The only event that even came close to that trek was the weekend when the folks from Anderson would come to Decatur. Both events were spectacular and had a Hollywood glamour element to them. There was singing, eating, shopping, and meeting new people who had joined the ministries since the last visit. The preparation for the trip to Indiana was a year-round process but when the date neared, everyone would shift into high gear. We would hold extra prayer services and choir rehearsals, and schedule group shopping trips to get our suits altered.

As the date for my second Indiana trip neared, I was excited. I had experienced somewhat of a spiritual revival the year before when we were there and my expectation was for more of the same. The difference this time was that I had a fiancée and I had engaged Lawrence by phone several times. Each conversation was short but it seemed we were making progress. He would say he was going to call, but never did. I would call him, he would offer his excuse, and I would apologize for him not honoring his word.

Two days before we were scheduled to depart for Indiana, I called Lawrence. He said, "Nice to hear from you, Cedrick. How are you?"

"I am doing well. Getting ready for a trip that is coming up on Thursday."

"Where are you going? Tahiti?"

"I wish. No. I am going with my church to Indiana for a few days."

"Are you driving?"

"No. We have chartered a bus."

"That won't be too bad."

"It wasn't bad last time but I will be better prepared with my snacks."

"Well, if you weren't going out of town this weekend, we could meet on Saturday."

My heart stopped as a lump formed in my throat. Most of our conversations involved him telling me he would call but he never did. This was different. He offered to meet without me putting forth a request. This was progress.

"I'm available Saturday."

"But you said you were going to Indiana this weekend."

"It's not this weekend. It's next weekend," I lied.

"OK. I misunderstood. So, we can do it Saturday morning."

"Yessir. That would be nice."

"Well, I have to get back to work. I will call you Friday to let you know where we can meet."

"That is good. I look forward to it."

I was elated. I called my pastor, Shelly, and my mom and told them the news. All three of them cautioned me against cancelling my trip.

My pastor said, "Bridgeforth, you have to be smart about this. I know you want to have a relationship with this man, but he has not told you one truth in all the conversations you have had with him."

Shelly begged me to go on the trip. She said, "Let him see what it's like when someone makes and breaks a commitment." She did not believe he would honor his word.

My mom said, "If he really wants to meet, he will make it happen when you are available. Call him back and tell him you will not be available this Saturday. Go on your trip."

I believed all three of them and I wanted to believe Lawrence. I wanted him to have another opportunity to do the right thing. I wanted every call I had made, every tear I had shed, and every pizza I had delivered to matter. Never mind the fact that grandma always told us that anything built on a lie would not stand. I had lied to force his hand.

The advice of everyone who knew of my ongoing saga with Lawrence fell on deaf ears because I cancelled my trip to Indiana. The charter bus left on Thursday; I spent that day at my apartment cleaning and rearranging the furniture as a way of keeping busy. I secretly held a fantasy that on Saturday after our breakfast, Lawrence would ask if he could see where I lived. I would escort him up the stairs to my apartment on Second Avenue above Gold's Gym—a mere two blocks from E.E. Forbes & Sons Piano Company and five blocks from the Morgan County Courthouse.

I would show him my Air Force uniform that hung in my closet, the hand grenade case I used as a coffee table, and the picture of my mom and siblings at my grandparents' fiftieth wedding anniversary. I imagined him marveling at the painting Jason had done of me that he gifted to me at our high school graduation. The thing that would be most impressive was how I had a window in my living room that opened to the roof of the gym below, giving me a massive balcony from which I could see most of the city. I would omit the part about sitting up there and watching the men cruise the local Greyhound bus station which was a local hookup spot. He would have to acquire his own Damron Guide for that information.

That Friday I drove to Huntsville to an art store and bought a drafting table so I would have it in my apartment, should Lawrence visit. I could show him some of my work and prove to him that I had some of his engineering skills or genes. I brought it home and set it up and spent the balance of that day drawing floor plans of homes no one would ever live in except the families I imagined in my mind. When the clock neared 6 p.m., the time Lawrence would normally be on lunch break, I checked every half hour to see if my dial tone on my phone was active. I double- and triple-checked my answering machine to be sure it was not malfunctioning. I stayed in my apartment all evening and into the night because I did not want to miss his call.

Chasing the Juice

The next morning, I was up and dressed by 6 a.m. I wanted to be ready when he called to let me know where to meet him for breakfast. What had been half-hourly checks the previous evening became quarter-hourly checks throughout the day. Whenever my phone rang, I would answer it midway through the first ring and terminate the call within thirty seconds.

My mom called around 3 p.m. to check on me.

"Hey, Ced. How are you doing?"

"I'm good. Can I call you later?"

"Why are you rushing me off the phone?"

"I don't want to tie up the line. I don't have call waiting on this phone. If someone calls while I am on here, they will get a busy signal and they may think I don't want to talk to them."

"Do you mean you want to keep the line free in case Lawrence calls?"

"Well, yeah! He said he would call."

"Ced, he told you he would call to schedule breakfast for this morning."

"Maybe I misunderstood. Maybe he meant he would call me on Saturday and that is when we would schedule breakfast."

"That is not what you told me the three other times you recounted that conversation. Look, you missed your trip and took off work this weekend. You have to let this go. You did what you could to be available and he failed to deliver on his promise."

I felt a need to defend him even more but her words rang with so much truth that I sat in silence and felt the phone grow heavier and heavier by the second.

"I know you want him to show up in some way, but he may not be capable of doing what you want him to do."

"Maybe something happened and he had to do something with his wife or his daughter." During one of my conversations with Lawrence, he had disclosed that he had a wife of many years and a daughter who was five years older than me. I charged forward with conviction. "You know things come up and I imagine he would not want to tell either of them that he was going to Decatur to see his secret son if there was any way he could avoid doing that."

My mom backed off of her efforts to get me to let go of the notion that he would call. She said, "I have always trusted you to do the right thing. I have to do that now. All I can do is pray that you see the light and move forward knowing you have done your best."

"I know. I appreciate it. I have to go now."

"Bye, boy. Call me tomorrow."

"Bye, mama."

I hung up and climbed out the window and onto the roof. It was a place that I found calming and secluded. I had lived there several months but that night I walked over to the edge for the first time. I allowed my toes to stretch out over the edge. I felt the breeze off of the Tennessee River that was a few blocks north. As it caressed my face, I looked up to the sky and prayed a simple prayer: "Lord, have mercy on me."

The manager position at Domino's was challenging but not much different from the people management and administrative tasks I had performed at Sonic Drive-In, for the Air Force, and at my church. My assistant manager was a former college football star. He had played a few pre-season games in the National Football League before he sustained a major injury that cut his football career short. The owner of the franchise we worked for was a long-time family friend and offered him a job.

That guy was lovable and he knew how to get the employees to perform at their peak. I learned how to engage the drivers and customers with a kinder and gentler approach by watching him. Maybe because he was almost seven feet tall and over three hundred pounds, he had mastered softening what could have been an intimidating presence. It worked for him and it started to work for me. Our location became a top performer within the company and the owners were pleased. By all accounts I was on the fast track within the company and could expect to be rewarded with sizable bonuses and other perks.

Most weekdays I would relieve the assistant manager at 4 p.m., but on Fridays, I would not come in until 6 p.m. because we were open later. On June 17, 1994, I called the assistant manager to let him know I would not arrive until almost 7 p.m. I had to go by the church to complete some paperwork for others to sign and I knew I would not have time to get it done the following day.

When I parked in front of Domino's, I could see inside past the blue-and-red signage on the windows. The assistant manager and several of the drivers were glued to the small television they had moved from my office to the front of the store. I walked in as the assistant manager yelled out, "Say he didn't do it, man! Say he didn't do it!"

"What are you talking about? Who?"

He pointed up to the television. "Juice. Tell me he didn't kill those people, man. This is crazy."

"I have no idea what you are talking about."

"O.J. is in that white Ford Bronco and the police are chasing him. They believe he is the one who killed his wife and her boyfriend."

I had slept in that morning and spent the afternoon at the church so I was not aware of the O.J. chase. The assistant manager was deeply invested because of his affinity with O.J. as a football player and as someone who was in a racially mixed marriage. That night's activities at the store were as unsettling as the images of O.J. being chased by the police. My memories of him involved him running through airports during Hertz commercials.

We had numerous undeliverable orders that night. One driver received a speeding ticket during his shift and another got into a minor car accident. The customers were unusually rude to the staff taking orders over the phone and more pizzas than I could count were made wrong, slowing our operation in the middle of our busiest hours. By the time I left that night, I wanted to get in my little red truck and ride off into the darkness, never to be found again.

Saturday's and Sunday's shifts were better but they were not back to normal. During our regular Sunday night worship, I sat next to Shelly. That was something we rarely did because she usually sat with the choir and I was either sitting with the ministers or doing something that required me to be near a door or providing support for someone. After the pastor's sermon, he called for those who wanted individual prayer to come forward. That was not unusual. In fact, it was expected that every time we gathered, he would lead the altar call by issuing a specific invitation.

There had been invitations to women who were looking for a husband, men who wanted to be delivered from homosexuality, children who wanted better grades, senior adults who struggled with their health, couples on the verge of divorce, and a host of categorical financial and legal needs. I usually served as one of the pastor's support ministers, so I did not get in the line. Instead, I helped keep the line moving and in order. That night I was first in line for prayer. I moved Shelly's hand from my lap, gave her my very heavy Dake Annotated Bible, and jumped up before I could question my actions. The pastor had an inquisitive brow as he looked deeply into my eyes and asked, "Do you know why you are in this line for prayer tonight?"

I shook my head and said, "No. I don't."

Tears began to flow from my eyes. He told me to lift both hands up as a sign of total surrender to God. He said, "You have been holding back too much of who you are and God wants to use all of you to make a difference."

I was nodding in agreement and as a way to help gravity move those tears from my cheeks and to another location. He continued, "You are very gifted. You are anointed. You want to see God's people do great things. You want to do great things, but you think you are in charge of your life. You think you have to have all the answers and all of them have to make sense to you before you will trust God."

I could hear him as clearly as I could hear those who had gathered around me praying aloud. He asked, "Are you open to allow God to do something miraculous in your life without you trying to control it?"

I murmured, "Yes. I am open. I am open to God."

He placed his hand upon my forehead and began to pray for me. The entire congregation prayed aloud for me with their hands outstretched toward me or touching me. They joined in prayer much like New Kingdom had done for me when I asked them to pray for my plans for the future.

There were many others who came forward for prayer that night. I did not stay to see how the service ended. I told Shelly I needed to go home and sit on the roof and meditate upon what had happened at the altar. She said, "I would not have it any other way. That was a lot for you to step up there and now you have to truly find your way of being open to what God is doing and will do. I love you. Let's talk in the morning."

As I sat on the roof thinking back over my life in high school, the Air Force, New Kingdom, my move back to Alabama, my engagement to Shelly, and my growing disenchantment with Lawrence, I anticipated starting Monday with a new attitude and a positive approach to the work. Even though I could not articulate what I was feeling, I knew something was definitely off-track and I needed to figure it out or move past it.

Shifts Change

Monday morning began with me waking up on the sofa. I had spent several hours on the roof and when I came in, I turned on some music and never moved from that spot. I got dressed, ran some errands, then drove to Domino's. I usually arrived earlier than I needed to so I could get everything set up before the morning crew arrived. I liked the quiet in the space before the phones, ovens, and fans crowded air. Just as the weekend had been different, so was this Monday.

I walked in and a stench that was probably there every morning but was masked by my need to feel significant and to prove my worth as a manager met me at the door. I paused next to the front counter. The dark gray tile under my feet had a hold of me and would not let me move forward. The air that was usually cold and crisp was heavy and hot. Everything within me was leaning toward flight over fight, unless it was to fight my way back to my truck. I prayed to God for deliverance in that moment, "Lord, have mercy on me. Lord, have mercy on me." As I prayed, I made my way to my tiny office and called Rick, my district manager.

He answered and before he could begin to speak, I said, "Rick, I need you to come take the store. I have to go."

He asked, "What are you talking about? Are you ok?"

"No. I am not ok. I need you to come take the store. I have to go now."

"Look, I have a few things to take care of this morning. I can get over there right after the lunch rush."

"I am getting up from this desk, placing the keys on the front counter, and walking out the door. I have to go now."

"Wait! I will be there in fifteen minutes."

When he drove into the parking lot, I was sitting in my truck. I waved good-bye to him and made a right turn out of the lot onto Fourteenth Street. Without discussion, thought, or even the semblance of a plan, I drove the seventy miles to Birmingham. It was my first time back in that city since Boys State. I remembered we exited Lakeshore Drive and went west to the campus, so I followed what I remembered until I came to the main entrance. I parked, walked into Samford Hall, and located the Admissions Office. The lady behind the reception desk asked, "How can I help you?"

I suppose she wondered if I had a delivery, since I was in my Domino's uniform, hat and all. I said, "I need an application for admission."

She gave it to me and told me I would need transcripts from all the schools I had attended, an essay, and $35 for the application fee. I asked if there was a typing room nearby where I could type my essay. She said, "We don't have a typing room. There is a computer lab in the library that you can use but you don't have to write the essay today."

"Yes, I do. I have to do this right now. How do I get transcripts from my high school?"

When she learned that I graduated from a high school in Alabama, she told me she could request it for me. I thanked her and asked for directions to the library. I walked from Samford Hall past the life-size statue of Ralph Beeson and up the center walkway as I took in the summer students tossing a frisbee on the quad and the high school students on campus for an event much like when I was there for Boys State. I opened the essay with details of growing up without adequate male role models, described being influenced by my grandmother, and included some experiences from my Air Force days. I closed it with:

I was always told that I would go to college but no one made provisions for that to happen. We simply lived with an expectation that has now turned to hope and probability. My reason for being here is to get what I need to live my life with purpose and meaning so that when my days are done, there will be evidence that I was here on this planet. I don't expect wealth, fame, or grand accolades. I just want what I contribute to the world to matter beyond me. I want those who have invested in me and those who may have learned from or worked with me to be proud of what we experienced, accomplished, and left for those who will journey onward with their hopes becoming probabilities.

On my way back to Samford Hall, I sat next to Mr. Beeson's statue and offered a prayer of gratitude for what was unfolding. I found my way back to the Admissions Office with my completed application, essay, and a $35 check. I presented the packet to the lady behind the desk and asked to speak with an admissions counselor.

The person who helped me was Dean Smedley. I told him my whole story and before leaving his office got a commitment from him that he would do all in his power to push for my admission. He was not optimistic about my prospects because the term was due to begin in just over six weeks. My next conversation, with the financial aid office, was even less promising, but I did leave with an assurance that if I were admitted for the fall, they would work with me to get financial support.

I sat in my truck and thanked God while also asking God what I had just done. No one knew I was in Birmingham applying for college. I wasn't completely sure how I had made the decision to walk away from my job and do that. All I knew was I wanted more than what I had. I felt I had to take a step forward and make a stand for myself. I ended up at Samford because I knew it from my time at Boys State and remembered how to get there.

On the way back to Decatur I had more questions about my future and how I would make this transition than I did about the decision I had made to potentially leave Domino's, Shelly, my church, and my family. My first stop in Decatur was Shelly's apartment. She was frantic.

"Where have you been? I called the store today and they said you left abruptly without any explanation. They assumed something happened to your mom. I called her and of course she didn't know anything so now she is worried."

"I will call her when I get home. I had something I needed to do today."

"What was so important that you didn't tell me or your mom?"

"I went to Birmingham. I applied for admission to Samford for the fall semester."

"What? Why would you do that? Doesn't it start soon? How could that even be possible?"

"The admissions officer assured me he would advocate for me to get in this term and the financial aid rep committed to help me once my application was approved."

Shelly struggled to listen to me that day. She felt she should have been consulted before I made the decision. She was right, but so was I. She did need to be a factor in the decision because we were engaged to be married and had plans to build a life together. I also had a responsibility to follow opportunities and options that would improve my standard of living and move me into greater understanding of my life's purpose. Domino's was not doing that for me. It was a reminder of what I was not accomplishing and of who I did not want to be in the world.

CHAPTER 6

BUILD A TEAM

Confessionless

By the end of my first semester at Samford University, I changed my major from Pre-Pharmacy to Religion. That was the handiwork of the Religion Department's formidable chairperson, Dr. Bill Leonard. I was enrolled in his Introduction to Church History course. One day after class he asked me to remain behind so he could speak with me. After the room had emptied, leaving behind faded archeological posters, books with tattered dust jackets, copies of ancient biblical manuscripts, my curiosity, and the two of us, he asked, "Why are you in my Church History class?"

I replied, "I believe I have a call to ministry"

"But your major is listed as Pre-Pharmacy."

"I plan to go to pharmacy school and graduate in a few years. With that degree I will be able to earn enough money right away to pay for a seminary degree."

It must have been blatantly obvious to this man that I was clueless, but whatever he discerned or imagined, he would come up short of knowing how little I knew about what I had gotten myself into. My grandparents and parents were not college-educated persons. They toiled the land and made products with their hands. College was a luxury they could not even grasp in their wildest dreams.

All I knew was that I would need a seminary degree to be in ministry. My best friend was a pharmacist. I knew he was paid very well upon his graduation from Pharmacy School. He did it and that convinced me I could do it too.

Dr. Leonard asked, "Would you be interested in a more intentional discernment process and regular vocational conversations about ministry?"

"Yes. I think that would be helpful because I do not know very much, but I do know I do not want to preach every Sunday."

"Well, what do you want to do?"

"I'm not sure, but I have been told I am a good Bible teacher and I know I have good administrative skills."

"We will work on figuring this out together. Let's meet a couple of times per month. I will give you some reading to do in between and when we meet, we will talk about it."

He introduced me to individuals who were educators and in other theological vocations. He explained how that was their expression of and response to a call to ministry. Dr. Leonard and other professors, like Dr. Penny Marler and Dr. Karen Joines, made it possible for me to engage with others in the theological field and in biblical studies.

The exposure to different ways of living out a call to ministry was a journey that called on the deepest and best parts of my being. I had to discern the ways that would work for me to serve in leadership and to facilitate learning without becoming rigid, dogmatic, or beholden to elements of the faith my grandmother wrapped neatly and delivered to me. I relished being free to explore without having to make excuses for my curiosity. I did not feel any of my college professors demanded or expected me to be anyone I was not.

Although I never disclosed my sexuality to them, I sensed they knew. Of course, I often made assumptions about what people did or did not know about me—especially in religious arenas. One time when I was sixteen, I almost told my grandmother that I was gay because I believed the evangelist already knew. My belief that he knew scared me to the point that I almost confessed to him and then to her.

Every year, a traveling evangelist and his wife would come to town and host the annual tent revival. My grandma would insist that my grandfather take her every night that tent was up. A curious reality about the revival was that it was the only religious gathering that was ever truly integrated, with white, Black, rich, poor, Baptist, Methodist, and holiness folks. None of those groups would dare gather together in any of their church buildings, but the pentecost moments under that tent were legendary.

One night my grandma wasn't feeling well and with nothing better to do, I went on my own. Toward the end of the service, the evangelist asked all the young people to come forward for prayer. I was frightened. It seemed everyone who went up there for prayer ended up passed out on the ground with him leaning over them praying louder and louder until the next person stepped up. I was committed to staying on my feet at all costs.

As he laid his very large, very sweaty hand on my forehead, I felt speckles of spit from his mouth land on my face. I wondered if anyone was behind me just in case I needed to turn and run. Suddenly he leaned in and spoke softly into my ear, "You don't have to be that way if you don't want to be."

I closed my eyes. He said it again and again before he asked me to look at him. I looked into his ice-blue eyes. He had a very stern and serious expression on his face. He said, "If you want to be delivered from that demon, God will deliver you tonight!" I began to cry and wondered how he knew I was gay. How did this man who had never met me know I was living contrary to what I had been told was the will of God? How did he know I struggled with my sexuality because I was ashamed and afraid? But in that moment, I was more afraid of his words than I was of going to hell or anything else. He kept his hand on my head and we stared at each other until he said, "It won't happen until you surrender your life fully to God." I wiped tears from my eyes and walked away, wondering if I had made a mistake by not confessing.

A few weeks later, my grandma asked me why I had been so distant—not calling each day or stopping back in the evenings. She said, "You can tell me what's going on."

I said, "Well, I think I am . . ." I caught myself from telling her my secret. Instead, I said, ". . . going to be off work the next two Sundays." That was my way of diverting the conversation to something that would make her happy instead of saying something that I feared would create distance between us.

I loved my grandmother. But I did not trust her enough to allow her to hold my truth with me. I did not trust that her love was unconditional and without strings attached.

It's strange because I did not see her as one who was overly judgmental. She showed up for people and advocated for their needs whenever such was warranted. She was nothing short of forgiving and understanding. Most notably I think about how she raised grandaddy's son by another woman as her own. I was almost an adult before I knew he had a different mother. So, why did I assume she would not be able to hear my truth and love me as she always had loved me?

Most times when I think of my grandma it is when I'm struggling to solve a problem or I just need a bit of wisdom to get me out of whatever funk I may have gotten into. She always had the right words at the right time. Even when I did not fully understand those words, I knew she was pointing me toward a truth or crucial realization. Although she was not physically affectionate toward me, I never doubted her love and commitment to my success.

I give her credit for opening my mind to the point that I could see great faults in others and not hold it against them. I saw how she took people in and nursed them back to health without asking for anything in return. The mentors, professors, lovers, and friends who expressed similar qualities are the ones who hold prominent space in my life. Working through issues of calling and finding an authentic voice as a teacher, preacher, and citizen of the world happened because I saw both good and bad examples of how to serve people. As my grandma would say, "God is not concerned with what you did or did not do. God is most concerned with whether or not you have been faithful."

Tango Birmingham

I was the only African American in the department and the first in decades. In some ways, that reality opened doors for me that otherwise would not have been opened, as faculty members leaned heavily on their dual role as pastors to help me navigate that space. That's really what Dr. Leonard did for me throughout that discernment process.

Walking into a racialized context at Samford did not concern me at first. I knew how to conceal my blackness in ways that allowed me to feel as though I fit in and not make white folks uncomfortable. I had not fully dialed in to the blatant—much less the subtle—race-based attitudes, policies, and accommodations at that institution. In the Air Force, it was made clear that any form of discrimination on the basis of race would not be tolerated. Racial discrimination was one of three offenses that could get an airman an immediate discharge. The other two were spousal abuse and homosexuality.

During my high school years, I was one of the popular students so I was not bullied or ostracized, except in eighth grade when I made the decision to quit the band and join the football team. I was often told, "You are not like other blacks." I would smile and feel a sense of pride, not realizing the level of violence and trauma that was being heaped upon me each time I heard those words and did not refute them. I was being set apart from others who shared my ethnic and racial identity much in the same way plantation masters would set apart "field negroes," who were of the darker variety, from "house negroes," who were usually the master's offspring. Either way, they were owned by the one who made the designations. It wasn't the slave's fault; it was the master's doing.

Much as I sidestepped issues of race, I deflected any discussion of sexuality. I knew how to show up and blend in with the crowd and stand out when necessary. I had learned to present myself as "one of the boys" in the Air Force, and I applied those same principles at Samford. Besides, if anyone asked, I could truthfully tell them I was engaged and broke off the engagement to pursue my education.

Birmingham, in general, and Samford, in particular, were not welcoming of ideas that might upset the status quo. I did not have enough courage to step into a space that might attract a spotlight. I chose to stand on the edge and observe with hope that I would find a rhythm that worked for me. Instead, the twin issues of racism and homophobia were to converge to a point where I could no longer dance around them.

Black Shirts

Many vestiges of Samford's racist past were present while I was a student there. The affiliation with the Southern Baptist Convention, the limited number of Black faculty and trustees, and the abundance of Black janitors and cafeteria workers were signs of that past that came into view over time. One of the programs for aspiring ministers and pastors was called "H-Day." It bridged the gap between Samford's origins as Howard College, a school that primarily trained Baptist ministers, and its present-day status as a modern university. H-Day allowed students to sign up to preach at a church in a predetermined area of the state for a weekend. Students on ministerial scholarship were expected to participate. The program allowed students much-needed practice in preaching in real congregations. It also allowed local churches to engage with up-and-coming students, while denominational leaders used it as an opportunity to recruit new talent.

When Dr. Leonard convinced me to change my major to religion. I went on a ministerial scholarship and that required me to participate in H-Day a few Sundays each semester. I also had a friend, Shawn Loscuito, who worked in the university chaplain's office, and he spoke very highly of his experiences preaching in various churches. I was struggling financially, and there was a stipend that would come in handy. My quest to maintain my scholarship, make some cash, and have some good experiences led me to H-Day.

Most of the churches I was assigned and the pastors I engaged were wonderful. I was always the only Black person present but I did not perceive that as problematic. Often after service the pastor would invite me to his home to join his family for lunch. They would ask a million questions about my story and how I ended up at Samford or with a call to ministry. Occasionally a pastor would take me to a restaurant for lunch instead of to his home. I never questioned whether that choice had anything to do with my race until I overheard the term "black shirts" one day.

The Beeson Divinity School was located at Samford University. Beeson had some international students enrolled from African countries and they were allowed to sign up for H-Day. We gathered at the appointed time to meet the pastors, determine carpool realities, and head to our various weekend destinations. The pastors were all there, lined up as they always were. The pastor who was responsible for making the pairings greeted us and began calling the names of the students to verify attendance. When it was time to pair up with our respective pastors, he looked at his clipboard and said, "I have four black shirts. Who can take those?" I looked around and I did not see anyone wearing black shirts. I did see four Black faces—mine and the three attached to the African students from the Divinity School.

I was shocked that this language was used in the presence of the students and without protest or correction from any of the pastors. I dropped my head with disbelief and waited to be called upon. Since the black shirts were only able or expected to go to certain churches, we were selected first and then the other students were paired with pastors.

The pastor who chose me for the day was a nice man who wanted to have a conversation along the ride from the rendezvous point to the church. While he spoke, I mentally replayed all of my other H-Day experiences. I realized that on each of those occasions I was the only student who was preassigned upon arrival. My over-inflated ego and assumption that I was special for reasons other than my race led me to believe I was preassigned because I had been requested. On this day, perhaps because of the larger number of "black shirts" present, the dynamics changed and selections were made on the spot.

The time when Shawn Loscuito shared the story about one of the pastors asking if "Loscuito" was Jewish was suddenly no longer humorous. It was racist. I saw that decisions by host pastors about where we would have lunch were probably race-based choices too.

I do not know what I preached about that day. I imagine I did the same thing I did the night of my high school baccalaureate service: I pushed aside my anguish and shame for the sake of fulfilling the role I had been assigned. It was a skill I had mastered throughout my lifetime. Deny myself, follow the expected path, prepare and perform even when all hell's breaking loose inside and around me. In this situation I damned racism and self-hatred while relinquishing self-respect and never exercising my own agency in the moment. No one else spoke up either. All of us went along in silence until I brought this incident to the attention of the university chaplain.

Dr. James Barnette served as university chaplain and was responsible for the H-Day program. Both he and his father were graduates of Samford and former participants in H-Day during their time as students. Dr. Barnette saw the benefits of the program for both student participants and local churches. It was also a vehicle used by Dr. Barnette to raise thousands of dollars each year for scholarship support. When he heard my account of what happened, he seemed appalled.

He asked, "Are you sure that is what they said?"

"Yes. We talked about it on our way back to campus. Shawn heard it and so did others."

"I am so sorry that happened to you. That is inexcusable under any circumstance."

"I don't hold anything against you, the other students, or the school for what they did."

"Thanks for saying that, but please know I will call and get to the bottom of this."

Again, I did not want to draw undue attention to my presence in the situation. I did not want to make things worse for any of my classmates or even for the pastors involved. I had not experienced any overt racism or racist behaviors during any of my previous H-Day engagements. It was a tradition that had its roots in the founding of the school. I did not feel strong enough or prepared to demand anything more than my release from any future obligations to participate in H-Day so that I would never have to be subjected to treatment like that again.

The silence or support of friends in the midst of adversity is always a key to what they value most—self-preservation or the dignity of every individual. This was true during the summer of 1996, when I, along with three others from Samford, were assembled as a mission team. We were two men and two women, appointed as summer missionaries to the sub-Saharan country of Botswana, where we would present music, drama, and Bible studies throughout the country. I was the only African American on my team and the only African American student missionary that summer.

We flew from Atlanta to London where we had a long layover and a need to switch airports. In between airports, we dashed around London to take in as many tourist sites as possible. Each of us named a "must-see" and we mapped an itinerary so we could get to all of them and make our flight to Johannesburg. We took the subway, rode a red double-decker bus, took pictures in a red phone booth, and gawked at the Brits' ability to drive on the other side of the road. We saw Buckingham Palace, Trafalgar Square, the

Tower of London, Westminster Abbey, Big Ben, Harrods, and the London Bridge. My must-see was the British Museum.

A semester earlier I had taken a course on Near East Archeology and one of the textbooks was published by the British Museum. I was troubled that all of those Egyptian artifacts were held and cataloged by the British. Every class session was like an awakening of something buried deep inside me. My racial consciousness and anti-colonialist sensibilities were being raised just as ancient ruins and kings' remains had been raided by their colonizers. As much as I wanted to see what I had studied, I also wanted to acknowledge the theft and cultural annihilation that was memorialized in that museum.

We left London on a thirteen-hour flight to Johannesburg with the plan of sleeping the entire time because we did not know what awaited us on the other end. During the flight I asked one of my team members, "What did you think about the museum?"

"I thought the artifacts were stunning and in such good shape to be so old."

"Didn't you think it was weird that the 'British' Museum was nothing but stuff from everywhere else in the world—namely Africa?"

"Well, to be fair, we did not see all of the museum."

"True, but the half we did go through was all African and Egyptian artifacts. They make money off of that stuff and they stole it."

"I'm sure it was expensive for them to bring it by boat to London and then to curate it for the museum. That costs a lot and it takes a long time to do all that."

"It would have been cheaper for them to build a museum in Cairo instead. Don't you think?"

That conversation was the first of many we would have throughout the summer. We touched down in Johannesburg and had one more flight to Botswana's capital city, Gaborone. We were met at the Gaborone airport with signs and banners held high by a fair-sized crowd. We had only learned a few basic phrases in Setswana, the national language of Botswana. Our limited linguistic skills made it necessary for us to commandeer one of our fellow travelers to be our instant interpreter. I asked, "What is written on those banners?"

He said, "*Masole a makoro.* That means soldiers of the cross."

"Thank you." We jumped around with excitement. We were prepared to be known as a music, drama, and Bible study team but they had given us a name.

As our translator exited the plane, he turned and said, "I bid you well on your crusade." We thanked him for his assistance and laughed at his calling what we were to do a "crusade."

Stepping off the plane into a sea of Black and brown faces with a few white ones floating among them was a reversal of every public space I had ever occupied outside of church and family functions. It was unsettling.

In one sense, it was empowering to be in the majority and I felt that in the same way I felt it each time I visited Atlanta and saw so many thriving Black people. I was proud and I felt stronger as a Black person in that environment even though nothing had fundamentally changed for me or about me. What had happened was an existential shift in my thinking of myself because of the environment.

In another sense, I felt the need to be overly apologetic when a Tswana person would address me as one of their own. When our team would present at a school, the children would scream whenever I would speak or sing in English. They would say, in their native language, "He is a ghost. He speaks as a white man." There was mass hysteria that teachers and the missionaries would have to calm. The older children and adults observed me with a sense of pride and connectivity that did not always require words. I wrote in my journal each day from the time we left the United States until we returned. The entry for June 21, 1996:

> At 7 p.m., we ministered at Zwenschumbe Junior Community School. It was a long program and the students really packed into that auditorium. We sang audience participation songs and the kids loved it! They touched my hair and found it was no different from theirs. They touched my hands with the expectancy of a different texture. But the expectancy seemed to intensify more for me today than it had the four weeks since we had arrived. I looked into their eyes seeking an answer. I wanted them to affirm something. I wanted them to see what I saw, feel what I felt, and longed to hear exactly what each of them was thinking. Once again, I left feeling as though I had not done enough to better their lives, but just as before, I was humbled and convicted by the whiteness I saw in the darkness. The glistening of their longing eyes and the whiteness of those ivory teeth told many stories of triumph, joy, and hope that no words could ever convey.

The young people of Botswana offered me hope and gave me a vision of a life that was not defined by materialism and what some deemed as proper diction. They saw hope in each other and in me. Seeing them smile and bring such joy to every space transformed my thinking. The experience of being or looking a part of the dominant culture grew on me throughout the summer and helped me interrogate my own notions of success, freedom, and blackness.

Strangely Familial

As we traveled through Botswana, Namibia, and the northern parts of South Africa, we would set up a large blue-and-yellow tent in each village. That became our sanctuary and our calling card to all the villagers that something special was happening in their village. We would sing, do dramatic skits, teach Bible lessons, and preach among the people. Our efforts wore on us toward the end of the summer. We went on holiday to Victoria Falls in Zimbabwe. While we were there, the man who cared for the garden where we were lodging invited us to his village for an annual tribal ceremony.

We gathered in the desert at dusk as the men prepared a very large bonfire and the women served us food and drinks that were customary for this event. I ate what they gave me and drank whatever was in that cup. By this point in the summer, we had eaten roasted pigeon, boiled liver from some animal, fried mopane worms, blue birthday cake, and grilled zebra. I learned to eat without asking questions.

The man who invited us was seated to my immediate left and Sally, our host missionary, was seated to my right. I asked, "What will happen here tonight?"

He told us, "The simple explanation is: this is where the boys become men and women learn who will be their husbands one day."

I understood the ceremony was an annual rite of passage, akin to a coming-of-age or naming-one's-faith ceremony common in many cultures. I had gone through baptism and confirmation at my church and had studied traditions of other religions, so this was not a far-fetched concept for me.

The young men were marched into the village and formed a circle near the bonfire. We, the spectators and other villagers, formed an even larger circle around them. There was drumming, singing, dancing, and chanting. I was captivated by the beat around that fire. I became one with the motion and the moment—I felt alive and a part of something that mattered to me. It was the same feeling I sought at those tent revivals. I got a taste of it in New Kingdom and when I was deeply in love. I felt it when driving alone in my car blasting "When Doves Cry" by Prince or "Simply the Best" by Tina Turner. Something deep within me had been awakened and made complete.

I looked over at Sally and could see she was crying. I asked, "Sally, what's wrong?"

Tears streaming profusely from those bright blue eyes, she flipped her blonde hair back from her face, and said, "My heart aches for these boys."

"Sally, why do you say that?"

"They don't know the Lord."

"We don't know that to be true. That's not what they are here for right now."

Sally's face reddened. She pointed a white index finger at me and asked, "Can you imagine what they are going through? What their lives will be without the Lord?"

"I can imagine what they are going through, Sally. I feel it. I feel revived by this ceremony in ways the church has never done for me. We don't know how they view God and salvation. This is their culture and I like it."

She stormed away and I turned my attention back to the beat of the drum. Sally returned with her husband and the rest of our team. They thanked the gardener who invited us and told him we had to leave.

The other members of the team had no idea what had happened and why we were leaving so abruptly. I tried to recount the exchange I had with Sally and they quickly understood the issue.

Back at our vacation lodge, Sally told me, "If your stay here wasn't almost over, you would be on your way back to Alabama first thing in the morning."

"Why? What did I do that was so wrong?"

"We thought everyone knew the purpose of our mission was to save these people. They have to know Jesus."

"I know that and I know I have not done anything wrong."

"You celebrated that demonic tribalism as if it were the same thing as them knowing our Lord and Savior."

"Sally, I don't know what they know or what they believe. I do know I felt something out there tonight that made sense to me and it did not feel demonic or wrong."

"Well, it is."

I was told I would not be allowed to preach for the remainder of the summer. I could participate in the skits and singing, but the white male on the team would handle all of the preaching. One day, in an act of defiance, I decided if I could not preach, I would not go with the team to any of the events. I stayed at the missionaries' home.

While there I began looking at the bookshelf and came across a book titled *Black Theology and Black Power*. I wondered why that book was on these two white missionaries' bookshelves if they did not believe those Black people knew any more about God than they did. I expected the book to be some whitewash of Christianity or of the Bible. It was the complete opposite. The words within that spoke of God being on the side of the oppressed and the power that Black people have to love and to liberate themselves followed the same percussive cadence as the drums around that fire in Zimbabwe. A liberationist was born.

When I returned to Samford for my senior year, I did not have to participate in H-Day and that was a good thing since I had discovered my voice in Botswana. I presented my proposal to the

Religion Department on Black liberation theology with full expectation that I would be allowed to write my senior thesis on a topic that was relevant to me and my heritage. My advisor rejected my proposal, stating, "This subject matter is too divisive. Please choose something more relevant to our current times."

I waged a protest for my right and need to do my thesis on Black liberation theology because I was about to graduate with a degree in religion and had not been exposed to any past or current Black theologians or scholars, except those I sought out to read on my own. An ally in this fight was Dr. Penny Marler, the first and only female professor in the Religion Department. Another supporter was an English Literature adjunct professor who had pulled me aside my first semester and given me a list of books by Black authors that she believed I needed to read. That same professor got me a ticket to hear Dr. Cornel West discuss his book *Race Matters* at the Sixteenth Street Baptist Church where four Black girls had been killed in 1963.

I advocated for myself as I had done to get a spot at Boys State, to keep my job at Sonic, and to get last-minute admission to Samford. I won some of those efforts and others appeared to be losses at the time, but grandma's words held me to my conviction: "If you never give up on yourself, you will always have at least one person on your side." I believed that eventually my advisor would have to succumb to the pressure. The refusal to approve my proposal because it was "too divisive" seemed equally as dismissive as the attempts to silence me in Botswana and to discriminate against me at H-Day.

The Tango Continues

If race was the first partner in the dance my life choreographed for me in Birmingham, then sexuality was the second. Samford had a "closed dorm" policy, which meant no one of the opposite sex was allowed beyond the common areas of the residence halls. On the nights when I would indulge or entertain other men, that policy actually served my purposes as a gay man more than any other rule the administration had in place.

I had become a master at hiding and denying my sexuality since I was a child and had an awareness of my difference. For the years that I believed my sexuality was not what God intended, I was supportive of policies and conversations that spoke ill of me in the same way I was silent and complicit in racist policies and acts that harmed me. My closeted nature became a veil that allowed me to pretend I was not gay. Well, I did not pretend I was not gay, it was more that I pretended to be heterosexual.

Southern culture and Baptist dogma permeated policies and defined relationships for students, faculty, and the surrounding community. There were gay and lesbian students but we were not allowed to acknowledge that publicly in any way. During my last year at Samford a handful of students tried to organize a gay support group on campus. None of them openly professed to be gay or lesbian, but they said they wanted to create a safe space where they could support each other in their efforts to support people who did identify as gay or lesbian. The cafeteria chatter rose to voluminous proportions to prevent the students from receiving any financial support from student fees. There were public debates and protests to ban the group from meeting on campus.

This topic came up during one of the weekly conversations I helped organize after the H-Day "black shirt" incident. A group of us gathered each week for a session called "Tolerance Talk" focused on racial matters and using a curriculum produced by the Southern Poverty Law Center. As the campus-wide debate about the gay and lesbian support group grew, it spilled over into our conversations about race.

The co-facilitators of the group were a psychology professor and Dr. Penny Marler, one of my favorite professors and one of the most progressive individuals on campus. Dr. Marler asked, "What have we learned in our conversations about race that may help us listen more intently in the conversations around sexual preference and identity?" That was the first time I had ever connected hate and disdain for people of color with hate and disdain for people who love those of the same gender. I had lived that double consciousness but I had never articulated it to myself. I listened as various students, mostly white ones, spoke up.

A petite white female student from Spartanburg, South Carolina, said, "People should be able to love whomever they choose." A male student wearing an Atlanta Braves hat nodded in agreement as he asked, "Who am I to judge?" Most of the white students rang a similar bell. Then a Black woman seated near me said, "I don't think it is right for men to lay down with other men. It is an abomination. God is not pleased with that." She received several "Amens!" and high-fives. Other Blacks, most of whom grew up in or around Birmingham, added, "Do what you want, just don't bring it around me" and "If they gonna be gay, they should all live in a gay dorm so we don't have to see that at all."

There was limited empathy and an absence of space for me to speak and name my deepest and truest self. I lived at the intersection of two identities and neither would find liberation or power at that institution. Neither my race nor sexuality were invited to dance.

Familial Stranger

Awakened to how my blackness needed as much care and advocacy as my queerness, I settled into the idea of leaving Alabama and moving to California after graduating from Samford. But old and unresolved feelings and relationships were not so easily left behind.

It was the week of my last round of final exams. I was walking out of my campus apartment preparing to host our last event of the year when my phone rang. The low-toned, very southern female voice on the other end said, "Hi! I'm trying to locate Cedrick."

Not being one who had paid all of his campus fees or car payments at that time, I asked, "Who is calling?"

"Is this Cedrick?"

"Well, that depends on who is calling, ma'am."

She let out a nervous laugh that let me know she was not calling to collect any money from me.

"This is Cedrick here. How may I help you?"

"I'm calling you because I received a letter that informed me that you are my brother."

Given the scribbles and parenthetical notations in the margins of the Bible that held our family tree, I was not completely shocked to receive a call like this. I had seen similar moments on television and in movies. I had friends who had been ambushed by revelations of a previously unknown sister, brother, or cousin. I took it in stride.

"Did the letter tell you how you are my sister?"

"What do you mean?"

"Sorry, it's not every day that I receive these calls. I am much better with bill collectors. I promise." She laughed again, this time in response to what I said rather than out of awkwardness. "Are you my mom or my dad's daughter?"

"We share the same father, Cedrick."

"Which one?"

"What do you mean, which one?"

"Well, that is complicated . . . who is your father?"

"Lawrence."

I found the nervous laughter that she had lost earlier. Although I had not reached out to Lawrence since he was a no-show the weekend of the Indiana trip, I had continued to think of him often. Two weeks prior to this phone call I was driving from Decatur back to Birmingham when I stopped at a Waffle House and wrote him a letter. I expressed my disgust with his lies and his unwillingness to even try. I told him how I was completing my degree in three years without his help, but with him as a motivating factor. I closed the letter with an ultimatum and declaration: If you think you might ever want a relationship with me, I need to hear from you before I leave for California on August 5, even if you want nothing more now than to leave the door open for some distant possibility.

"Lawrence is your dad? Wow! What is your name? I guess I need to know my new sister's name." Our laughter merged.

"Sittra. My name is Sittra."

"I'm speechless, Sittra."

"I can't believe I'm actually talking to you. This is so weird."

"I know." There was a knock at the door. I yelled, "I'm on the phone. I will be there in a minute!"

Sittra said, "I'm sorry I called at a bad time. We can talk another time."

"She wants me to help grill some hot dogs. That can wait a few more minutes. I'm curious about the letter you mentioned."

"You wrote it."

"Wait . . . you read my letter to him? I think that is a crime of some sort."

"Not if he left it in a spot where I could see it."

"That is true."

Three hours after that phone rang, we ended our conversation with a plan to meet the following Saturday at Madison Square Mall in Huntsville.

I arrived at the region's largest mall on the appointed day approximately fifteen minutes ahead of schedule. We were to meet in the food court in the middle of the mall. I found a seat on a nearby bench that gave me full view in both directions. As I sat there a panicky feeling came over me because it occurred to me that we did not discuss how we would recognize each other. This was a Saturday morning and the mall was already extremely busy even though it was only 10:30 a.m.

I looked in both directions, trying to see a Black woman who could be my sister. As luck or reality would have it, while I was sitting there, my cousin Charlotte and one of her friends saw me and came over. We greeted and she asked why I was in Huntsville. I said, "I'm here to meet someone before I get over to Decatur to visit my mom." She said, "Oh, tell your mom I said hello and I would love to catch up with her at some point."

We hugged and exchanged salutations. They walked down the corridor and I went back to scanning both directions. When my cousin and her friend reached the ramp in front of Footlocker and the Hallmark store, they stopped to greet a woman wearing a green jogging suit. My cousin was pushing a stroller and the woman bent over to see the little one. My head continued to swivel until I realized that the woman in green was now approaching me and calling my name. "Cedrick!"

I recognized that stranger's familiar voice. I said, "Sittra!"

We embraced, looked at each other as though we were taking in the finer points of our own being. I was overcome with joy and awe as I realized the striking resemblance we shared. Her face was like mirror unto me and I could see parts of myself that only Sittra could reflect.

We sat on that bench and she said, "I just saw my sorority sister down there. She asked me where my kids were and how I'd gotten out the house without them on a Saturday morning."

"She's my cousin and she was drilling me about why I was here, too. It's a mall and it's Saturday. There's nowhere else to go at this point."

Sittra and I talked as long on that bench as we did earlier that week on the phone. In the midst of our conversation, I excused myself to call my mom to let her know I would be late. When I greeted her, she said, "Cedrick! I have been trying to call you all morning."

"I drove up to Huntsville for something and then I'm coming over to Decatur."

"You may want to come now because George just had a stroke. They have taken him to Decatur General Hospital. I am going there now that I have talked with you."

"I will get there as fast as I can."

I hung up the phone and told Sittra, "My dad . . . I mean, my other dad . . . just had a stroke. I have to go."

She said, "I understand. Please be safe driving."

We hugged before I left in full sprint from the food court to my dirty red truck.

The journey from the bench where I sat beside my sister by the man who refused to connect with me to the bedside of the man who gave me his name was an emotional lift that I never knew I had the strength to endure. I ran into the hospital and passed the main reception area. I knew a more expedient route to the fourth floor. It was the back stairwell I used to rendezvous with Shelly on those nights when we both worked the late shift.

Decatur General Hospital was where I was born, where I had my first real job after the Air Force, where I met my only fiancée, and now it was the place where I was brought face to face with my feelings about the man who raised me. Sitting next to my dad's bed, not knowing if he would fully recover from that stroke, put Lawrence's empty promises in perspective. I could long for what

I never had or cherish that which was right in front of me—both were real, but only one was there.

Grandma would often say, "You know what people are made of when they go through tough times with you." My dad had gone through some tough times and he took us through some, too. He was a heavy drinker, a womanizer, and a very poor gambler. After the divorce from my mom, he remarried and eventually divorced her too. All of that, along with my incessant self-interrogation about why I felt different from my siblings, led me to maintain emotional and physical distance from him.

While I was living in Decatur and scrambling around between my many jobs, he would sometimes just stop by my apartment unannounced. I would ask him why he came by. He would say, "I saw your light on" or "I saw your truck out there and figured now was as good a time as any to check on you." Many times, I would lament his visits because they were not from Lawrence. George's kindness created a deep inner conflict for me that I never resolved or confessed to him.

When he died almost eight years after his stroke, I remembered the sergeant's words: "The longer you live, the closer death comes to you." He was right. At the age of thirty-five I sat on the front pew as a son of the deceased. He was a person who did not work at hiding his flaws or bad behavior. That was apparent as the three pastors who presided at his funeral did all they could to keep him out of Hell. They could not utter the normal funeral tropes: "George is in a better place," "He was such a good man," "George loved everybody and everybody loved George." I sat there knowing that though I did not have his DNA, he would be with me always because he gave me his last name. He demonstrated for me what it means to show up. I later learned that he made a choice very early in my life to put aside any doubts or questions he may have had about my paternity. He was equally as loving and biting toward me as he was toward any of his children. He, like my grandmother and grandfather, found a way to move ahead and keep the family together as long as possible.

Good News

By the time I was preparing for graduation from Samford, I found myself drawn to family members, teachers, professors, commanding officers, colleagues, lovers, and friends who shared the qualities I admired most in my grandmother. The appeal of those qualities for me would increase as the years progressed and I began to function as a mentor to others.

It was a mentor relationship and a page out of Mentoring 101 that led me to California. Dr. Leonard introduced me to Dr. Claudia Highbaugh, chaplain at Harvard Divinity School. When I was considering prospective graduate schools of theology, she invited another Samford student and me to stay with her in Boston while we toured Harvard and Boston University. During our visit she said, "You keep saying B.U., but I hear Claremont."

I took a slow swig of my first-ever Samuel Adams and asked, "What is Claremont? Where is it?"

"It's my alma mater. It's in Southern California."

"I am not applying to any school I have not visited and I can't afford to fly to California."

"I think you ought to check it out before you make a decision. That's all."

When I returned to Birmingham, I had a voicemail from the Claremont admissions office, saying that one of their prominent alums had suggested I would be a great fit. They were sending me a viewbook and an application, and hoped to hear from me soon.

Within four weeks of that call, I was on a flight to Ontario International Airport to participate in scholarship interviews and a weekend seeing the sites around Los Angeles. One of the outings I chose that weekend was to attend worship at First African Methodist Episcopal Church where Reverend Cecil Murray served as pastor. The other option was Crossroads/Njia Panda United Methodist Church in Compton. I chose to go hear Dr. Murray because I recognized his name from news reports following the L.A. riots. I was able to meet Dr. Murray between services.

After I moved to California, I attended a few services at First A.M.E., but that ceased after Cynthia, a classmate and friend, invited me to attend the church where she was on staff. I asked, "What church is it? I can't handle anything long or boring."

She said, "Oh no, my pastor is not long-winded and the church is definitely not boring."

I agreed to attend that Sunday under the condition that we go in separate cars because I did not want to be held hostage at some strange church in Compton. Plus, since I was going to be close to Los Angeles, I could make a visit to West Hollywood before driving back to Claremont later that evening.

From the moment I exited the 105 Freeway and saw a sign for Watts Towers, my interest was heightened. It rose to another level when I stopped at an intersection and saw Charles Drew College of Medicine, followed by a sign for El Segundo Boulevard. I knew Charles Drew from Black History Month presentations on medical pioneers. I knew of Watts from hearing about the 1965 riots and that was where Fred and Lamont lived on the show *Sanford and Son*. I had assumed "El Segundo" was made up but here was a major street bearing that name. As I waited for the light to change, two men approached that intersection on horses. I noted they were observing a small two-seater plane overhead. I would later learn that the pilot of that plane was most likely one of the licensed teen pilots training at Compton Airport.

Crossroads was not like any church I had ever visited. Most of the congregants were wearing African garb and bright colors. The music was sacred, soulful, and fit for any major stage in the country. The pastor, Dr. Lydia Waters, preached a powerful message about dignity and hope. What resonated most with me was the way she conducted the benediction. She grounded it in African traditions and family-focused unity by asking the men to encircle the sanctuary and face inward as the women repeated an affirmation about the strength and determination they admired in the men. The men repeated a vow to cherish the women and children and protect them from all hurt, harm, and danger. I shed tears as I received and offered affirmations. It was as though that was the ending of a ceremony I never completed in Zimbabwe.

Before I was able to slip out the side door and head to West Hollywood, Cynthia invited me upstairs to meet Dr. Waters. If I had only heard her on the radio, I would have pictured a preacher who stood about seven feet tall by the way she commanded the room. Barely five feet, she embraced me upon our introduction. She said, "Son. You are beautiful and God is all over you. Do you know that?"

My eyes filled with water and there was no energy available to dam the gates. I replied, "I don't know anymore."

"God has already worked things out for you. Son, you are going places and you will have people follow you. I can see that you are smart and you are a spiritual person."

She laid hands on my head and prayed for me. I cried. She cried. Cynthia cried.

When the prayer concluded, Dr. Waters said, "I want you here. I need you on my staff."

Without hesitation, I said, "Yes ma'am. You got it."

By accepting that job at Crossroads, I now had to do what I had done when I first returned to Alabama—I had to figure out how to juggle multiple jobs. Part of my financial package at school was a job as a counselor in the admissions office; now I added a position as Minister of Youth and Men at Crossroads. I made it work.

Dr. Waters was a nationally known preacher and she traveled extensively, so I was scheduled to preach at Crossroads on Sundays when she was out of town. Because she was such a dynamic preacher, scholar, and activist, I felt great pressure standing in for her, but the congregation encouraged me and helped me hone my preaching skills. Dr. Waters was all about prayer, worship, and community service. Like my grandmother, she taught and exuded excellence in everything she put her hand and heart to.

When it was time for me to select a site for my field work, I told the coordinator, Dr. George Walters, a retired, white clergyman that I wanted to remain at Crossroads for my education credit. He said, "They don't have enough money at that church to pay for an internship."

I told him, "They pay me $125.00 every two weeks."

"That is not even close to what they would need to pay an intern. It would be better for your career if you left Compton and served in a more affluent place like Pasadena."

His words stung like those old assertions that I was "not like other blacks." In times past, I would have smiled and nodded in agreement, but I couldn't do that this time.

I said, "I'm not concerned about a career move. I plan to teach anyway. I'm not going to be anybody's pastor, so it should not really matter where I do my internship."

He said, "I won't approve for you to serve at Crossroads. I will set up interviews for you with Pasadena."

I hung up the phone in disbelief of what was happening to me at one of the most politically and theologically progressive graduate institutions in the world. It was like standing in the parking lot of that diner hearing "black shirts" all over again. I told Dr. Waters about the exchange with Dr. Walters and she said, "Son, just be prayerful. God has this under control. People are always trying to do Compton wrong. They are going to learn the hard way that God is not pleased with that."

My interview with one of the pastors in Pasadena ended with him telling me that he did not believe I would be a good fit, but he would be willing for me to interview with the other pastor. When I met with her, she explained that most of her duties involved visitation and care ministries with the senior members of the congregation. She was very warm and engaging but I had to be honest with her. I said, "I appreciate you taking time to share with me, but my grandmother spent her entire life cooking and cleaning for elderly white people in hopes that we would not have to. She would roll over in her grave if I were to serve in a role like this. I can't do it. Thank you."

When I spoke with Dr. Walters again, he relented and signed the approval for me to serve at Crossroads in Compton for my internship. I had gone from admonishing myself for being too Black in some circles and too gay in others to speaking up for what I wanted and needed. My grandmother encouraged us to speak up and to speak out. Sometimes she landed on the wrong side of an argument but she never wavered from her faith in God and belief that all people should be treated with dignity and respect. Those qualities were also present in Dr. Waters.

The same was true of Jim when he brought me into his circle of friends and taught me the finer points of how to use a Damron Guide. I was a gay man who was not fully accepting of his own sexuality; Jim helped me see I was not alone on that journey. And it was true of Dr. Leonard, who helped me discern a deeper sense of my call to ministry and explore service beyond the local church context. All I had known was one way of being in ministry. Dr. Penny Marler modeled inclusivity and spoke up on my behalf when I wanted to write my thesis on a subject that was deeply personal and necessary for me. These mentors showed me a more expansive view of what it means to serve others. They exposed me to people who looked like me and thought like me—Black people, gay people, and others trying to find their way in the world.

Good Man, Bad Feet

I have always been a joiner and a helper. Those two traits were in full effect the day of my dear friend Reggie's funeral and they would usher me into the ranks I would join that day. The turn my life was about to take was not on my wish list but it was one that had long been in the making.

Reggie was one of the first people I met when I moved to Los Angeles. He was a debonair and dashing man who expressed great confidence in his walk and in his talk. He was an avid churchgoer and never questioned my theological perspectives or expressed any contradiction he observed or considered to be present in me. He had a way of seeing and seeking the finer things in life and in those around him. He lived to travel and to host themed parties.

I told my best friend about Reggie as soon as I met him. As others encountered Reggie, they wondered why we were not an "item." We seemed so good together. I brushed that off and continued to enjoy his company at movies, dinners, and walks on the beach. We discovered new watering holes, planned trips, and shared our best-kept secrets. Whenever Reggie wanted to connect, I would make time to do so unless I was deeply involved with work or whomever I happened to be dating. Now, we did not talk very much about our dating escapades and that should have been a sign.

We'd been friends for more than a year when he invited me to attend his fortieth birthday party. I hadn't realized he was nearly nine years my senior. I had heard of Reggie's legendary parties, so a milestone birthday bash was surely not to be missed.

It was a dinner party at Stevie's Creole Café in Encino. I'm pretty sure it was my first time driving to Encino because I recall being aware that it was the home of the Jackson family compound. I wondered if I was near that Tudor-style mansion that I often saw pictured in *Ebony* and *Jet* with all of the Jacksons gathered out front. I had thoughts of the level of difficulty involved if I were to try to locate the Jackson compound to take a picture.

As I walked from my little red Chevy S-10 pickup and neared the restaurant, I could hear music and the yelps of the crowd inside. It sounded like the scene in *The Color Purple* that night Shug Avery premiered her act at Harpo's Juke Joint. The rumbling of the trumpet and riffs from the sax along with a melodic alto voice belting one of those early Chaka Khan songs was just what I needed to calm my nerves and let me know I was in for a great time.

I walked into this establishment and the volume told me what was in store—everyone was eating good food, drinking stiff drinks, enjoying friends, and reliving some sho' nuff good times through the music provided by the live band. I quickly scanned the room and my eyes met Reggie's. He smiled and motioned for me to come in his direction. For some reason I kept my eyes glued to his. It could have been because I didn't feel comfortable joining the party late. It could have been because I realized I left his birthday card on my coffee table and I was showing up empty-handed.

I scooted around various patrons enjoying fried catfish, baby back ribs, collard greens, and macaroni and cheese until I reached Reggie. We embraced as I mustered up my best impersonation of Bette Davis in *All About Eve* when she wished her beloved Bill a happy birthday. I moved in near his ear and said, "Reggie, it's your birthday. Happy birthday!" He chuckled and said, "Thank you, Miss Bette."

I quickly acknowledged that the card I had for him was at my house and he would get it the next day. He looked deeply into my eyes with a sly grin and remarked, "I know I will." He then directed me to sit in the lone vacant seat at the table. It seemed odd to me that there were probably twenty people seated with this party and no one had claimed the seat across from the honoree. I took stock of the group and quickly realized that every eye at the table was directed at me—especially the two owned by Reggie's mother. With a jolt, I realized what he was proclaiming by seating me directly across from him at his fortieth birthday party. Reggie was letting everyone there, including me, know that I was his man.

When all of that settled upon my mind, a primal battle began within. In one instant I was flattered and intrigued. In the next, I was ready to turn and bolt out the door.

Reggie and I eventually made peace with the fact that our best option was that of friendship. We loved to laugh, shop, watch movies, and cook together, but he wanted someone who was ready to make a lifetime commitment and I was not at that point in my life. He was the type of guy most people would move heaven and earth to have as their life partner. He checked all the right boxes. There was one problem that I have not been able to work through in all my years of living, dating, and undergoing intense therapy. He did not have pretty feet. They weren't Robin-Givens-in-*Boomerang* bad but he did have one black toenail on his left foot. The moment I saw that, I knew the best I could offer was friendship.

Reggie loved being around people so much that just shortly before he died, he invited me to come hang out with him and a few friends at the Mondrian Hotel on Sunset. I told him I had plans with some friends visiting from out of town.

He said, "Tell those queens Reggie is more important than those boys they are planning to chase in WeHo. You better get over here." He insisted that I come and that I bring them with me.

When my friends arrived to pick me up for our night out in West Hollywood, I told them we needed to make a quick stop by a friend's kickback on Sunset. I explained that my friend had been ill for a while and was feeling much better. He liked doing nice things for himself and others, so getting this swank suite overlooking the city was his way of healing himself and bringing joy to those around him. My friends did not know Reggie, but when they walked into that suite it was as though he had known them since kindergarten.

We never made it to West Hollywood that night. Most would have been content in a regular suite with a city view, but Reggie booked the penthouse. It was Reggie in every way, with plush white furnishings and pops of color throughout. There were tall, clear vases of long-stemmed white roses adorning every table. The music was kept at a low volume but there was no mistaking the rousing beat and rumble of house music. We spent our evening there laughing, dancing, and listening to one another's stories.

It wasn't long after that night at the Mondrian that I received word that Reggie was gravely ill and was at Cedars Sinai Hospital.

At that point, Reggie had fallen in love with a wonderful man named Oliver. It was Oliver who called to tell me Reggie was sick again. He also warned me that Reggie's mother was not permitting any visitors. I dropped everything and raced to the hospital. Once there, I circumvented the no-visitor rule put in place by Reggie's mother by stepping into my clergy role and asking the hospital chaplain to assign me to that ward. She made it possible for me to get into Reggie's room and spend a few quiet moments alone with him. I thanked him for always making me feel and know I was special. I thanked him for being a true and loving friend. I thanked him for showing me how to be a better man.

When he died less than two weeks later, I was heartbroken. He was someone I loved. I question fate and I question notions and doctrines of predestination because they seem so limited and passive. Yet, when I think about how I met Reggie and maintained a bond with him until his death, I wonder how and why it all turned out the way it did. Was I supposed to look past his black toenail and fall madly in love and commit to living a life of bliss and adventure with him? I don't know the answer to that, but I do know that his story and mine are forever linked. Even as he rests in eternity, I can never ever tell my full story without including him in it—because on the day we buried him I made a series of choices that would move me closer to my own grave than I could even begin to imagine.

We gathered for his funeral, followed by a private repast for his closest friends at which we laughed and cried for hours. Eventually the crowd dwindled to just a few of us. One of the stragglers was leaving at the same time I was leaving, and he asked directions to the 405. I told him I was going in that general direction and he could follow my car. We left Leimert Park and headed toward the freeway. As we crossed La Cienega, I motioned for him to continue west. He waved thanks and I made a quick right turn so I could return in the opposite direction and get to my house. I'd lied when I said I was going in that man's direction. I just wanted to be helpful. I was channeling Reggie and what I believed Reggie would have done. He would not have told him how to get there, he would have shown him how to get there. That is what I did.

That one act of kindness, extended in the spirit of one of the kindest persons I have ever known, brought sure horror to my doorstep. But I was not to realize that yet.

Facing the Streets

All of the decisions I have faced as a leader have been reached after much prayer and planning. I have witnessed stalwarts in the faith, beginning with my grandmother, make momentous strides by remaining true to what they understood the gospel reflects of Jesus's teachings. These teachings emphasize the need to liberate all persons and peoples held in bondage to laws and practices that oppress them. As a child, I did not understand why grandma would let women who had children and a husband stay at her house. She was helping to liberate them from abuse, whether physical or mental. I did not know that when she kept envelopes of money for people and would not give it to them just because they asked for it, she was helping to liberate them from debt by keeping them from wasting it.

Seeing her walk alongside people in need without judging or ridiculing them was transformative for me later in life. During my three-year term as chairperson of Black Methodists for Church Renewal (BMCR), from 2013 to 2016, there was an open season on Black men and women on the streets of America. I had lived most of my life with a belief that if a person did the right thing, then right would come their way. I believed the police existed to serve and to protect all citizens. However, when thrust onto a national platform as leader of an advocacy group that centers Black people within the United Methodist Church, I quickly realized that our

focus had to be much more expansive. We had to pay closer attention to Black communities and what was happening to our people
with respect to health, healthcare, wealth, welfare, and economic
stability.

The model of ministry that had me walking the streets around
Bowen Memorial instead of hiding inside the building was the
same tactic I had to bring to my new role. I found role models in
others who had served by holding the needs of the community to
be served, heard, and empowered while challenging the systems
and policies that legalized and sanctioned poverty and poor health.
One of the first public addresses I issued as chair of BMCR was in
response to the slaying of Michael Brown:

> ... Lives have been lost. Families have been destroyed.
> Communities have gone up in flames. All the while, America
> fights wars around the globe to ensure freedoms and liberties
> for people who have been pushed out or otherwise annihi-
> lated due to their religious, ethnic and/or economic realities.
> There were tanks in Ferguson and people were outraged by
> the presence of such machinery and weaponry. Questions
> were raised about the necessity of such fire power, but all one
> needs to do is watch the news reports coming in from around
> the world to see that this is the response waged against sup-
> posed terrorists or those in opposition to whatever regime is
> in power or attempting to gain power.
>
> The presence of those tanks were tangible signs or even
> poignant expressions of the laws stacked against the disen-
> franchised of this nation and the certain acknowledgment
> that Black people rising up and speaking out are in fact ene-
> mies of the State. Those tanks roll when empires are threat-
> ened. Those tanks roll when economic engines are at stake.

Those tanks roll when young people challenge the status quo. While the tanks roll so do the cameras and rhetoric about change and the need for justice and unity. Now the tanks are gone and so is the hope of some who saw this as a way for people of America to wake up and to own up to its need to do better and to be better.

It seemed that every few weeks I had to issue a statement or gather our leaders to discuss a response to violence waged against Black folks. People who were instrumental in forming BMCR had marched with Dr. Martin Luther King Jr. and others who put their lives on the line for freedom and liberties to be extended equitably to all people, long before I was born. Like others before me, I had to speak out and challenge systems and institutions that benefited from Black people's oppression.

Mentoring Matters

I did not seek out or campaign to lead BMCR any more than I had campaigned to be dorm chief in basic training. There was an election but there were no flyers, buttons, banners, or ads. During the months leading up to the election, I led the organization through a strategic planning process. Since BMCR's inception, the most notable leaders in the United Methodist Church have served in the organization's leadership. Everyone knew that.

The strategic planning committee presented the plan and it passed without any alterations or amendments. There was jubilance in my soul and in the auditorium. The next item on the agenda was final nominations for new officers. The presiding officer called for nominations from the floor for the office of chairperson. He recognized a speaker. She said, "I nominate Cedrick Bridgeforth." Mass hysteria broke out in the room. Some were celebrating the nomination and others were questioning it. The questions arose because there was an unwritten rule that leadership of the organization would alternate between clergy and laypersons each term. The outgoing chairperson was clergy, and the expectation was that the next leader would be a layperson—presumably the current vice chairperson.

The debate over whether or not the organization was bound to its tradition went on for several hours. Folks eventually accepted that the election would go forward and the results would reveal the will of the body and the direction the organization would take. During the balloting period, the other candidate for chairperson was seated next to me. I put my arm over the back of her chair as we stared ahead and tried not to be distracted by all that had centered around us. I thought it imperative that we be seen together in those moments and show a unified front for the good of the organization. She leaned over to me and whispered, "I should just withdraw and make all this go away."

I squeezed her arm and said, "No. Don't do that. They are having a lay-versus-clergy conversation, not a conversation evaluating us as potential leaders. We can't short-circuit that. We won't learn better if we don't do better. We are in this together."

She said, "Thank you. That means a lot."

We leaned into each other and allowed our heads to rest together.

When the results were announced I was elected as chairperson with a clear mandate to implement the strategic plan and move the organization forward. I became a student of the organization and all that it had accomplished up to that point. Somehow in all my years of serving on the board, I had missed the fact that Dr. James Lawson was the first chairperson of BMCR and Dr. Cain Hope Felder was the first executive director. This was a powerful legacy.

Dr. Lawson was one of those mentors who appeared in my life without solicitation from either of us. I had read about him and knew of his teachings of nonviolent resistance that led to desegregation within this country. I knew of his long tenure as a preacher-activist-scholar in Nashville, Memphis, and Los Angeles. The ways in which he went about knowing, engaging, and teaching demonstrated a depth of spirituality and courage that spoke to something deep within me. It was like when I first encountered Sergeant McRay and saw something in him that I wanted for myself. Neither man asked me to emulate them but their character and practice of life beckoned to me.

Prior to my election to lead BMCR, I was appointed as a district superintendent. That meant that I had to leave my pastoral appointment at Crenshaw United Methodist Church to assume responsibilities for multiple churches in the Los Angeles area. The members insisted on having a celebration to mark my transition. I insisted that it be limited in budget and scope. Carolyn Lane put herself in charge of the event. She forewarned me that it would be conducted as a roast and I needed to be prepared for that.

Those seated on the dais that night were the individuals Carolyn and others knew would tell my story best. I was elated because my mom was there next to me for the celebration. I appreciated everything everyone said about me—good and questionable. What added to the solemnity of the event for me was when I stood to offer my remarks and I saw Dr. James and Mrs. Dorothy Lawson at the middle table alongside Dr. Cornish Rogers, one of my former professors. I thought, "Who am I that these giants would spend a Saturday at the Proud Bird Restaurant to celebrate?" I shared my delight with my mom. She said, "They know who you are and whose you are. It's an honor you can't take lightly."

My voice for justice and liberation grew over time as I served as pastor, educator, and board member with several nonprofits. I wrote one such call for equity in 2015, on the subject of Black masculinity:

> ...we can perpetuate the myth and stereotypes that shape our realities or we can write new scripts that allow for a confluence of narratives that devalues your need for comparisons and measures that no longer have relevance in my context. Black male masculinity will be challenging as long as we lack variety and validation of our identity and emotions.

To get from here to there we must become and esteem role models who embody and embrace varying ebony hues, "round the way" theologies, and hardheaded diplomacy, while we dismiss all "mother may I" democracies. There are too many of us, Black males and males in general, who do not know how to feel deeply about something or someone and express it without fear of being labeled. My mentors cry. My father figures weep. My true brothers embrace me when I need a hug. All of them tell me they love me and they inspire such within me.

The multifaceted consciousness that comes to bear as a Black, male, Christian, gay leader in any arena calls for some tough choices when so many conversations sound more like single-issue monologues. I can't advocate for right treatment along the basis of race yet turn a blind eye to homophobic practices. Equally, I am less than who and what my grandmother taught me to be if I ignore the plight of women from whatever station I find myself occupying.

When Bishop Mary Ann Swenson invited me to serve as a district superintendent, I had to bring all of who I am to the role and I had to commit to serve all people. Just as I had observed

Reverend Lawson and claimed him as a mentor, I did the same with Bishop Swenson. She lived her faith in front of the world when she appointed women and persons of color to the highest offices possible within her sphere of control.

On January 7, 2008, I thought I was being reprimanded for firing two musicians and a choir director who were wreaking havoc at the church I was pastoring. Instead, she invited me to lunch to have a different conversation. We ate our meal in a leisurely fashion. She asked about my family, my dog, and my recent travels before pitching the primary reason for the lunch. In a very casual tone, she said, "I want you to consider serving as a district superintendent on my cabinet."

I suddenly had deep regrets for not having the glass of wine I had been offered earlier. With humility and disbelief, I asked, "Bishop, are you sure?"

She took a sip from her glass and offered as calm of a response as any native of Jackson, Mississippi, might ever offer, in a Southern accent that was certainly undeniable. She said, "I am very sure. I want you to serve the people of the Los Angeles district."

"Then Bishop, I would be happy to serve as you have asked."

She was taking a risk by going outside the "norms" and reaching into a population for leadership that is all-too-often overlooked when leadership decisions are being made. I had only been ordained for about eighteen months and was by far the youngest person to serve in that role in recent memory. I was gay and the denomination was not quiet about its anti-LGBT stance, even though in our region it was a non-issue. When I accepted that appointment, I served on a cabinet alongside one of those pastors with whom I had interviewed ten years earlier and was the direct supervisor of the other one. It had all worked out.

CHAPTER 7

WORK IT OUT

Cali Confessions

As I prepared to move to California in 1997, my pastor, Reverend John Porter, the only African American member of Samford's Board of Trustees, mentor of Dr. Claudia Highbaugh at Harvard, and close friend of Dr. Leonard, invited me to preach at Sixth Avenue Baptist Church. I attended Sixth Avenue while at Samford and participated in the College and Career Sunday School class and I was in awe of Reverend Porter's legacy as a civil rights leader. He was a giant of a man and that sanctuary beckoned for grandeur and poise as much as any world stage in our modern era. As he concluded his introductory remarks, he said, "Cedrick is heading off to study theology in California. We always look to the West to let the rest of us know where we are heading. He is going to be on the frontlines of theological and political thought for the next few years . . ."

Reverend Porter not only marched with King; King preached his installation service at Sixth Avenue when he became pastor. Now this civil rights icon spoke highly and favorably of the path I had chosen. His words would join the mixtape that included the teachings of my grandmother, vibrant expressions from Auntie Eunice, admonitions from my mom, and the words of that sergeant who spoke about the proximity of death.

On my drive from Alabama to California, I had everything I owned underneath the unlocked camper shell my stepfather had given me, a credit card with a $300 limit, and the prayers and hopes of all my ancestors. I spent my first night near Columbia, Missouri, in a motel that was situated so I could back my truck up close enough that no one could open the camper shell while I was asleep. My next stop was Oklahoma City where Hanes and his family had relocated. His wife was expecting a child during the time of my visit and I hoped to be there during the birth. The only time I had alone with Hanes was when he drove me downtown to see the wreckage from the bombing two years earlier. Our conversation were strained, at best. My relationship with his wife was much richer as we talked often and she kept me abreast of what the kids were doing.

I experienced some jealousy when they moved to Oklahoma because my relationship with her shifted. After they had been there a few months, she told me, "I met Quinton at the Base Exchange and he is just like you. He is funny and he takes time to listen to me. Since he is here, you may get replaced."

I said, "You and I both know I am the original and anything else is a mere copy that can never compete."

On my visit to Oklahoma City, I met Quinton and I was not impressed and I did not see the similarities. In fact, it was when Quinton came over to visit that I insisted Hanes take me to see the Federal Building. I did not want to be around the person I presumed had moved into every space I once occupied.

I was only scheduled to be in Oklahoma for three days but I remained for five and that baby showed no sign of movement.

I had to get on the road to arrive in California by August 5. As luck or fate would have it, when I stopped the next evening to sleep and called Hanes to check in, he had just returned from the hospital. Apparently, she went into labor within an hour after I left Oklahoma City.

That was the last time I saw them. We only spoke on the phone over the next ten years because Hanes was often on deployment and my schedule was relentless with work, school, church, and community service. I maintained connection with them until the day I called to let them know I might be able to visit them the following month. She said, "Your friend will be on deployment. Plus, I don't think having you come around is a good idea."

She and I often joked about cutting each other off when we went too long between conversations. I said, "Girl, it has only been a month since we last spoke. Stop it!"

With a sternness that I had never heard in her voice, she said, "He told me everything, Cedrick. I can't believe you didn't think enough of me to tell me."

I was beside myself. Why had he told her about us? We ended our sexual behavior prior to their nuptials and he vowed he would never tell her. I said, "That was something that happened a long time ago. We moved on and I never did anything to interfere with what you two were building. In fact, I have been your biggest cheerleader since day one."

"But you know if I had known how deep things were between you two that I would have gone about this a different way."

"I'm sorry. It was not my place to tell you."

"I disagree. I think you owe me your side of the story. I have his. What's yours?"

I felt so horrible that I had caused this woman pain. She really was a good friend to me and I was one to her. From the day I learned of their engagement I embraced her and worked to build a good relationship with her. During that conversation I went all the way back to the very beginning when Grumbault invited me to New Kingdom and concluded with the night I learned of their engagement. I ended by saying, "I am so sorry you have to feel pain about something we did before the two of you even met."

She paused and allowed silence to speak into the thick atmosphere created by my rendition of my relationship with the man she married. Then she said, "Thank you for telling me the truth. I never would have gotten him to confess."

"What? I thought you said he told you everything."

"He did. He told me everything about everyone except you. He never mentioned a relationship with you and it did not make sense that the two of you were as close as you were and there was nothing there."

"Wait! I don't think . . ."

"No. You told me the truth and I thank you for it."

"I told you because you said he told you. I am so sorry . . ."

"If he had told me the truth, I would not have needed you to tell me anything. I'm disgusted with both of you. Please make this the last time you call my house to speak with me, my children, or my husband. You are no longer welcome in our family."

For someone who had made family or a semblance of one everywhere I went, her declaration of my expulsion hurt. They were my lone connection with the folks from New Kingdom. I shared the accounts of that conversation with my best friend. He said, "Well, now you don't have to carry that secret any longer. If you have others as old and tawdry as that one, you may want to put them out there too."

I didn't have other secrets quite like that one, but I did have truths about myself that I did not readily share with people. I felt like California was big enough for me to explore my identities in separate spaces, but I quickly learned that much of Los Angeles, whether the church realm, the Black community, or the gay world, functions like the small town I grew up in. There is great autonomy but little anonymity.

The relationship with Hanes was one of many that were cloaked in secrecy and shame because of the theological and ecclesial mandates that spoke against such loves. It was impossible for me to fully be with someone when the core teachings I espoused said, "Your lifestyle is a sin." Essentially, every time I looked upon the man I loved, I sinned.

That reality did not keep me away from men; it kept me from embracing and expressing my full identity beyond small cliques and circles of folks who did not hold my humanity against me. The horror and fear of it all was as prevalent in the gay spaces as it was in Black spaces. One of the most terrifying questions a person can ask me, in a gay bar, is, "What do you do?" If I say, "I am a pastor," the music suddenly stops and all eyes are on me for holding a cocktail in my hand and for being in a gay establishment. Two of the church's taboos collide in that space.

The next question is, "How can you be a pastor and be gay?" I could explain the church's long and complicated history of homophobia and heteronormative ideologies that are not fully supported by scripture. I could explain that the verses in the Bible that are used to condemn gay people are surrounded by edicts and mandates that no one would ever take seriously now. I could explain that God is love and anything not borne of love is sin, so as long as my actions and intentions are rooted in love, I am fine in the eyes of God. I could go into all of that but with the go-go boys dancing on the bar and $5 drink specials on a timer, I prefer to simply say, "God and I have a deep understanding about who I am."

For many years I did not date Black men because of the assumption that all Black people were religious people and all religious people think being gay is a sin. I did not want to deal with anyone who brought that into my space. I lived with that assumption until I heard Bishop Melvin Talbert speak as vehemently against homophobia as he did racism and sexism. He and many around him opened me to recast my sexuality in a context of love and embrace authenticity.

The self-hate that I inflicted when white folks would tell me I was "acceptable" because I was different from other Black people was just as detrimental as the silence I maintained when Black people would tell gay people they were going to hell for being gay. I felt a call to speak out against injustices but I felt ill-prepared because I was not whole. I did not feel adequate to say anything to anyone else about harming others when I was doing harm to myself. It wasn't until I became active in Black Methodists for Church Renewal that I acquired the language and platform to express my intersecting oppressions and identities along the lines of race and sexuality.

As I did more justice work, I began to see how the views I held of myself were more damaging than any words anyone ever spoke to me. I recalled a phrase I heard my grandma say to my uncle when he was complaining about my aunt. She said, "You cannot love pieces and parts of people." I had to apply that to my own image and knowledge of myself. I had to love all of me before I could expect or demand others to do the same.

Protests

Anyone serving in a pastoral role in Los Angeles has cause and opportunity to raise awareness about issues of poverty, houselessness, educational disparities, and episodic blight. Like many communities in America, Los Angeles is one of those cities where one block is pristine and quiet with well-manicured lawns but the next is littered with trash, furniture, and discarded cars. Most people in Los Angeles avoid going through or knowing about areas they do not live in or frequent for entertainment.

In my time in the City of Angels, I have served as pastor of four churches. In each community where the churches were located, the demographics and economies were very different. I was called upon to address issues of violence and gentrification, whether I was speaking to homeowners concerned about their property values or people without homes concerned about finding affordable or secure shelter. Both groups loathed gentrification. They could spot the early signs—white women driving through the neighborhood during the late evening, couples walking their miniature dogs, and police calls to report nonviolent behavior, like three Black men standing on the corner. Another sign was when the corner strip mall lost its fish market, check-cashing place, and liquor store and gained a ramen spot, Wells Fargo, and a wine and spirit shop.

My presence at those community meetings and block club conversations was usually more as a referee or additional set of eyes and ears. Very seldom was I a direct participant in what was happening. There was a frequent call from clergy coalitions and community groups for me to don my clerical collar and participate in a march or press conference to support the causes of those who were living on and beyond the margins. Most often if there was some action that might antagonize the police, I chose to sign a petition, write a statement, or broker a meeting between parties. I made it known that I don't participate in public protests.

When my Auntie Eunice died in 2003, the reasons I had always said no to public protests became even more salient for me. We gathered at her home after the funeral service. Although she was not there in body, we played her old albums, danced on her worn light blue shag carpet and laughed at ourselves in the beveled mirrors in her living room. We ate and drank the way she would have insisted we do it if she were present. It was bittersweet to realize that she would never sit in the wobbly rocking chair by the window and take slow deliberate sips from her ice-cold can of Miller beer. Those days were gone.

We concluded our third or fourth round of the electric slide and my sister said, "Wow!"

I passed her a glass of red Kool-Aid and asked, "What are you wowing about?"

My sister has eyes that change with the season. Sometimes they are light brown and at other times they reflect a hint of green. Regardless of the hue, they are always sparkling with curiosity. Without looking at me, she scanned the room and said, "Of all the male cousins in here right now, you are the only one that has not gone to jail."

I surveyed that same room and said, "That means we have work to do with the next generation."

My commitment is to provide an alternative example and counternarrative for the next generation of men in my family. This includes not going to jail. I could have easily landed there or even in prison if I did not learn some early lessons about drug use and taking care of my financial responsibilities. In my family, incarceration is an ever-present reality. We see it at every family funeral when at least one cousin is accompanied by a marshal and cannot do more than attend the actual service. It's a reminder that we are not all free to go and do as we please.

My refusal to protest was in service of my desire to show Black boys and girls someone from the same place with similar circumstances as theirs who did not end up in the penal system. But when the killings of Black men and women on the streets of the United States by police began to reach epidemic proportions and non-Black people could see the ills of what was happening to us, my reasons for not protesting increased.

In 2013, my bishop invited me to participate in a protest against the country's immigration policies. The protest was a national effort orchestrated by church leaders and it was scheduled to take place in front of the White House. When the request came from my supervisor, I said yes without much hesitation.

The morning I was due to fly from Los Angeles to Washington, D.C., I had called my Uber and was waiting on my front porch. I sat on the top step with my blue Tumi carry-on bag between my legs. The bag became my altar as I prayed, "Lord, you know my heart. You know I want to do what is right. I want to support causes and people who can benefit from my voice and presence."

Just as I had the experience of hearing "go home" when I was preparing to move from Cheyenne to Fort Collins, it happened again, but now the message was "stay home." The difference this time was that I did not consult others; I did not question the validity or efficacy of the prompting. I accepted it as the nudge I needed to support those who could most benefit from my voice and my presence—and that meant Black boys and girls, in general, and my family, in particular. I cancelled my Uber and rolled my Tumi altar back inside the house.

It dawned on me that I needed to inform my bishop of my decision not to join her for the protest. I sent a text and let her know that I had cancelled but wanted to explain my reasons for doing so. She called a few minutes later and said, "You want to tell me why you made this choice. I am listening."

I said, "Bishop, I don't protest because I am the only male of my generation in my family who has not gone to jail. I don't want to give that up. I want to hold to that as encouragement for my nieces and nephews."

She was very affirming of my position. I continued, "In addition, I don't trust that if I am arrested, I will be able to pay $85 and walk out of the police station like everyone else."

She said, "I understand, my brother. Would you mind sharing your reasons with the organizers? I think it would benefit them to know your perspective on this matter."

In the midst of civil unrest and the rise of the Black Lives Matter movement, I have questioned whether there is nobility in my stance or simply fear. The trauma of seeing Black people pulled over for minor traffic violations—or for no reason at all—who now have websites and hashtags calling for justice for them, sickens and frightens me. But I am not silent. While I do not participate in gatherings, marches, and protests that could potentially attract or antagonize the police, I use the power of my pen, phone, and connections. The organizations that I engage as a pastor, educator, consultant, or board member all have economic, social, racial, and gender justice and equity embedded in their work. Providing support for them is my form of activism—it allows me to be an example within my family and still use the network I have built over the years as a resource and agent of change and transformation in and beyond Los Angeles.

My work to see communities, families, and individuals experience liberation and know what it means to live healthy lives is a quest that has its roots in the care I saw my grandparents extend to others. They used what they had to inspire and assist folk who needed to know there was someone in the world who loved them and believed in them. Many times, all my grandparents had to offer the wanderers and drifters who came their way was the assurance that their integrity and compassion would not waver. I saw firsthand how 706 McGaugh Street would seem to be at its capacity with three or four extra people living there, but that little round kitchen table would expand as wide as it needed to so that everyone who hungered was fed. Grandma would fold two of her handmade quilts into the shape of a twin bed on the floor. She would form what we knew as "pallets" until there was a place for everyone to lay their head.

As dorm chief in basic training, I would wake up a few minutes each morning before the trumpet would sound revelry. After whispering a prayer of gratitude for another day, I would scan the dorm and see the rows of men on their bunks and marvel at how sleeping on my grandma's living room floor prepared me for those moments. That went along with her insistence that all of us, boys and girls, learn to cook, clean, iron, make beds the right way, and do laundry. She would say, "Learn what grandma teaches you because this will make good husbands and wives out of you."

She taught us how to contribute to the household. As a result, I was more than adequately prepared to succeed in the structured environment of the Air Force. I learned to welcome and trust strangers before questioning their character or level of truth. I learned to lead by listening to what was not being said as much as to what was. I became self-reliant and independent. Perhaps my openness to accept people and not to judge them because of their circumstances made me susceptible to becoming attached too quickly. I welcome and include others in my life without full knowledge of their story and without them having access to mine. This could be perceived as a flaw, but the opposite can lead to a callousness that is beyond the bounds of who I can be in the world.

To my grandma, family was not demarked by biology. After all, she married a man whose paternity was always in question. She had to reconcile that her children would never know their father's family. Even though there were speculations and rumors that continue to this day, there was never any conclusive answer as to who was my grandfather's father. The answer could have meant clarity and connection for his children, but it could have torn another family apart for having to own the atrocity that some white man fathered a child with a Black woman in that community.

U-turn

Every decision has a consequence. My decision to show Reggie's friend how to get on the freeway after we celebrated Reggie's life was not something I planned in advance. I wasn't looking to meet anyone new that day. In fact, I had just met met several fascinating people at the repast that afternoon. The right turn I made to get home was in fact the wrong turn for me because it caused me to make eye contact with a caramel-colored man with a bright smile upon his face. He was sitting at the stoplight as I made my right turn onto the street where he was waiting. As I drove past him, I saw him. He was the most gorgeous man I had seen in ages. I was certain he saw me too because I turned my head to look back at him, and found he had turned around to look back at me.

Though this was the first time we set eyes on one another, we would soon discover we had been on a course to meet for more than a decade.

If anyone were watching what transpired next, they would have assumed it was a scene being filmed for *National Lampoon's Vacation*. I looked. He looked. I made a U-turn as he made a U-turn. When I realized we both made U-turns, I made another one and so did he. At this point we had made several big circles in a small intersection of a ritzy residential community. I pulled over to the side of the road out of embarrassment and shock.

I was embarrassed by my driving and shocked by my reaction to this man. At this point all I knew was that he was gorgeous, and he drove a silver Volkswagen convertible. He pulled up next to me and since his top and my windows were already down, he said, "Well, hello sir!"

I responded, "Hello to you, sir! Where are you speeding off to?"

"I'm going to pick up my daughter for a rehearsal. What's your name, handsome?"

"No, my name is not handsome, but thank you."

"Seriously, I have to know your name and I have to get your number."

"My name is Cedrick. Why should I give you my number if I don't know your name?"

"You should give me your number so I can call you tonight. My name is Evan."

I gave him my number. He asked if I wanted his and I told him I would have it if and when he ever called me.

We sat there at that intersection for what seemed hours but was really only about five minutes. He told me he had to pick up his daughter for a session with their vocal coach. I was expected for an early evening event with my estranged partner. His disclosure that he had six children and my disclaimer that I had recently ended a relationship were clear signs we had too much going on to pursue anything of great depth.

Evan was true to his word. He called that evening and we spent hours on the phone. We began to connect regularly, but always during daytime hours. Our lives were hectic and complex, so being alone with someone who was not asking very much of the other was refreshing and welcomed. It felt good to be with him. Not only was he easy on the eyes, but he had a midrange baritone voice that would melt butter. Well, it melted me every time we spoke and especially when he would bless me with a song. Like butter, I would melt because the sensual and spiritual connections were almost otherworldly.

We found that we had many things in common. One was that I had served in the Air Force and he was a member of the Air Force when we met. The irony was that back when I was asked to join Tops in Blue, had I done so I would have met Evan. If I had said yes the first time I was asked, I would have been on the technical team with him. If I had joined the team the second time I was asked, he would have been the show's master of ceremonies. The third and final time I was actively recruited, a yes would have landed me under his command as he was the showrunner. This felt like more than coincidence—it was destiny. We had been in each other's orbit for years and now we were in each other's worlds.

We had what most would define as a whirlwind romance or fling. It was what we could handle at the time because I was rebounding from my last relationship and he was still quite closeted, in the Air Force, and a father of children ranging in age from twenty-one to seven years old. I was not exactly what anyone would call "out" either. Evan's family, military situation, and insistence on daytime rendezvous lacked possibility for any long-term considerations. We maximized the moments we could steal between his acting auditions, vocal training, and time with his children.

Once, while sitting on the bed in his apartment, he turned to me, flashed that winning smile, and asked, "What are you most afraid of?"

I thought for a moment before I responded. "Right now, I am afraid of you, Evan."

He looked puzzled and then hurt. "Cedrick, why would you be afraid of me?"

"You are limited with what you can offer me by way of your life."

He interrupted, "You have limitations too."

I continued, "Yes. I do have some limitations, but the more time I spend with you, the less any of that seems to matter."

The pain of Reggie's death and the simultaneous dissolution of the romantic relationship I imagined would last forever helped me open myself to Evan. I was more vulnerable and transparent with him in a few months than I was with the man I dated for four years and broke up with prior to meeting Evan.

I inhaled whatever carbon dioxide he exhaled. He pulled me into his perfectly chiseled chest, kissed the top of my head, and said, "Never be afraid of Evan. You have had my attention since I first said hello to you."

That "hello" on the day of Reggie's funeral became part of the soundtrack that got stuck on repeat in my brain. From Evan's "hello" the day we met to the "Hey you" and "Hey handsome" salutations that began every conversation we had, whether we were making sandwiches for lunch in between his rehearsals and daddy duty or showering after passionate moments in his bedroom, his voice would lull me to his whims.

Evan became like a drug that would soothe any ailment or at least push it to the recesses of my mind. His charms helped me forget the anguish and depression I hid from most people and from myself. My life lacked focus and balance. I surrendered my empty emotional reservoir for Evan to fill. My existence mattered and I was sustained because he quenched my thirst. He told me how much he adored me and enjoyed our time together. He told me how much he missed me when we were apart. He told me how invigorating he found our conversations about art and God. He told me about each recent escapade of all of his children. He even told me about his roommate's late-night booty calls.

He never told me he lived with HIV.

Keaver

The tryst with Evan ended during the summer of 2006, almost as quickly as it began, because he accepted a job outside of California. I went from the end of a four-year relationship and the disappearance of the deep connection with Evan into an emotionally charged relationship with Keaver. He was everything Evan was and more. Within two months of meeting, Keaver and I became roommates and within three months we became lovers and launched a home-based art business together.

I was introduced to Keaver at a party hosted by my friend Erik. Well into the night of cocktails flowing and laughter rising, Erik joined a conversation I was having with Keaver about a vacation Erik and I were taking to the Dominican Republic in January. After Keaver and I became serious, he expressed concern that I was going to the Dominican Republic without him. He said, "I know you planned the trip before you knew you would fall madly in love with me. I trust you to keep us in mind while you are there."

I brushed my hand across his freshly braided cornrows and down his cheek as I said, "Thank you for being so understanding and loving."

Since I moved to California, I made a practice of getting tested for HIV frequently. My friend Bison also got tested often and he was terrified of the process. I would go with him and I would get tested each time he would so we could truly be on the journey together. One day, a few months after Evan had moved away and I had become involved with Keaver, I sat in the clinic parking lot waiting for Bison to show up for our regularly scheduled testing appointment. He was habitually late for everything but almost an hour had passed and he was never that late. I wondered if he had gone in ahead of my arrival and was sitting in the lobby waiting for me. I walked in and looked around but he was not there.

The clerk asked, "Are you here for testing?"

As I scanned the lobby once again, I replied, "I am here for a friend to get tested."

He said, "Honey, since you are here it won't hurt you to go ahead and sign in for testing too."

I completed the paperwork as I did every time I visited that clinic and I took a seat in the back corner where Bison and I would usually sit and people-watch while waiting to be called for testing or results.

When I spoke with Bison later that evening, he told me he had car trouble and he had no way of communicating that with me. He said, "I'm sorry. I hope you didn't waste the trip up there and you went ahead and got tested."

I said, "I did. When are you going?"

He said, "So we stay on the same cycle, I will go today right after work. Since you went by yourself, I will go by myself this time, but we're going together to get my results."

At this point in the evolution of HIV testing, the process had progressed from blood draw to mouth swab, but it still took two weeks to get results. During those two weeks I would pray more than ever. I would make deals with God that I hoped I would be able to fulfill. I would not go out to the clubs and I would refrain from being intimate with anyone—even in conversation. I would mark the fourteenth day on my calendar so I would know when my agony would end.

On day ten of my fourteen-day waiting and bargaining cycle, I received a call from the clinic director asking me if I could come in some time that day or the next. I said, "Of course. Is there a problem?"

She did not respond to my question. She asked, "Can you come in today or tomorrow?"

I slowly replied, "Today. Three o'clock ok?"

"Yes. Thank you. Ask for me after you sign in."

I did not reach out to Bison to tell him about the call. I did not bother Keaver with that detail either because he was busy preparing for a big audition for a movie role. After all, I reasoned, this appointment could only be for her to tell me I had been exposed to HIV in some way or that I needed to take the test again. I could not imagine any other option so I drove myself to the clinic and arrived an hour early. The four hours from the time she called to the time I found parking outside were far worse on my psyche than the normal two-week waiting period.

I signed in and asked to speak with the clinic director. She came out into the lobby and escorted me through a door that I had not noticed on any other visit. How had I missed the little white door with the framed yellow sign that read "Counseling"?

She took her seat behind the desk and asked me how I was feeling. I asked her to dispense with the niceties and get to the reason for calling me in early. She said, "Your test came back positive."

I looked directly into her eyes and asked, "What? How is that possible?"

She said, "Well, it could be a false positive, but I don't think it is."

"How could you even say that to me without being sure?"

"I understand this is difficult, Cedrick, but we have a process and we have support for you."

"I want to be tested again. Can we do that?"

"That is part of our normal protocol. That way, if we get two positive results, then we know for sure."

She gave me a stack of pamphlets to read and recommended I also reach out to my doctor to get a blood test in the works while we waited for the second test results. I used a pay phone in the lobby of the clinic to call my primary care doctor to tell him what had happened. He called in a lab request and directed me to go to the lab right away. I followed his instructions and I read all the pamphlets. I catastrophized how my life would be one of immobility, shame, and hopelessness. I wondered how quickly Keaver would leave me for even having to tell him I had false positive result. I did not want to scare him without cause and I wanted the time between my test and the results to be calm between Keaver and me.

Those were long and complicated days because I thought about how my relationship with Keaver would come to an end and much it would hurt. I thought about Jason, Andy, Hanes, and the others who had come and gone. I thought about Evan and how fully I had given myself to him and how freely he had received me. On the surface things were good between Keaver and me but internally I was a mess. I hated keeping this information from him but not as much as I worried about losing him.

In what seemed like record time, I received the results from the blood test. My doctor called and said, "We have the test results. Can you come in tomorrow?"

I said, "No. I leave for the Dominican Republic later tonight. Can I come now?"

I left my half-packed suitcase on the living room floor and drove myself to my doctor's office. While I sat on an exam table waiting for him, I refrained from my usual bargaining with God. Instead, I prayed for the strength to live with the consequences of whatever he said. He walked in and got right to it. He said, "Your test came back positive."

His words filled the room so much that they plugged my ears. He asked if I had questions, scheduled a follow-up visit, and gave me a copy of the test results, a yellow carbon copy of the pink and white pages he had on his clipboard.

When I returned home, Keaver was there. He had gathered a few items he thought I should pack for my trip. We greeted one another. He looked closely at me and asked, "What's wrong? You should be excited about everything except being away from me for a week."

I couldn't speak. I just handed him the yellow paper that my doctor gave me. Keaver read it, looked up at me in confusion, and asked, "What does this mean?"

I said, "It means I am HIV positive, K. That's what it means. It also means if you want to leave, I understand." With the weight of those words now lifted from me, I fell like a stone onto the large gray sofa we often cuddled on while watching television.

He nestled himself beside and then behind me on the sofa. He positioned his lips next to my ear and his strong arms around me. He whispered in a melodic baritone cadence, "I ain't going nowhere you ain't going. You good with that?"

I nodded.

He moved slightly so that our cheeks were now touching. He repeated, "You good with that?"

I said, "Yes. I am."

We stayed in that position until my arm went to sleep and the pain became too unbearable to ignore. I stood up from the sofa and looked down into his chestnut-colored eyes. "Thank you," I said. "I love you."

"I know. I love you too. Just tell me what you want to tell me and tell me what you need from me."

"Right now, I need you to help me finish packing so I don't miss my flight."

Keaver helped me pack and he made snacks for Erik and me to have on the plane. I placed the snacks in my backpack alongside the yellow paper the doctor gave me a few hours earlier. As soon as Keaver dropped me at the airport and drove away, I wondered if what was so broken in me that had allowed me to open myself to Evan the way I did was healed. Was Keaver only good for managing symptoms or was he the cure? I thought about Evan's first "hello." That simple word following what I intended to be a good deed had changed the course of my life.

Condi Rice

When Erik and I landed in Santo Domingo's airport, thoughts of Evan faded a bit. I was relieved and grateful to be in a new environment, but then I remembered the crumpled yellow paper tucked away in my backpack with my passport and wallet. Erik and I made our way through the passport checkpoint, picked up our luggage, sipped the complimentary Brugal rum even though it was 6:30 a.m., and found the taxi to our resort.

On the bumpy two-hour ride from the airport to Boca Chica, my mind played and replayed snippets of the Evan reel that began the day of Reggie's funeral. I went from shock to hurt to questions. The questions were a mix of voices that sounded like Nina Simone and Grace Jones taunting me all at once. I wondered why Evan had been completely silent with me about his HIV status. I wondered if I had ended the four-year relationship I had before meeting him for the wrong reasons. I wondered how Keaver was so calm when I shared my news with him.

All of those questions crashing and clanging in my mind were probably why, when we finally reached our resort, I was so preoccupied that I left my backpack in the taxi. I did not realize this error until Erik and I were checking into our hotel and the clerk asked for my passport. When I realized what I had done, time stood as still then as it had the day before when the doctor said, "Your test came back positive."

I thought, "Damn it, Reggie! Why did you have to die?"

I said, "Damn it, Evan! Why would you try to kill me?"

Those were two hauntingly intertwined questions that lingered throughout that trip, and, dare I say, for many more days. The hotel staff was less concerned about the backpack than about my emotional reaction. They assured me that I would get the bag back. They knew my identification, passport, and money were in the bag, but they did not know my secret was in there. I was not consoled by their certainty. I was afraid someone, anyone, might unfold that crumpled yellow paper, read it, and reveal my status in some nefarious way before I had a chance to share my own narrative.

The clerk assured me, "Sir, the taxi driver will find your bag and he will return it to you."

I exclaimed, "If he does not realize it is there before he picks up more passengers at the airport, he will not know who it belongs to."

She laughed. "You are very funny, sir."

Her laughter caught me by surprise. This was a moment of sure panic for me.

She said, "Of course he will know who it belongs to. Your beautiful picture is inside your passport."

She was right and I joined in with a slight laugh that lessened the external tension while doing absolutely nothing to calm the wild fears bubbling inside me. She continued, "He keeps a log of all the names and hotels for all his passengers. He will bring it here."

That made perfect sense, but then I started thinking about other passengers rambling through my bag. I envisioned a drunken bunch of travelers taking it with them when they disembarked the taxi. All of my versions of the story ended with strangers reading the words on the crumpled yellow paper and doing something that would hurt me. I thought about confessing to Erik what was in the bag along with my wallet, money, and passport, but I did not want that news to interfere with our vacation more than it already had.

My patience had dwindled to near nonexistent. Maybe it's because I prayed, "Dear Lord, grant me patience while I wait for this backpack." I should have known that was not a good idea. Grandma always told us, "Be careful when you pray for patience. God stores it on the other side of Hell and you will have to go through Hell to get it."

Spending every waking hour with Erik, away from Keaver, while harboring the secret that was in my backpack somewhere in Dominican Republic felt like hell. I was more concerned about others knowing and telling than I was about figuring out how I would live with this new reality.

On the third day of our trip, we got up early in the morning and boarded what is called a "local taxi"—basically, an unlicensed minivan. These crowded vehicles seldom had doors and packed in as many persons and small animals as possible. The fee was very low and no tourists were allowed.

The bellhop told us about the local taxi after we gave him a tip. He said, "Do not wear your best clothes. Dress like the locals." Most of the persons riding the local taxi would be on their way to work in the city. He also said, "Do not speak a word to anyone."

I asked, "How will they know when we want to get out, if we do not tell them?"

He said, "Stay there in the taxi until you hear 'Condi Rice,' then you get out."

We boarded the taxi at a stop near our resort and did exactly as the bellhop had instructed. I was terrified the entire ride, because this minivan meant for a family of seven had no fewer than fifteen people in it. At one point, the number of passengers was reduced by four but increased by two live chickens in plastic bags, carried on by an older woman. After what seemed an eternity, about eight passengers remained on the van when I heard, "Condi Rice!" I nudged Erik to move toward the door. The lady with the chickens said, "We know you are Americans. Have a blessed day!" We laughed, thanked the driver, and hopped out.

The line at the U.S. consulate was already long and the office would not open for at least an hour. We found a little café nearby and ate some breakfast before heading back and getting in line. When I finally entered the building, I saw a life-sized portrait of Secretary of State Condoleezza Rice hanging in the entrance and smaller versions of the same photo in every waiting area. Erik was not allowed inside because he was not transacting business, so I had my own chuckle right there. I now understood why the local taxi driver had shouted "Condi Rice." But that begged the question: What did they call it when Colin Powell was Secretary of State?

My day at the consulate was spent shuttling from waiting room to waiting room, without much semblance of progress. It was late in the afternoon before I realized the reason no one was giving me any answers. As it turned out, the information I was given by others while waiting outside on line was incorrect. Unknowingly, I was in the line for Dominicans applying for an emergency passport.

I kept my eye on the door through which I saw staff enter and exit. There was one woman who passed through about every fifteen minutes carrying a stack of papers. I overheard her speak with another employee and she did not have even a hint of a Spanish accent. Upon her next entrance, I intercepted her.

I said, "Excuse me, Miss. I have a question."

She twirled around as though she had reached the end of the runway at New York City's Fashion Week. She was wearing a red skirt with cream-colored triangles the size of a dime, a cream-colored blouse with red stitching around the collar, and little peep-toe red pumps. She said, "How may I help you?"

I told her why I was in the consulate and my concern that it would be a wasted day if no one really understood my situation. She invited me to have a seat as she took notes of my social security number, birth date, and current address. She smiled, "This should not be a problem. Give me a moment." She disappeared for a few minutes, then returned and escorted me back to the waiting room where I began that morning. I was told to have a seat behind the red tape and wait for my name to be called. I thanked her. She laughed and said, "I love California. That is why you are getting help right now."

I asked, "Why do you love California? Have you been there?"

She was already walking away, but she twirled back in my direction and said, "I'm a Valley Girl. Couldn't you tell?"

Within thirty minutes of her intervention in my case, I had paid a hefty fee and was ready to depart the consulate with my temporary passport. I was mystified by the process but elated that my problem was solved. My elation was soon dissipated by two realities. The first was our need to take a regular taxi back to the resort. The local taxi was much more interesting and far less expensive.

The second came by way of the Expedia travel agent who had a service desk in our resort's lobby. When we arrived back at the resort, we stopped by the front desk, as we had every day since our arrival, to ask, "Did anyone deliver my backpack today?"

We knew the answer, but we had to ask. But this time, before the desk clerk could answer, we heard someone shouting across the lobby: "Mr. Cedrick! Mr. Cedrick!"

It was the Expedia guy. We did not want to hear any sales pitch for excursions and we did not want a discount on our next visit. We wanted to avoid that guy and get to the bar as quickly as possible. Erik, trying to hide himself behind me, said, "Please answer him before he totally embarrasses us in this lobby."

I said, "Yes. I am Cedrick. How may I help you?"

As we approached him, he stood from behind his small pecan-stained desk and extended a hand. We shook hands before taking a seat. He said, "Why haven't you responded to my notes?"

We looked at each other because this was clearly the intro to some sort of scam. I asked calmly, "What note? We have not received a note from you."

He looked quite dumbfounded at us and asked, "Didn't you leave your backpack in the taxi?"

"Yes, but the hotel staff knows about that. We didn't know we needed to share that information with you."

"But I have information. That is why I have left notes at your room each morning."

"I don't understand?"

"I have your backpack, Mr. Cedrick."

"What? You have it? Why didn't you turn it in to the hotel desk?"

"I wanted to give it to you myself."

"I have spent the entire time here worried about that backpack."

"I believe you, Mr. Cedrick. The taxi driver discovered it. He knows I work here so he gave it to me to give to you. I put a note on your room the first day, yesterday, and today."

"We did not receive any notes, sir."

"Room 6125! That is where I left the note."

"We are in 1625!"

Erik was suspicious. He abruptly asked, "How did you recognize Cedrick now but not before?"

He replied, "Today was the first day I looked into the bag. I saw your picture and when you came in, I recognized your face."

He pulled the backpack from his desk drawer where he said it had been since the first evening of our arrival. He asked for the chocolates I had in there and a small tip for his troubles. I thanked him and gave him the small amount of cash in my wallet and the chocolates Keaver had packed for us.

I told Erik to go ahead to the bar and I would join him after I put the backpack in our room. Upstairs, I ripped through the bag in search of my secret. At first, I could not find it. My heart was pounding like a drumline on the fifty-yard line at any historically Black college's homecoming game—it was loud, fast, and fierce. I emptied the bag onto the bed and rifled through the contents until I found that tattered piece of yellow paper.

When I read it this time, I was smiling. I was happy to have the paper in my possession. But it held less power now than it had when I received it a few days prior. I was oddly more concerned about how others might react to the information than I was about my own health and well-being. My habit of hiding in plain sight was still deeply ingrained.

In my distracted effort to conceal the paper I was holding so tightly, I somehow misplaced it again for several days. Learning to live with my new truth did not come in an instant. But for now, the worst thing that had occurred as a result was the loss of time and money spent in a building that resembled a shrine to our Secretary of State. My world did not come to an end that day.

Speak for Myself

I thought learning of my HIV positive status would be the worst news I would or could ever receive. When that was not the case, I thought having to disclose the information to current or future partners would be humiliating or debilitating, but it was not. In fact, I grew to accept that what I had in my blood stream did not define me, nor would it place any unjust limits on me. But nothing could prepare me for what lay nine years ahead.

In the summer of 2016, I was nominated as a candidate for the episcopacy. That means I was chosen by my peers to be considered in the upcoming election for bishop. It was a great honor; it meant that my colleagues thought enough of me, my gifts, and my relationships with them to cast their votes for me.

They did not know what had gone on behind the scenes. They did not know I had been at the center of an internal investigative process that threatened to end my ministry and terminate my service to the church. They did not know that someone who had been a close friend, not affiliated with the church, had filed a formal complaint against me citing that I had willfully engaged in unsafe sex with him, his partner, and a host of others. That was the subject of the email Bishop Dale called me about in late 2015. The only people who knew about the allegations were my closest friends, the person who filed the complaint, and the church officials involved in processing and investigating the complaint.

When it all crashed in on me, I had a moment of reckoning. I had truly done something horribly wrong for my life to have taken such a drastic turn. I had to look inward and come to grips with where my life was not in alignment. I had offended someone so deeply that they felt justified in disclosing my personal medical condition to strangers in an email that could destroy my career. I had to own what I had done and make amends for the offenses I committed, and I had to be clear about those of which I was not guilty. It was apparent, as my grandma would say, "There was fire nearby. The fire has burned or it will. Just wait." I had created smoke by not fully honoring my ordination vows and not honoring celibacy, and I did not conform to heteronormative notions of marriage and intimate relationships. I did take my sexual health and medical diagnosis seriously from the very first day I received that yellow piece of paper from my doctor.

All of that had to be disclosed and discussed with my superiors and some colleagues as part of a grueling process that seemed to go on for an eternity. Throughout the process I trusted it would all work out the way it was supposed to work out. Yet the rounds of interviews, accusations, counseling sessions, and pulling back the curtain on my entire sexual and relational history reinforced my own questions of significance and validity.

Throughout the time I was involved in this investigative process, the United Methodist Church was in upheaval about issues of human sexuality in general and homosexuality in particular. The biggest question was whether persons who identified as LGBTQIA+ could be full participants in the church. That debate was the latest in a string of discriminatory practices, postures, and edicts that had kept the church on the verge of dismantling for over four decades. Considerations of gender equality, racial equity, and the vestiges of colonialism abroad were also being brought into the conversation. I felt my intersecting identities were uniquely fit for the moment.

When I stood on that stage to accept the nomination in front of the delegates who would potentially vote for me to be their spiritual leader, I don't know if I was standing up straight. I had been told only a few minutes before the speech that I needed to withdraw my candidacy because of the investigation I had been involved with.

As I took the podium to deliver a four-minute speech, there was prayer covering me in so many ways. I was wearing a stole with colored handprints all over it, signifying a laying on of hands by those who made the stole. Those artists were hopeful that their efforts in making the stole would yield a favorable outcome for the candidates and for the church. They were local missionaries and artisans who believed in the efficacy of prayer. They were present in the colored handprints that adorned the stoles but they were also representative of the larger community that joined us in the event.

I began speaking. "I am committed to justice and equity for all people. The church is at a crossroads, just as I am at a crossroads. The church is trying to figure out how it will live up to its calling and I am trying to do the same for myself." My voice trembled and quaked as the words left my larynx and entered the microphone.

I let the internal battle wage while I presented a sense of calm and deliberateness that would allow me to hear most clearly the voice, guidance, and assurance I needed. I delivered an underprepared and unrehearsed speech, trusting that somehow it would all work out. Throughout the remainder of that evening, I went through interviews and interrogations about my thoughts on issues facing the church and about what kind of bishop I thought I might be. By the time the final reception ended, I was drained. Two dear friends slipped me out a back door and drove me to my hotel. Once there, I showered and considered ordering room service. Instead, I opted to sit in silence and pray. I don't know what I prayed exactly but it was for God to speak clearly enough so that I could hear and know what to do.

That hotel room with its lone king bed, small desk, inoperable dorm-size refrigerator, and Arizona desert-themed canvases adorning the walls became my own Garden of Gethsemane. In that dark moment I wanted and needed others to join me in prayer, but I was alone—except for the presence I felt with the stole of praying hands that rested on my pillow next to my handkerchief, Bible, and agenda for the week. No matter what course I chose, it was certain a life-altering decision and series of events would take place the next day. I had to make a decision. I had to know which path would bear my footprints.

What happened in that hotel room was not much different from what I remember seeing my grandmother do in good and bad times. She would kneel by the bedside, fists clenched and eyes closed. I sat in that same posture that night—on my knees, fists clenched—but I kept my eyes open. I wanted to be as present in that moment as possible. Even in the dimness of the room, I could see the outlines of the hands on the stole. It was as though they were joined with mine as I prayed.

After prayer, I sat in silence. In the midst of the silence, I not only heard but also felt a small voice acknowledge that I was called to serve. I could serve, but this was not my time to serve. I heard it. I felt it. I welcomed that deep sense of awareness and clarity. It was deeper than intuition and not as definitive as prophecy, but it was as present and as affirming as those hands on the stole that I held tightly as I felt a sense of peace and calm permeate my body.

This was the certainty that I had longed for since I was first nominated. I had a sense of calm and peace now that I knew what to do. The silence in that hotel room moved me to peace as soon as I saw that the calling to serve was not bound by a four-year election cycle. There was too much at stake and so much to heal and learn. It was similar to the calm I felt when I made the decision to return to Alabama instead of matriculating at Colorado State. It was akin to the calm I experienced as I stood in my Domino's uniform and submitted my application for admission to Samford University. I was as resolute in the peace I felt in withdrawing from that process as I had been in my protest against H-Day and my insistence in knowing the truth of my father's identity.

I can say I was clear. I felt free. I felt a great sense of peace. I knelt beside my bed and prayed the most earnest prayer I had prayed in almost a decade. I expressed gratitude for what I had received that day. I had been affirmed. I had been admonished. I had been under the shadow of humiliation. I had answered many questions about leadership and the future of the church with great precision. I saw that I could serve as a bishop, at least from that vantage point. But in the stillness of that brown hotel room, I saw light burst through my soul and illuminate what I must do to be whole. I was humbled by all of it.

With my newfound clarity and sense of humility, I sent a text to the presiding officer to inform him of my decision. I knew I needed to withdraw from the process before the first ballot. My ego and the pressures from others might be too great if I allowed even one ballot to pass before eliminating any possibility of my continuance as a candidate.

A few hours later, I stood at the microphone before that same crowd who had heard me decree, just one day before, "I was born too early." This time I had more news and a deeper revelation. I said, "I stood before you yesterday. But today, I say: this is not my time to do this. I want to remain in the conversations and work around justice and equality . . ."

My dream and aspiration were to be a part of history. Within thirty hours we elected one of the other two openly gay candidates as a bishop—the first in our denomination. That was a moment and a message so many had labored to see and to be a part of for decades before I arrived on the scene. I had the privilege of participating in that historic election. I began as a candidate, discerned my appropriate role, and went on to help make history.

I would love that the story ended with me withdrawing from the election process and everything was smooth from that point. Soon after my withdrawal from the bishop election process, I was informed that all of the charges that had been made against me, resolved, and adjudicated were back on the table. The first time all this was brought to me, I was hurt. This time, I was angry and felt betrayed by the system and those who used its rules to pursue this campaign against me. I would have to go through the entire process again, detail by detail, and no one would make it stop.

I recall grandma saying, "Don't ever let them know they can get along without you or they will." That came to mind as I eventually felt I could not continue in my role as a pastor and fight this fight again. I opted to take a leave of absence, which felt like an abdication of my calling and a loss of what defined much of my identity. I had to reassemble a livelihood and a life that made sense. My ministry was no longer an option. That is how I ended up working as a Lyft driver.

My major concern was being recognized. Every time I would hear the ping of my phone alerting me of a ride, my prayer was, "Lord, please don't let this be someone I know." My second prayer was, "Lord, let this be someone who is not interested in talking to me or asking a million questions." My partner was correct, I did not like being a Lyft driver. It was not fulfilling any purpose except that of making money and that was not in alignment with who I wanted to be or how I wanted to live.

Several months before going on leave of absence and becoming a Lyft driver, my therapist made a recommendation that caught me off guard. He said, "I suggest that you find an organization or experience to be part of where you have no chance of being the leader." My therapist was a very tall man in his mid-to-late sixties with a gray handlebar mustache and beard that made him appear more like a model in a Harley motorcycle ad than a therapist. He may have ridden a Harley or belonged to a leather consortium, but the gentle care he offered me through my professional and personal crisis changed everything I ever thought about the exterior of a person. Of course, my grandparents and parents told us, "God looks on the heart, not the exterior of people," but those words did not take on flesh until I met this therapist who defied every stereotype I had about outward appearances.

At his advice, I attended a meeting that brought together military veterans and agencies seeking to serve veterans and their families. It was a very large gathering and it fit the bill as something I could not lead. It was my first meeting so I attended an informational session for first-timers. The person seated next to me introduced himself: "My name is Carlos. I am the new recruiter for veterans who want to become teachers in the district." Carlos and I exchanged information before the presentations began. We kept in touch via email for a few weeks while trying to schedule a time to meet for lunch. His adjustment into his new role and my responsibilities involved with managing the church's case against me made it impossible to honor any of our lunch appointments.

Weeks later I emailed Carlos. "Hello Carlos! It's been a while since we attempted to connect and I'm bummed we never got to have that lunch . . . I would like to talk to you about the possibility of becoming a substitute teacher in the district. Let me know when you have some time to discuss my options." Within five weeks I was walking into a transitional kindergarten class with six four-year-old special needs students as their substitute teacher.

Substitute for Myself

When I stood before that crowd in Texas in 2017, my biographical statement was incomplete. The person they invited to speak was there, but so much had changed in the eighteen months that passed between the invitation and the delivery of that speech. The introductory remarks centered on what they knew from my public persona, peripheral personal experience, and what they could find on the internet. A year and a half had passed since this group first reached out to invite me to speak. My life had been turned upside down in that time. When first contacted, I was president of a national advocacy group, a district superintendent, a member of the General Board of Pensions, a leading voice in the global conversations about the intersecting harm being done to LGBTQIA+ and people of color, and a presumptive longtime and future leader in the church.

My opening words centered on wisdom learned from my grandmother, like "Don't mess with people who don't have as much as or more than you to lose" and "Be careful when you pray for patience because God stores it on the other side of Hell." The title of the speech came from her nuanced phrase: "There is the church and then there is the church." She uttered the first "church" in a positive and exuberant tone, while the second was said in a tone of wary caution. She meant that there was a difference between the institution, the buildings themselves, and the people who came together to form congregations. How they presented themselves determined which inflection best fit. These words had guided much of my life and work. It seemed that this group of justice-seeking, theologically progressive United Methodists deep in the heart of Texas might resonate with the most southern aspects of my upbringing. I was less sure of how they would react and respond to a perceived fall from grace.

I was no longer leading a national organization, I was not on any boards or agencies that they were aware of, and I was serving a church that was not considered a premier placement. I had all of that on my mind and it churned in my soul as I leaned on and shared the only thing I was certain of in that moment: I was a Black, gay, ordained clergyperson speaking to a group of United Methodists in the same hotel as many who were leading the charge to have folks like me expelled from the denomination. I had no sense of what was next, but I trusted that all I had gone through would not be in vain. It would all work out.

I took a risk and chronicled aloud the arduous path that had led me to that moment—the missteps, lessons, and disappointments of a life lived as one who was, from birth, a target of derision, often without even knowing it. I had willingly stepped into leadership roles within a denomination that I chose knowing it was a hostile environment. As in every other arena I lived, loved, and worked in, I gave the best of myself and I said "yes" when it seemed the right thing to do. I closed the address with the following:

> Saying yes to all those things came at a price. Staying in those conversations [about racism and homophobia] and finding ways to make them work together came at a price. Working to end racism and assuming legislative means, whether incremental or monumental, was work that came at a price. Believing stronger wills and enlightened minds would prevail

and justice would be wrought with a stay on church trials came at a price.

The price for me is that I woke up not too long ago in the throes of a process that I wish upon no one. I woke up and am no longer serving in any of the capacities previously named, but I am still African American, male, gay, clergy, United Methodist, southern by birth, western by world view, committed to full inclusion, but committed to doing so from a place and with a voice of wholeness and integrity.

So, in my woke state, I have decided to take a leave of absence. Not because I am one without hope that racism and homophobia can be eradicated from the hallows of the church. It is quite the opposite. My quest is to repent of my wrong. In my woke state, I see my wrong is not that who I am "is incompatible with Christian teaching." It can't be unless what I also believe about being fearfully and wonderfully made is also not true.

I woke up to find that in all my doing I was really doing church work. I was more committed to church work than I was to doing the work of the church . . . So, the next season will be about re-centering and recalibrating. I believe this is a necessary reality for me and maybe for others who are weary and worn.

I woke up and realized what my grandmother taught us was true: "Don't let them know they can get along without you, because they will," "Don't mess with anyone who has less to lose than you do," and last but not least, "Learn how to read a room."

There were many applauses that followed the speech as well as additional invitations from others to share my story. It seemed the surrender of my silence and the confluence of what my grandmother, faith, and life experience taught me touched the hearts of those who heard my story.

Two days later I walked into Room 4, a bungalow filled with four year olds near a small enclosed play yard, and I thought about how different my life had become. In one arena I was a Black man stirring up trouble in the church and in another, I was a Black man bringing calm to children who missed their parents and wanted to play most of the day. When I would take them out to the play yard, I would sit under the very large tree that the asphalt hugged tightly and remember days gone by when I was younger and would play under the large maple tree in my grandparents' front yard.

A Strong Foundation Will Not Crack

In 2015, when the life and career I had spent almost twenty years building began to crumble, all I had to rely on was my faith in God and trust that those whom I had supported would come to my rescue if I asked for help. I trusted that I had done right by people to help them get jobs, find housing, and start their lives, whether in Los Angeles or somewhere else. I trusted that all the good I had done within the organizations I worked for and in the communities I served would matter more than any rumor, misdeed, or accusation that might come to light. It wasn't a truth I ever wanted to test, but test time came.

In spaces where I have had opportunity to pour into others as mentors, elders, and saints have done for me, I do it. Whenever asked and whenever possible, my answer is yes. As a result, I have a cadre of friends and mentees around the world serving as executives, writers, investors, actors, and educators. I have received much and I have given much in return.

I serve on nonprofit boards and work with nonprofits that share my personal values—the dignity of individuals and liberation of persons from exploitive work and systems. Those are the values my grandmother held when she encouraged many to take a stand whenever they saw something that got in the way of a person, family, or company living up to its highest potential. My mom worked for General Motors for over thirty years, but when she first started there, she got involved with folks who wanted to unionize the plant. My grandma was scared for my mom because she did not want her to lose that "good job." However, she told my mom, "You do what you think is best and trust that it will work out, because if you are doing it for the right reasons, it will."

My mom worked tirelessly to get that plant and many others unionized. Our living room, the same one where she and I had most of our late night and early morning gut-wrenching talks, was the meeting site of organizers who made at least six local manufacturing plants go from low-wage to living-wage workplaces. As a teenager I was not focused on the details of what they were doing, but I knew they drank a lot of Bacardi Rum, ate too much KFC, and prayed and stood with workers who endured retaliation and termination. Their efforts were a reflection of how we were raised to give of ourselves to make the world a better place for all.

The lessons learned since early childhood have shaped me and informed how I show up in the world. There are those who celebrate with me and there are those who do not understand why I do what I do. I have tripped over just as many obstacles as I have overcome.

There is one curious thing that I will carry with me for whatever will be my eternity. That is the question of why I learned so much from my grandma—so much that I have sought to emulate her in every aspect of my life, and repeat and share her wisdom everywhere I go—but I do not hold one memory of her ever saying, "I love you."

I don't know if she ever spoke the words to me. She communicated her love by teaching me to trust that if I give my best, then everything will work out. This truth has proved to be a strong foundation that has never failed me.

Brick Wall Averted

Driving for Lyft and substitute teaching were things I could do to support myself after I fell out of the good graces of the church and questioned whether we might ever reconnect. They kept me moving but I was moving in place, not forward. Then came a period where mom was on life support for almost two weeks, my stepfather was battling chronic kidney issues, and I had no prospects for my future in 2017. I literally dropped what little I had going on in Los Angeles and stayed in Texas as long as I could to support them and nurse them back to some semblance of health.

Once they were safe and set up with health care options at their home in the Dallas area, I returned to Los Angeles to resume the task of figuring out how to put my life back together. I returned to substitute teaching but I refused to turn on my Lyft driver app. Over time the dinging sound it made when I had a passenger began to feel like a noose that tightened with every ding.

I made a conscious choice to list early elementary and special education as my preferences for substitute teaching assignments because those were high-need categories in South Los Angeles schools—especially for men to fill them. It worked well for me in that there were very few days that I did not get an assignment if I wanted it. This was an arena where my race was a bonus and my sexuality was not central to scrutiny or debate.

One day when I was leaving an elementary school where I had taught a special needs pre-K class, I felt like driving into the brick wall in front of my car. That was not the first time I felt that way. Just then, I received a phone notification that I had an email from Reverend Sherry Daniels. I quickly skimmed it: "Dr. Bridgeforth, I will be in Los Angeles this coming week and I need to meet with you while I am there." It was curious that a church colleague would send me a request like this. Didn't she know I had stepped away from all of my church relations and responsibilities? We were friendly but we weren't friends. Why would she want to meet with me?

I replied, "Cool. Let me know when you will be free and we will set something up while you are here." I did not expect anything to come of that because people often report that they will be on the West Coast and never follow through.

A few days later, I received a reply from her: "I am available Saturday for lunch. Will that work for you? I want to go somewhere nice and look cute."

I responded, "I have plans to meet Dr. Larry Hygh on Saturday because he will also be in town. Is there another day or time that might work for you?"

Undeterred, she said, "Great! I need to speak with him too. Can we all just go together? That way we can all have the same conversation and get this done."

I reached out to Larry, and asked him to secure a location. On that Saturday I picked up Sherry and drove to a hotel with a rooftop restaurant situated by the pool. It had rained earlier so the sky was the blue it should always be but seldom is. We had a full view that stretched from Santa Monica across the Century City skyline, the Hollywood sign, the Griffith Observatory, and all of the construction cranes downtown. It was one of those Los Angeles postcard photo ops.

We had our meal and chatted about current events and denomi-national gossip. As the meal extended far beyond the length of time I expected, I began to worry that the reason for this invitation was really just to catch up. The check landed on our table and disappeared as quickly as it appeared, as Sherry said, "This is a business lunch that I arranged with the two of you to discuss some business. Now that we've gotten all our personal stuff out of the way, let's get to it."

I leaned back in my chair now that the reason for this meeting was about to be revealed. She looked at me and said, "I am going to end what I say with a question mark but it really isn't a question. It is more of a calling or a divine assignment with your name on it."

With sweat beads moving down my spine and thoughts swirl-ing around in my mind, I listened as she continued. "I have watched you do your work for years. You are smart. You know how to talk to people and people listen to you. They believe you and they believe in you. Because of that and because I know you have even greater work to do, I have a project I want you to consider."

She went on to share the details of the work she had in mind and invited Larry's input and participation as well. She was on my team and I didn't even know it. My answer was an immediate yes.

With that request from her, I began to work more intentionally as a coach for pastors and churches. That work led me to self-pub-lish my third book, and receive inquiries and contracts from others seeking coaching services. Her request and my yes was the genesis of what is now a thriving consulting firm with several sub-contrac-tors and contracts across the country. My crisis of faith was not limited to my faith in the church, in God, or in those I had trusted as friends. It was also about losing my belief in myself.

I was making a date with a brick wall when an email disrupted my plans and led me back to ministerial and service work with nonprofits that I loved and longed to do. Sherry knew me through my work as a district superintendent and as chairperson of BMCR. A few years earlier I was in her area during Easter weekend for my Alpha Phi Alpha fraternity brother's wedding and I decided to visit her church. I arrived without telling her I was coming and she called me up during the service to share some words with the congregation. I could not have known that my gesture that day would connect us in ways that would have her in position to throw me a lifeline that she didn't even know I needed several years later.

My life now is one that was only made possible by those experiences of deep loss and disconnection from everything that I had allowed to define me. I had to get to a point in life where revelation of future possibilities and repentance for past wrongs occupied equal space in my machinations.

It hurt to be in a space where I did not want to go to church and I did not trust the institution that I had given so much to. It helped to realize my work had to focus less on those serving the institution and more on those being served by it. It hurt to have those I had claimed as close friends deleted from my phone and nowhere near my prayer list. It helped to know those who remained through my toughest times were the ones I could always trust. It hurt to want to be present with others but be incapable of doing so when my own pain bore down too much for me to move. It helped to remember that all of us have times when we need support, even when we cannot give voice to that need.

Having someone on my team remind me that I had worth and that my life mattered awakened me to a pathway that I had not seen. Saying yes to the offer that came my way helped me acknowledge my losses, let go of my self-loathing, forgive myself, and re-vision the good I believe I was created and crafted to do in the world.

Dear Grandma,

This letter, like all the stories of my journey, may never be fully complete. So much of my life has been about full-circle moments, experiences, and relationships. I came into this world and have moved through it with a big question mark over my life. When I was born premature, there were questions about whether or not I would live. As I grew, I questioned my paternity. I did not know who to ask about it and I did not want to draw any undue attention to myself. What if I was wrong?

I did not know how to express what I was feeling toward or about other boys, but I knew enough to know it was not safe or acceptable for me to do so. I heard the murmurs and admonishments about boys acting like girls or being soft. I was aware that anything that did not align with actions and choices other boys around me were making was not in my best interest or should be kept secret. All along I knew I was different from most of the other boys, but not different from all, because some of them liked me back. But it was all a secret that I held tightly yet lived out loud.

Much as I tried to conceal my sexuality, I also tried to deny my race. I did not pretend to be white or pretend not to be Black. I put energy into believing race did not matter and anyone who made an issue of race was divisive, racist, or small-minded. That was because I had not had to grapple with systemic and overt racism enough to recognize it for what it was. In high school, when others were selected to attend Boys State instead of me even though I was the one promoting the opportunity, I attributed it to the fact that their parents were deeply involved with the school. I did not even see that two white boys were selected while the lone Black one was dismissed. After the black shirt incident, my trip to Botswana, and the denial of my senior thesis topic, my eyes were opened as wide as Adam and Eve's were opened after taking a bite of the forbidden fruit.

After experiences of dating Black men, moving to a Black community, and committing to serve a Black church, the realities of oppression and self-hate left a bitter taste in my mouth. I could hear those preaching and proclaiming freedom for Black folks speaking hatred and damnation against queer folks. It seemed as I found footing and voice in one of my identity, the other was being stamped out. Trying to liberate only a portion of one's being is to no avail. I had to find community that valued the intersectional nature of my identity and I had to own being Black, Southern-born, Methodist-ordained, same-gender-loving, West Coast-grounded, and open to serve the world out of the abundance of who I am.

It has taken me to this moment in my life to fully embrace who I am and know that I am not defined by what I do, what I have, or what others say about me. I am defined by what makes me whole, complete, and compassionate. I am defined by what I offer to the world and what I receive from it in the most humble and symbiotic relationships. The wrongs I have done and words I have left unspoken have impacted me but they do not define me any more than the good I have rendered and the statements I have made define me.

How shall you judge me?

Cedrick

ACKNOWLEDGMENTS

Many thanks to the members of my village who made a conscious and unrelenting decision to love all of me even while I was looking for the better parts of my being. It all began with the love extended to me by my maternal grandparents, Clifton and Premina Griffin, and passed to me and my siblings by my mom, Doris. Thank you, mama, for being my number one fan and for always finding a way to push through your own pain and past your own need to ensure I had what I needed. Marcus and Quanza, you two do not get half the credit you deserve for helping me learn how to share and to give. Both of you are natural comedians who love life and gifted the world with beautiful children. Lamont, Georgetta, Pauletta, and Sittra, share in the shaping of my story and know parts of it that can't always be understood or expressed. I love you all and hope you are proud of who I am and what I attempt to add to the world. Ron, I shall forever sing your praises. Henry, Charles, and G.W., I am grateful for you calling me "son" and always introducing me to others with pride.

In life if there are a hand-full of people who say they are your friend, that is a blessing. If there are several who span multiple decades and arenas of life, that is a miracle. Darin, Terako, Ed, Larry, Derek, Pierre, Erik, Will, Jamie, Kathey, Cynthia, Adrienne, Brian, Craig, Catie, Tom, Tim, and Mark, thank you for being friends who loves at all times.

Dr. Lydia Waters, Dr. Bill Leonard, Dr. Penny Long Marler, Dr. James Barnette, Rev. Jim Conn, Rev. Ed Hansen, Rev. Clayton Hammond, Bishop MaryAnn Swenson, Bishop Grant Hagiya, Rev. Dr. Cornish Rogers, and Rev. Dr. James Lawson, thank you for being spiritual leaders and mentors who saw me as one worthy of investment.

I offer thanks to every layperson, staff member and clergy colleague who has served alongside me and offered nothing but grace at every turn. Bowen Memorial, Crenshaw, Santa Ana, and Grace United Methodist Churches accepted me as their pastor and never insisted that I be anyone other than myself. Thank you for entrusting me to journey with you through life's mountain top and valley low experiences.

Susan Shankin, Sara Volle, Ruth Mullen, and Darcy Hughes, as the newest members of my village, you now know all there is to know about my life and the folks and experiences that brought me to the point where you could graciously and compassionately read, edit, and promote this unfolding story that is my life. The ways you helped me put words to emotions and descriptions to faded memories was nothing short of genius.

Speaking of genius, Linda Furtado is an amazing artist. Thank you for listening so intently to the address, "Unnatural Disasters" I delivered February 2016 at Upper Room Ministries/Discipleship Ministries, and for sketching what was the only obvious choice as the image to grace the cover of this book. Your artistry captured the spirit of the moment five years ago and shall encapsulate the most revealing of messages I have ever written.

All of you referenced in these acknowledgments has a special place in my heart. Some of our shenanigans, triumphs, and entanglements appear in the pages of this book, but there are no words that can truly express what your willingness to do life with me has meant to me.

Finally, those named and unnamed here and in the text of this book: I want you to know your presence in my life gave me light and hope until courage came and found me. Thank you.

ABOUT THE AUTHOR

CEDRICK D. BRIDGEFORTH, EDD, is an ordained minister, author, educator, executive coach, consultant, public speaker, and the founder of 20/20 Leadership Lessons. A native of Decatur, Alabama, Cedrick is a U.S. Air Force veteran and holds a Bachelor's degree in Religion from Samford University, a Master of Divinity Degree from the Claremont School of Theology, and a Doctorate Degree in Organizational Leadership from Pepperdine University. He is a former District Superintendent in the California-Pacific Conference of The United Methodist Church, served as Director of Academic Programs at the Ecumenical Center for Black Church Studies at the University of La Verne, and is a member of Alpha Phi Alpha Fraternity, Inc. Prior publications include *Thoughts and Prayers* and *20/20 Leadership Lessons: Seeing Visions and Focusing on Reality.*

Made in United States
Troutdale, OR
10/28/2023

14097657R00188